MAD TOM'S RISING

IAN BRECKON

MAD TOM'S RISING

THE REVOLUTIONARY MYSTIC
SIR WILLIAM COURTENAY
AND THE LAST BATTLE
FOUGHT ON ENGLISH SOIL

ICON

Published in the UK in 2026 by
Icon Books Ltd, Omnibus Business Centre,
39–41 North Road, London N7 9DP
email: info@iconbooks.com
www.iconbooks.com

ISBN: 978-183773-228-9
eBook: 978-183773-227-2

Text copyright © 2026 Ian Breckon
The author has asserted his moral rights.

Every effort has been made to contact the copyright holders of the material reproduced in this book. If any have been inadvertently overlooked, the publisher will be pleased to make acknowledgement on future editions if notified.

No part of this book may be reproduced in any form, or by any means, without prior permission in writing from the publisher.

Typeset by SJmagic DESIGN SERVICES, India

Printed and bound in the UK

Appointed GPSR EU Representative: Easy Access System Europe Oü, 16879218
Address: Mustamäe tee 50, 10621, Tallinn, Estonia
Contact Details: gpsr.requests@easproject.com, +358 40 500 3575

CONTENTS

Prologue – Bossenden Wood ix
Introduction xvii

1. 'An Outrage upon Common Decency' 1
2. 'Truth Bears off the Victory' 29
3. 'Sir William Courtenay … Has Become Insane' 59
4. 'Low Persons of Suspicious Character' 85
5. 'From the Bonds of Satann' 113
6. 'The Earth Shall Rise Up' 139
7. 'To the World's End' 169
8. 'I Have Jesus in my Heart' 197
9. 'Mad Tom of Canterbury' 221

Notes and References 251
Bibliography 267
Acknowledgements 273
Index 275

PROLOGUE
Bossenden Wood

I first came to Bossenden on a warm grey afternoon at the end of May 2018. I was searching for the scene of a battle, but my only guides were a 180-year-old sketch map and a vague sense of intuition. From the outside, the wood does not appear in any way distinguished or unusual: just a tract of scrub along the verge of the old A2, the Canterbury Road, cut off now by the Boughton Bypass. Step off that road and you are among coppiced trees, low bushes, a path of bark chippings leading into the deeper thickets. Little here to show that this woodland is older than England.

Bossenden is the westernmost surviving patch of the great forest of the Blean, which once covered the high ground between Canterbury and the Kent coast to the northwest. In many places the trees were never cleared for cultivation but instead kept for their wood, the oaks and hornbeams and beech coppiced, cut back to grow tall slender rods; in the glades between them charcoal burners once worked and pigs foraged for acorns and beech-mast. This country lay outside the parish boundaries, outside the law in many cases; it was the home of smugglers and squatters, broom-dashers and sheep-stealers, masterless men. The sort of place where the imagination could take hold, and one might dream of a different sort of world.

In the first year of the reign of the young Queen Victoria, these woods were the scene of a bizarre and bloody clash: the last battle ever fought on English soil, as subsequent historians called it. Less a battle, perhaps, than a skirmish, or an ambush, but no less violent and terrifying for those caught in its grip, no less lethal for those who were shot down or bayoneted among the coppice glades. The last time that the common people of England rose in armed insurrection against the state. The last time that regular troops have marched out to crush a revolution.

Strangely, this uprising was not led by a normal sort of political figure. Not by a normal sort of man at all. Instead, the rebellious farm labourers of 1838 massed behind a muscular bearded eccentric they called Sir William Courtenay, *alias* John Nicholls Tom, *alias* 'Mad Tom'. He had until recently been the inmate of a local asylum, but he claimed he was Jesus Christ returned from heaven, that he could work miracles and protect his followers from gunfire, and that he had come to herald the end of the world. Stranger still, a great many people took him at his word. Many of them followed him to their deaths.

Old coppice woodland can have a strange effect at times. It appears relatively open, the narrow tree trunks rising in slightly slanting verticals, the ground between them clear and flat. But as you move deeper into Bossenden Wood, the sounds from the road are quickly deadened. The stillness is eerie, tranquil but unnerving. All around rise the narrow trees, bar upon bar of them, shutting out the horizon. The ground is a dense mat of dead leaves, soaked by rain, spongy underfoot and absorbing all sound. Here and there stands a thicker older trunk, black oak or hornbeam, or ghostly silver birch. And between the trees, away from the bark-chip path, the open glades are choked by low brambles that catch and drag, tough clusters of nettles, rotting deadfall underfoot mulching down into the leaf mould.

In the silence – the stillness that feels now more like a shocked pause in time, with even the birdsong cut off and the sound of your footsteps consumed – you might begin to imagine that little has changed here since that afternoon of violence 180 years ago. Easy to conjure the closeness of the past in such a place. You begin to feel, perhaps, that time itself might be permeable, and that if you train your eyes you could suddenly bring everything into focus. At any moment you might hear the shouts of the combatants and see the red-coated soldiers surging through the thickets ahead, the flash of their bayonets catching the refracted light.

You remember the accounts you have read of what happened: the engagement lasted barely three minutes, but the troops fired over 80 rounds of musket ammunition. Imagine the noise of that amount of gunfire, blasting apart the silence. Imagine how much smoke it would have produced, the acrid black-powder fumes hanging between the trees. One newspaperman who visited the scene the next day described the ground still saturated with blood, pooled in the wet dirt even after a night's rain, the undergrowth all around trampled and stripped by souvenir-hunters who had flocked to the scene, both the faithful and the morbid, to collect scraps of bloodied cloth and hanks of hair, and to gouge the lead musket-balls from the trees, ripping away even the bark and the leaves in their desire for relics.

But in the stillness of the woodland, nothing remains but an empty hush, and the imagined echo of violence. Those narrow trees clustering all around you feel oppressive after a while, all those slanting verticals inevitably suggest a standing figure, a watcher in the middle distance. The sketch map makes no sense, the paths you have been following – paths that seem to have vanished underfoot – have not led you to any identifiable site at all, but only into fantasy. Blink, and you are standing in an English wood in the middle of a Thursday afternoon, a silvery overcast sky shedding a shadowless half-light through the foliage, and the past is far away and lost to comprehension.

And it is at that moment that you see the figures moving between the trees, and you realise that you are not alone here after all.

I first read of the strange events in Bossenden Wood when I was in my mid-teens, in a history magazine that one of my father's friends got on subscription and then passed on to me, knowing I was interested in such things. The story was fascinating and baffling, and weirdly horrible. It did not seem to fit into any conception I then had of England's past. The familiar pageant of kings and queens and battles and conquests held no place for this bizarre frenzy, this impassioned delusion and bloody chaos. Perhaps even then I began to think of the story of Sir William Courtenay, the impostor messiah, as part of some alternative national history. A parallel past, submerged far beneath the one that we think we know.

The magazine article was illustrated with grimy reproductions of sketches and etchings from the period. One showed the corpse of the slain John Nicholls Tom, laid out on a trestle table, another the bodies of his followers, those of them who had died with him, arranged in a row on the straw of a stable. There was a woodland scene, with a rather genteel group of men on horseback observing ranks of soldiers in shakos and crossbelts marching off down a lane to confront the rebels. The juxtaposition of the images felt troublingly incongruous. As if the figures from a biscuit-tin illustration or a comfortable Victorian nursery scene were about to erupt into savage murderous rage, and to start slaughtering each other in a muddy clearing. A grisly and furious nightmare, it seemed, with a gruesome conclusion.

What was it about that story that lodged in my mind? For many years it trailed along in my imagination. Needless to say, I never met anyone who had heard of Sir William Courtenay, or John Nicholls Tom, or Bossenden Wood. I could almost have believed that I had dreamt up the whole thing myself. Around the time I left college, I first conceived the idea of writing a novel about the Courtenay revolt. Although I could remember almost nothing of what I had once read about it, I believed that I could summon up enough of the details, and perhaps just invent the rest. Like so many of my ideas at that time, it floated tantalisingly across the surface of my mind and then sank swiftly back into the murky depths.

But why did this story return to me, decades later still? Perhaps it was merely the social and political state of the nation at the time. That strange frenzy that had gripped the labouring people of Kent in 1838 and led them into riot and rebellion no longer seemed as curiously incomprehensible, as fundamentally *un-English*, as once it had. Both the UK and the wider world buzzed and seethed with violent energies, mobs surged in the streets beneath banners and placards, angry confrontation and upheaval threatened to blast away any comfortable notions that our country, our democratic society, held any inherent immunity from chaos. At such a time the stranger tracts of the past, the buried or submerged avenues and pathways of history, begin once more to shimmer and to gleam.

Normality loses its grip. Distorted memory and fantasy, dream images, folk horror and superstition gather a greater charge. In the remembered drama of the Courtenay revolt, I began to discern the shape of something I could excavate and explore, something I could possess and make meaningful, here in the twenty-first century.

But once I began to reconstruct the events of 1838, the volume of historical data quickly became overwhelming, crowding close around me like the coppiced trees of Bossenden Wood. I needed to get away from the glowing electronic screen and the printed page, and in the last week of May, as the 180th anniversary of the battle approached, I went to Kent, to the countryside around the villages of Boughton, Dunkirk and Hernhill, around Bossenden and the Blean, to see these places for myself.

Already I had visited the church in Hernhill, where the vicar Charles Handley read the Sunday service a few days before the uprising. I had visited Handley's former residence at nearby Mount Ephraim, too, and sifted through the bewilderingly various collection of Courtenay artefacts kept there: original documents and items that included the rampant lion flag that the rebels once carried before them, and a grimy photograph of the madman's heart, preserved in a jar. The 91-year-old owner of Bossenden Farm, Tom's last headquarters, had shown me around his property, and together we had paced the lawns outside to determine the exact location of the murder that ignited that final day's violence. Only then did I enter the woodland that bordered the farm, searching for the site of the battle marked on the 1838 sketch map.

It was only once I had walked almost entirely through it that I recognised my mistake. The western half of Bossenden Wood, I realised, had been cleared. The broad tree-covered

Prologue

tract shown on the old maps, a spreading pair of lungs divided by a stream or rill, was now split into a woodland reserve on one side and open fields on the other. The battle site, in a clearing close to the bank of the stream, had once lain at the very heart of the woods, but was now at its westernmost fringe. The trees and foliage thinned along the stream's edge, which was now the boundary of the woods, and opened to the fields beyond.

The disappointment was only momentary. I had, at least, found the right place. The maps made sense, too, now that I could position myself correctly. But who were the other men I glimpsed away to my left, moving through the trees? And why was one of them dressed as a Victorian farm labourer?

'Are you for Courtenay, or the government?' they asked, as I joined them. There were three of them, and they had made a fire in a split log, stuck a loaf of bread on a pole just as Tom's followers had once done, and opened bottles of beer.

'Courtenay, I suppose,' I told them. He was, after all, the reason I was there.

The men lived locally and came to this place every year. At one time, they told me, the memory of John Nicholls Tom and his uprising had been an embarrassment in the district. Most of the local people had family members who had been involved, on one side or the other, and they knew too well the long trail of recrimination and suspicion that had followed those events, right through into the twentieth century. A sad heritage of murderous fanaticism and collective madness, best forgotten, seldom mentioned. But more recently, they said, the people of Dunkirk and Hernhill had gained a fresh understanding and appreciation for what had happened. A pride in it, too; this was a unique place, with a unique and strange claim to historical significance. They were trying, these three men, to get the site of the battle marked by a monument of some kind and marked on the Ordnance Survey maps, too. John Nicholls Tom – Sir William, as they called him still – was no longer a grim figure from the turbulent past, but a local hero.

One of the men had a bag of blank shotgun cartridges with him. He rigged them to the coppice trunks, and when the exact moment of the battle arrived, we drank bottled beer as the shells exploded and toasted the memory of Sir William.

It was around then, as the smoke and reek of the gunpowder lingered between the trees, that I realised that the story of the Courtenay uprising was too large, its roots entwining too many diverse narratives that already pushed at the boundaries of the fantastical, to be effectively encompassed by the novel I had intended to write.

Instead, if I wanted to capture the full resonance and potency of those events, I would have to try and reconstruct them as they happened, expanding the narrative to glimpse their meaning in the society of the times, and in the experiences of those forever marked by them. By summoning a multiplicity of voices and viewpoints, I might be able to reflect the deep confusion and dismay – the passion and elation, too – felt by so many during that strange and bloody day in Bossenden Wood. The book I wanted to write, I decided, would present an alternative vision of late Regency and early Victorian England as a place of mystical religious enthusiasm, riot and disturbance, arson and uproar. It would describe a society far more nervous and fragile than it might have appeared, and the violent overreaction of a state terrified of popular revolt. It would be a story of faith, fanaticism, and the uncanny power of the imagination.

This, I hope, is something like that book.

INTRODUCTION

News of the killing reached Hernhill only a few hours after daybreak, carried by a boy riding bareback on a plough horse. Up the hill he rode, past the churchyard and square flint tower of St Michael's. As he passed the green that lay between the church and the Red Lion pub, he saw Edward Butcher, local farmer and publican, and shouted to him as he cantered by.

'Courtenay has shot Mears,' the lad cried, 'and he'll shoot a hundred more of you buggers before night!'[1]

It was the last day of May 1838, a week after the nineteenth birthday of the young Queen Victoria. A fine warm morning in the depths of the Kent countryside, albeit with a heavy feeling in the air that threatened rain to come. The railway and the electric telegraph would not be seen for many years in these districts; news travelled as it had done for millennia, at the speed of a galloping horse. The main artery of communication was the London to Dover coaching road, the old Roman Watling Street, which ran its arrow-straight course between Faversham and Canterbury with barely a deviation. Along this road the messengers carried news in both directions, and the word went spreading across the countryside, along the lanes that burrowed between the rippling hills and traced the narrow valleys, steady as the tide covering the mudflats of the Thames Estuary to the north. Men called from field to field, house to house, along the lanes in the first light of morning. *Courtenay has shot Mears*, they cried.

Edward Butcher carried the news back down the lane and across the valley to the brick mansion of Mount Ephraim, which for two decades had been the home of the Reverend Charles Richard Handley, vicar of Hernhill. Handley may have been expecting it for some time. He knew that the man the local people called *Sir William Courtenay* was in reality John Nicholls Tom, impostor and lunatic, bizarrely dressed mountebank and political agitator, seducer of men and perverter of religion. Three days previously, Handley had been 'astonished' to learn that 'Thom[*] with 15 to 20 others was going about the country exciting the people' ... Now the impostor was a murderer, too. Handley knew at once, or so he later claimed, what this killing foretold. A 'wicked conspiracy' was in progress, he believed: 'an insurrection of the labouring classes.'

Half a mile to the south, where the village of Boughton Street straggled along the verges of the coaching road, Handley's fellow clergyman Mr Marsh had already heard the news. The elderly vicar had it from his own servant, who had ridden from the scene of the killing. Marsh lost no time in sending word to his neighbour, the retired military man Colonel Groves, and together they despatched messengers to the nearest magistrates in Faversham, to all the local gentry and landowners, and to the authorities in Canterbury, requesting prompt aid and assistance in quelling an imminent uprising.

....

[*] Writers of the time had difficulties with this name, which often appears as Thom or Thoms. The man himself signed his marriage certificate in 1821 as John Nicholls Tom; this is the spelling I have used in this book.

Introduction

A few miles away, at his country mansion of Provender, between Faversham and Sittingbourne, the magistrate Norton Knatchbull heard the news from Boughton as he was preparing for breakfast. Knatchbull was a young man, not yet 30, and eager to prove himself. Only the previous evening he had learned that the impostor John Tom was 'parading about the country with 60 to 70 persons,' and trying to incite a disturbance. Later that morning he would hear that another thousand or more labouring men were rumoured to be marching from the districts all around, intent on joining the insurrection. He slipped a double-barrelled pistol into the pocket of his riding coat, bade farewell to his young wife Mary, and called for his carriage.[2]

Before the hour was out, the news had reached the Reverend Dr John Poore, Knatchbull's fellow magistrate and Justice of the Peace, at his rectory at Murston on the outskirts of Sittingbourne. Dr Poore, too, was well aware of what the news meant. The previous evening he had written out warrants for the arrest of William Courtenay *alias* John Tom and three of his associates. Until that point, he had resisted the calls from agitated landowners and local gentlemen to proceed more vigorously against Tom and his men; a magistrate could not act until he had received sworn testimony that a crime had been committed. Now there could be no further hesitation.

Dr Poore soon discovered that the murdered man was not, as he might have assumed, John Mears, plumber and parish constable of Boughton, but rather his brother Nicholas Mears, sworn in as an assistant constable only the day before to help execute the warrants of arrest. Mears and his brother, together with a third man, Daniel Edwards, had set off at sunrise on Friday, 31 May for a place called Bossenden, an old farm where John Nicholls Tom and his followers were reported to be staying. Bossenden lay in the extra-parochial district of Dunkirk, up the steep hill from the straggling settlement of Dunkirk Ville and tenanted by a small farmer named William Culver. It was an isolated and decaying place, surrounded by woodland – the name appears as Bosenden on older maps, and local people pronounce it *Bo'zn'dn*. A later Parliamentary report called it *Bousden*, while Norton Knatchbull referred to it as 'a farm in Dunkirk the name of which I can't spell.'[3]

It was there, outside the farmhouse itself, that Mears and his two assistants had encountered Tom, armed and apparently intent on murder, and Nicholas had died only moments later. After making his escape from the scene of the crime, John Mears had raced all the way back to Faversham to make his report at the office of the magistrates' clerk. His brother had been shot dead in cold blood between six and seven o'clock that morning, he reported, and he himself would have been killed had he not immediately fled the scene. John Tom and a gang of his followers were reported to be moving westwards, through the woods towards the hamlet of Dargate.

The only body that Poore and Knatchbull could call upon to uphold the law were the parish constables, civilian officers like Mears who served for a yearly stipend and bonuses, or the temporary expedient of assistant or special constables, sworn in for duty in times of trouble. In 1838, there were no professional policemen in the rural areas of England; Canterbury already had a small constabulary, but almost two decades would pass before the formation of the regular Kent force. If the limited capabilities of the parish constables were exceeded, magistrates could summon military assistance – either from the part-time volunteer Yeomanry cavalry or the regular army – 'in support of the civil power'. Troops had been used in this way against a political demonstration in Manchester in 1819,

Introduction

leading to the infamous 'Peterloo' Massacre. Similar violence had occurred when the army was sent into Bristol in 1831, during rioting after the blocking of the second Reform Bill. But with no available force to draw upon between the truncheons of the untrained special constables and the muskets, bayonets and sabres of the army, magistrates like Dr Poore felt they had little choice. He at once addressed a letter to the authorities in Canterbury, requesting the assistance of troops in putting down an armed revolt in his district.[4]

Shortly afterwards, in the town of Faversham, a young man named George Catt, the owner of a beershop called the Good Intent, took the oath as a special constable and was handed his truncheon. He was eager to serve, having heard a rumour that the capture of Sir William Courtenay, *alias* John Tom, carried a reward of ten pounds. As the sole provider for his mother, his widowed sister and two nephews, Catt needed the money. If nobody else would arrest Tom, he boasted, he would do it himself.[5]

By mid-afternoon he would be dead, the back of his skull blown apart by a musket ball.

The Mears brothers and their assistant had not been the only men lurking around the perimeter of Bossenden Farm that morning. Several other observers, who had been concealed in the fringes of the surrounding woodland, had witnessed the attack on the constables and the killing that followed, and had already run off to make their reports. Hernhill churchwarden and farm supervisor Edward Curling had been prowling the vicinity of Bossenden for several hours, mounted on a horse and dressed in a labourer's smock as a disguise.

Curling had visited the farm the evening before, demanding the return of several men contracted to work on his land, whom he believed 'Sir William' had enticed away; he had earlier been one of the first to swear an affidavit to Dr Poore that criminal offences had been committed. His visit had not been a success, but Curling had been suspicious enough of activities at Bossenden to remain in the vicinity, perhaps hoping to creep closer and observe what was going on. Now, with the news of the killing confirmed, he sprang into action. Still wearing his smock, Curling set off at the gallop.[6]

Canterbury was the home of the county magistrates and banking partners Richard Baldock and William Henry Halford. It was also a garrison town, and the barracks at that time were occupied by the men of the 45th (Northamptonshire) Regiment of Foot. Curling arrived around eight in the morning and went straight to see Mr Halford, who told him that he would need a signed statement from a magistrate on the scene before authorising military assistance to the civil power. Undaunted, Curling rode the five miles back up onto the Blean ridge. At the turning to Bossenden he met his son, also named Edward, who had just come from the farm and had seen the body of the murdered man lying in a ditch. Mounted on his father's horse, Curling Jr rode down the hill to Boughton to find Dr Poore. Then he saddled up once more and went hammering all the way back to Canterbury with Poore's letter. Suitably authorised, the Canterbury magistrates at once alerted the commander of the garrison.

Among the officers of the 45th was a young Irish lieutenant, Henry Boswell Bennett. A 'fine looking young man' with the reputation of being 'a perfect gentleman', Bennett was popular in Canterbury. He was officially on furlough in May 1838, but was visiting friends in the city when the news arrived of the disturbance in the districts around Boughton. The 45th had recently returned from a long posting in India, and many of its officers had seen action in Burma. Bennett, however, had only transferred to the regiment after that war was over, and had seen no active service. Perhaps that was why he was so eager to volunteer for special duty that morning. A few hours later he, too, would be dead, shot through the heart, the first military combat fatality of Queen Victoria's reign.[7]

The magistrates of the Hernhill and Boughton districts and their supporters among the gentry and landowning classes had plenty of experience of unrest and discord in the neighbourhood; the English countryside in the early nineteenth century was not a peaceful place. The previous decade had been more than usually fractious and violent, as the competing forces of reform and conservatism, modernity and tradition surged and struggled for control of the nation. This was a time of rage and revolutionary threat, of popular upheaval and furious invective.

Those hoping that the reign of the young Queen Victoria would mark an end to a tumultuous decade, and inaugurate a new era of tranquillity, harmony and growing prosperity for the United Kingdom, would have been disappointed at the first reports of the bloodshed in Kent. But the outrageous conduct of 'Sir William Courtenay' and his followers was a form of violent disorder quite different, it soon appeared, to earlier outbreaks. This was an eruption of mass delusion and religious insanity, inspired by a man who believed he was Jesus Christ returned to earth and who had exhibited to his disciples the wounds of the crucifixion upon his flesh. The evening before, Norton Knatchbull's stepmother Lady Fanny – niece of the novelist Jane Austen – had written in her diary, in a neatly miniature script, that 'the poor Madman calling himself Sir W Courtenay' had 'assembled a party of 50 men and began rioting at Sittingbourne, saying he was <u>The Saviour</u>!!!!'[8]

While Charles Handley, the vicar of Hernhill, had quickly decided that the threatened uprising was a 'wicked conspiracy', a political insurrection and an attempt at class war, others in the surrounding area had quite different ideas about what was happening, and about the true identity of Sir William Courtenay. At Fairbrook, a neat brick farmhouse between Hernhill and Faversham, the yeoman farmer George Francis was still very undecided in his allegiances. For over six years, the socially ambitious Francis had been a close friend and supporter of the man he still called Sir William. He had stood bail for him after his arrest on a charge of fraud in Canterbury in 1832 and had escorted him from Barming asylum after his release five years later. Sir William Courtenay had been a guest at Fairbrook over the famously cold winter of 1837–38, and during that time Francis's faith and belief in the man he had first taken to be a political visionary were cruelly shaken. But while Sir William had ultimately disappointed George himself, others in the household were still devoted to him: Francis's eldest daughter and sister-in-law were among his most ardent admirers and had reportedly given him large sums of money.

George Francis would have passed an anxious Friday morning, then, after learning not only that his former friend had apparently murdered a man, but that he was now rumoured to be advancing on Fairbrook at the head of a large gang of his followers. Still, he was determined to take a neutral course; surely it would be possible to reason with the man, and to persuade him from any rash course of action? He was unaware that at that very moment John Nicholls Tom was boasting to his followers that he would go to Fairbrook on Saturday and murder George Francis and his entire family, shortly before or after burning Canterbury to the ground.

Others, too, had received communications from Tom's followers. One local man reported that a letter had been sent to him the day before, 'threatening him with death by shot, if he did not become a follower of Thoms [sic], whom the writer insisted was Jesus Christ.' Faversham lawyer and landowner Julius Shepherd later claimed that he had narrowly avoided encountering John Tom and his little army that morning; he expected that if he had done so, he would have 'received a bullet in the thorax.' A neighbouring farm manager, the irascible Scotsman William Kay, had sent out a general warning to Tom's supporters several days beforehand, stating that he had 'a good piece, the contents of which I will empty into the first individual who presumes to force an entrance to my dwelling.'[9]

While violence, and threats of violence, hung in the early morning air, others were energised more by hope than by fear. Henry Hadlow, the boy who had ridden through Hernhill and shouted his warning to Edward Butcher, had been working in the fields with horse and harrow when he heard of the killing at Bossenden; if he was close enough to Boughton at the time he may have picked up the news from one of the messengers sent out by Mr Marsh and Colonel Groves. But he acted promptly, unhitching his horse and riding up and over the hill through Hernhill towards his home. Hadlow was the son of the bailiff of Lavender Farm in the hamlet of Waterham, one of Julius Shepherd's properties. His mother, Lydia Hadlow, had been at one time mistress of a local Sunday School, and was a devoted follower of the new messiah. Young Henry rode straight to tell her the news, and to pass on the rumour that 'Sir William' and his supporters had emerged from the woods and were marching towards Waterham; they would soon be needing breakfast. The killing of Mears had been the signal that the day had come, the promised 'glorious and bloody day' of violence and retribution, when Sir William would lead his followers against those that oppressed them – the gentry and landowning class – and bring the Millennium, the thousand-year reign of Christ and his saints, and heavenly justice for those who believed in and followed him. Within the hour, Lydia Hadlow 'gave her son her blessing' as he marched with John Nicholls Tom and his band, and 'sent her husband, whom she controls, to join him in the same mad expedition.'[10]

Others, too, were swept up in the crusade as Tom and his followers made their way along the lanes and through the hamlets. As he passed through Dargate, Tom's followers saluted him with leafy green oak branches, flourishing them before him in what the correspondent of the *Times* would later call 'another impious mockery of our Lord.' Not all those who joined Tom and his followers did so with such open enthusiasm. Tom himself had several times threatened dire punishment on all who failed to heed his summons; he would invoke fire and brimstone upon them, he told his listeners, and they would be sent directly to hell. One man living nearby rose on Thursday morning after a sleepless night of turbulent fears, and told his wife that he had no choice but to join Sir William, 'for if he did not he was convinced that a shower of fire would come down from heaven and burn him and his children to ashes.'[11]

By late afternoon, the first reports of disaster were reaching Canterbury. There had been a riot – a *battle*, in fact – in the woods close to Bossenden farm, between the followers of John Nicholls Tom and the soldiers of the 45th Foot. Both sides had taken casualties. Initial reports put the number of dead at twenty, later revised to eleven. One army officer was dead, another badly injured. John Nicholls Tom himself and several of his followers had been killed, many more were critically wounded. Aside from their leader, Tom's men had been armed with only sticks and fists in their confrontation with a fully equipped military detachment that outnumbered them by more than two to one. It did not take long before people started mentioning 'Peterloo'.

The Union mail coach left Canterbury that evening heavily loaded with passengers. Most travelled only a few miles, to the top of the Blean ridge and an isolated roadside public house called the Red Lion. From there, tracks led into the surrounding woodlands, to Bossenden farm and to the scene of the fighting. It was to the Red Lion, and to another pub down the hill in Boughton Street, that the bodies of the slain had been taken. There, in a low outbuilding, the corpses were laid out on straw, before the gaze of their families, their neighbours, and the gawking spectators alike. By the following day an artist had appeared, from the *Weekly Chronicle*, to sketch the scene.

News of the bloody events in Bossenden wood travelled in the other direction, too. Henry Ward, a Canterbury journalist, had followed the troops from the city. When the firing commenced, he had immediately taken cover in a roadside ditch, but as soon as the noise of battle ceased he scrambled aboard the first passing coach to London, and on his arrival that same evening went directly to the offices of the *Times*. Determined to get an exclusive account of what had happened in Kent, the newspaper's managers ordered Ward to be locked in a room while he wrote his full report. In the House of Lords, the assembled peers were coming to the close of an extended debate on the Irish Poor Law bill when the first intelligence reached them. The conservative Lord Winchelsea 'rose in great agitation and announced the horrible fact of a battle having taken place'; he asked the Whig leader of the government, Lord Melbourne, whether he knew anything more about it. Melbourne did not but told the house that a messenger had arrived from Kent that very moment and was waiting to provide further details.[12]

It was Melbourne himself who brought the news the next day to the Queen. Victoria had been out the evening before at the opera, enraptured by a performance of *Don Giovanni*; now the reports of 'this atrocious riot' left her deeply shocked. 'It's dreadful,' she wrote in her journal, 'really quite dreadful, *all* this useless bloodshed is, and all caused by a wretched madman, who, Lord Melbourne said, got great power over the people's minds.'[13]

Henry Ward's initial report on the 'FATAL RIOT NEAR CANTERBURY' had appeared in the *Times* that morning. 'Intelligence of this serious riot reached us at a late hour,' the editor's introduction stated; 'of the death of the military officer and constable, as well as that of the insane instigator of the mob, there can be no doubt.' *The Champion and Weekly Herald*, a Sunday newspaper run by the sons of the late political reformer William Cobbett, was more dramatic in its coverage: 'We stop suddenly to insert an account of an awful poor law battle that has just been fought in Kent!' Little detail was available to print at that point, but the outcome was clear: 'It is an awful state of things!'[14]

The journalist's assumption that this was a 'poor law battle' was widely shared, at least initially. The New Poor Law – or the Poor Law Amendment Act of 1834 – was the hot political topic of the era, and even the threat of its introduction had already led to rioting in Kent and elsewhere. With the full implementation of the act's provisions only having commenced the year before, any outbreaks of violence in the countryside could easily be attributed to its effects. While the opposition – both Tory and Radical – at once blamed the Whigs for the injustice of the bill and the violence it had caused, the Whig press and the government in turn accused the opposition of having stirred up violent agitation with their inflammatory rhetoric and encouragement of unrest. 'Have the chiefs of the Tory party nothing to answer for,' the editorial of the *Examiner* asked on 3 June, in discussing the recent events in Kent, 'who have omitted to raise their voices against the incendiary practices of their partizans?'

It rapidly became clear, however, that little evidence existed to tie the uprising to the opponents of the New Poor Law. While John Tom had allegedly promised to demolish a workhouse at one point, and Dr Poore's first statement had reported his claim that the labouring community 'were oppressed ... particularly by the New Poor Law, and that if they would follow him, he would rescue them,' this was based solely on hearsay. The new ruling otherwise barely featured in Tom's voluminous bizarre pronouncements. Instead, it was these very pronouncements – amassed by newspaper correspondents in their interrogations of local people or quoted during the trial inquest on the surviving 'rioters' – that now became the focus of public scrutiny.[15]

Tom, in his assumed guise of 'Sir William Courtenay', had, it transpired, been a well-known character in the districts adjoining Dunkirk and Bossenden several years before. Rather than 'coming down from heaven on a cloud,' as he claimed, he had in fact appeared in Canterbury back in 1832 (albeit rather mysteriously) and had even stood for election to parliament in December of that year. Several months later he had produced his own newspaper, or political broadsheet pamphlet; largely ignored at the time, copies were now located and their contents extensively quoted in national newspapers, scrutinised for clues to the genesis of his political and messianic appeal.

Stranger still, it was soon revealed that Tom – in fact a former maltster and wine merchant from Cornwall – had been for several years the inmate of a lunatic asylum, from which he had only recently been discharged after being granted a free pardon on the accession of Queen Victoria. Here, too, the political partisans found fresh ammunition; had this pardon and discharge been politically motivated? Had the Home Secretary, Lord John Russell, been petitioned or influenced by the MP for Truro, an ally of the government who at one time had been Tom's employer? A Parliamentary Select Committee, convened in July of 1838, failed to uncover any evidence of malpractice. The release of 'Mad Tom' had, it seemed, been a mistake, but not one based on political influence or cronyism.

Long before this, however, the focus of media speculation and opinion had shifted from the political to the religious. What had happened in Kent was, the *Examiner* proclaimed, 'a scene of fanaticism ... without a precedent in England since the days of Cromwell and his blaspheming followers.' Only ten days after Tom and his supporters were cut down in a blaze of gunfire, the editorial of the *News and Sunday Globe* declared that 'the sanguinary conflict which converted a spot in the neighbouring county of Kent into a battle field' had not been a result of any action by the government. In fact, 'the peasants who were engaged in resistance to the law were not, as first reported, dissolute characters, smugglers, or discontented paupers, [but] labouring peasants, yeomen, and cottagers, usually industrious and habitually peaceful ...' Their rebellion was motivated 'not by any political grievance, real or fancied – not by any hatred of the New Poor-law,' but by an outbreak of mass religious fanaticism inspired solely by ignorance, and permitted by clergymen neglectful of their duties and responsibilities:

> Such, it appears, is the state of things in 'enlightened England' and in the nineteenth century. Within sight of the towers of the cathedral whence the first hierarch

of our Established Church derives his title ... exists a race of men so dangerously ignorant, so utterly incapable of reasoning, so innocent of all knowledge of what religion is, that when a notorious madman comes among them with pistols in his hands, and tells them he is the saviour of the world, they believe him implicitly, rise in a mass and follow him ...[and] fight like wild beasts to the uttermost, holding in death the belief that they cannot be slain ... Throughout the region where such things can happen there must reign a vast unbroken atmosphere of ignorance – a 'darkness which may be felt.'[16]

In the meantime, correspondents from the major national newspapers flocked to Boughton, Hernhill and Dunkirk, hoping to probe this vast darkness of local ignorance and discern, if possible, exactly what had happened there. Over successive days the newspaper-readers of England were fed an extraordinary diet of information, speculation and anecdote about this previously obscure corner of the country, and about every aspect of the uprising, whether attempted revolution or episode of mass religious hysteria, which had blazed for so many days there, unobserved and unnoticed. What had caused the ordinary people of these parishes to fall such easy victims to what the correspondent of the *Times*, in a telling phrase, called 'the infection of fanaticism'?[17]

England in the early nineteenth century was in the grip of a religious convulsion. The Evangelical movement within Anglicanism, and the various dissenting and nonconformist sects outside it, had together created a new mood of anxious and impassioned religiosity quite at odds with the more complacent spirit of the preceding century. English people of the 1830s might feel inspired to attend open-air prayer meetings or find themselves intensely moved by the blazing sermons of celebrity preachers. Among the biggest draws in London at the beginning of the decade was the Church of Scotland minister Edward Irving, whose fiery pulpit delivery packed out Hatton Garden's Caledonian Chapel with a congregation that included senior government ministers and members of the aristocracy – and, it would later emerge, John Nicholls Tom.

Coupled with this dramatic new sense of popular spirituality were ideas that might have been considered alarming or absurd only a few decades beforehand but now found wider acceptance. Millenarianism – the expectation of the second coming of Jesus Christ, to be followed by the glorious thousand-year reign of the saints, the Resurrection and Last Judgement, and the end of the world – was a profoundly-held belief across all levels of society at this time. Its exponents included the Reverend Mr Irving of Hatton Garden, and also John Nicholls Tom – although in his case he would eventually declare that he *was* Christ incarnate.[18]

Irving fell from grace rather rapidly after 1830, when his sermons began to be enlivened by members of the congregation 'speaking with tongues', and the pastor himself was found guilty of severe doctrinal error. Irving's descent into what the *Times* called 'blasphemous absurdities' underlines the peril of this new spiritual sensibility; religion in the 1830s could be an explosive, transformational force, but its power might prove dangerous. It should not, many felt, become too *exciting* – especially for the lower classes. Piety could easily tip over into religious 'enthusiasm', which was only a step from 'fanaticism'. A speaker like Irving – or like John Nicholls Tom – could easily 'act upon the minds of the weak part of his flock' to create 'a kind of epidemic madness.'[19]

Introduction

In John Tom's case, of course, he was literally mad: a certified lunatic and the former inmate of an asylum. The educated classes of the early nineteenth century were both intrigued and appalled by madness and fascinated by the workings of the mind more generally. Popular pseudo-sciences of the day reinforced this fascination; proponents of Physiognomy believed that by accurate observation and measurement of the facial features one might gain an index of character, temperament and even destiny, while the disciples of Phrenology claimed that by palpating the crania of their subjects they could discern the hidden truths of the individual psyche. Both practices were at the height of their popularity in the 1830s, and reports on the inquests on John Nicholls Tom's followers feature several physiognomic observations. The cranium of Tom himself was sadly unavailable for palpation, having been sawn off so the surgeons could examine and measure his brain, but a plaster cast had already been taken of his face.[20]

As an attempt to palpate the crania of an entire community, so to speak, the investigations and interrogations of both newspaper correspondents and magistrates had already been successful in diagnosing many symptoms of fanaticism's infection. But the reports go much further than that; in the polyphony of reportage, of quotation, allegation and anecdote, they provide a reverberating and often dissonant choral backdrop to the events of Tom's uprising. Successive repetitions of the same testimony either reveal or obscure details, confusing times and dates and places. Individuals identified in one source are rendered vague in the next. Words fly from one mouth to another. As the relentless enquiries of the newspaper correspondents take them from the inquests on Tom's surviving followers to the funerals of their slain messiah and comrades, and the trials of those accused as ringleaders, the sheer volume of detail becomes baffling, almost defying understanding.

The sympathies of those reading these reports in full from one day to the next would have been sorely tried.

The nineteenth-century British public – or those of them with the means, the education and the leisure to read widely – were increasingly interested in people who might previously have fallen below their notice. The same newssheets that carried, in the first days of June 1838, the reports of the insurrection in Kent also reviewed the latest instalments of *Oliver Twist*, Charles Dickens's serial successor to *The Pickwick Papers*. Those enthralled by the grim picture of urban criminality and rural poverty, and the grinding injustice of the workhouse regime, need only have cast their eye across the page to read, depending on their political inclination, of the effects of injustice elsewhere in the country, or of the bloody results of madness and inflammatory rhetoric.

As never before, educated Britons were inspired to peer into the homes of the labourers, into the hovels of the poor and destitute, into the hearts and minds of the lower classes generally, and try to perceive something more subtle and acute than the generalised picture of a 'brutalised peasantry' conjured in many of the early reports on Tom's followers. A decade of reformist politics, shaping towards if not yet embracing ideas of democracy; a decade of social unrest and fervent debate on poverty and poor relief, on the rights of the agricultural workers of Kent and the mill-hands of Lancashire, had instilled in the liberal class of Britain a new-found curiosity about the lives of those at the lower end of the social establishment. Perhaps even a nervous scrutiny of those who may soon enough, or so the traditionalists thundered, rise up to overthrow that social establishment entirely. There are strong suggestions of surveillance in the newspaper reports from the 'disaffected areas' following the revolt, just

Introduction

as there are in the recorded activities of the local gentry and landowners in the days leading up to it.

Some of the investigations into the Kent uprising approach the qualities of early social anthropology. In the summer of 1838, the barrister Frederick Liardet visited the districts of Boughton, Hernhill and Dunkirk to compile a report for the Central Society of Education 'respecting the late extraordinary occurrences in Kent.' While Liardet's conclusions are somewhat foregone, and replete with the standard sanctimonies of his class and era, his findings are invaluable in the detailed picture they present of life in an English agricultural community of the period. More of a still-life than a snapshot, however: besides a few anonymous locals who give their own views on proceedings, most of the people Liardet describes have already been killed in the conflict or are in prison.[21]

Besides collecting anecdotes of the uprising and scraps of speech as the newspapermen had earlier done, Liardet compiled statistics on local employment patterns, wages, land ownership, and background details on the men who died. He went into their cottages and tramped about their gardens, asking questions and noting down everything he found: How many pigs and cows did their families own? How many rooms did their homes contain? Were they literate? How many books did they possess, and of what sort? How many pictures did they have on their walls, and what did the pictures portray? Again, we sense the viewpoint of the establishment, taking stock. Liardet gains mastery over the 'peasantry' merely by close observation of their habits and habitat, and draws conclusions as to their improvement. One can only wonder what he missed, or what might have been deliberately concealed from his surveilling, appropriating eye.

Liardet's report, published the following year, nevertheless provides invaluable evidence on the background to John Tom's revolt. Many journalists in Kent had been fascinated by the antics of 'Sir William Courtenay' for years beforehand as well. Shortly after the events of 1838, an anonymous writer in Canterbury calling himself 'Canterburiensis' published a lengthy history of Courtenay/Tom, his background and the uprising that he led.

The Life and Extraordinary Adventures of Sir William Courtenay was probably written quickly to cash in on the celebrity of its subject. It is a strange hybrid text, partly composed of cannibalised extracts originally printed in the *Times*; quite possibly 'Canterburiensis' was local journalist and publisher Henry Ward, and he had originally written much of the material himself as the chief correspondent for the London newspaper. Appended to this narrative are full transcripts of the various trials of Tom's supporters, and correspondence between his family and others: all solid and worthwhile material, and much of it supported by available contemporary documents. But the first half of the book comprises a lengthy and detailed account of the impostor's childhood and earlier years, including a colourful travelogue of his journeys in eastern lands. All, or at least most, of this is total fantasy. Many of the dates in even the less fanciful parts of the narrative are faulty, too, and only when the author starts quoting directly from newspaper reports do we reach firmer ground.[22]

More reliable witnessing comes from a series of interviews undertaken by the Parliamentary Select Committee investigating Tom's discharge from Kent County Lunatic Asylum. Also published in 1838, the committee's report is rich in individual testimony, much of it unmentioned elsewhere. While the newspaper coverage sketches out the wider narrative of the uprising, official depositions and testimonies fill in the details, and the anecdotes and personal statements taken down by journalists lend texture to the picture. Surgeons' reports on the bodies of the slain, subsequently printed in the national press, provide what seems today a startlingly intimate account of the wounds inflicted in the brief frenzy of the battle: the effects of bullets and blades on flesh, the track of a projectile inside a human body, the shattered bone and burst internal organs, all noted with cool steely precision.[23]

Combining these sources with Liardet's social study, the published writings of John Nicholls Tom himself in his 'Courtenay' guise, and the various letters and unpublished accounts by participants like Charles Handley and Norton Knatchbull, we might consider that we have a complex panorama of the uprising and its aftermath, from multiple points of view. The first modern study of the events, Philip G. Rogers's 1962 *Battle in Bossenden Wood*, relies almost entirely on these textual sources, and takes us down a broad and solid highway through the thickets of the historical narrative, with plenty of colourful incidents along the way.[24]

We must ask, though, as we might with Liardet's observations, what we are missing in these accounts. The writings of John Nicholls Tom were published five or six years before his death; his sayings and statements in the days before he died are reported by others. They are the lines spoken by an actor on a stage, albeit one performing in deadly earnest. What he might really have thought or believed himself to be doing in his constant self-invention and reinvention remains obscure to us now. While the private accounts by Handley and Knatchbull, together with the first reports by Dr Poore and the military officers involved, offer more immediate testimony, they are the statements of the establishment, shot through with the desire for self-exoneration. Liardet's detailed probing into the lives of the people can touch only the surfaces, without entering the depths of human truth.

In the newspaper coverage, as in Liardet's report, there are frequent quotations from people of the lower classes, those who had known Tom or who were related to his followers. Reading them, we can pick up a flavour of local speech, pronunciation and dialect. But, whether recording the words of an anonymous woodcutter or a labourer's wife, or the father of an unnamed man wounded in the battle ('Lord, Sir, my son is an *unlarned* man like myself; he can neither read nor write, and how was I or my lad to go for to gainsay such a great scholar as Sir William?'), or an Irish infantry soldier ('O by the powers I'd no notion at all that you Englishers fought so cruel hard!'), or noting down exactly – with colourful spelling errors – the graffiti painted on a barn door, or a plaintive scrap of naïve verse apparently penned by one of Tom's closest disciples, these are essentially efforts at literary mimicry, similar in their effect to the lower class 'voices' captured by Charles Dickens in his contemporary *Pickwick Papers* and *Sketches by Boz*. The real voices of the people concerned, of Tom's followers and their families, are lost to us. Lost, too, are their reasons for doing what they did, for all the vague excuses they might have provided to the importuning gentlemen of the London press. Their voices, and their views, are no longer available; unlike the bloodied and confused survivors of Tom's ragged army, they cannot be *apprehended*. In most cases, the only real records left by the poor of the early nineteenth century are those taken down by the police and the magistrates' clerks.[25]

In more recent years, historians have paid a lot more attention to these lost voices, these *subaltern* lives, or what we might be able to reconstruct of them. Barry Reay's 1990 book *The Last Rising of the Agricultural Labourers* is a sober and finely detailed social analysis of the background to Tom's rebellion and the political forces that might have driven it. With its painstaking attention to family structures and the patterns of local allegiance and identity among the labouring community, Reay's scholarship is vital to understanding the events of the day. My own current effort would have been impossible without it. But – perhaps sensibly – neither his book nor Rogers's earlier work extend their focus much beyond the immediate radius of Tom himself, his followers, and their families.[26]

By the late nineteenth and earlier twentieth centuries, John Nicholls Tom had been transformed into a fantastical bugbear, a semi-mythological figure better placed in the world of folklore, or perhaps a quaint manifestation of English eccentricity turned violently unruly. Today, however, things appear rather differently. Like the early nineteenth century, our own epoch has a Millennial feel. John Nicholls Tom might today be called a cult leader. His claims, so eagerly and wholeheartedly believed by those who gave their lives for him – the evocation of a miraculous world in which belief can repel bullets, men descend from the sky upon clouds and shoot stars from the firmament, and deadly fire rains from heaven upon the unfaithful – might be called magical thinking, or conspiracy theory. As such, he is no longer the inhabitant of a distant era or an unimaginable moral universe. In his reinventions of identity, his blurring of the real and the fantastical, and his passionate revolt against modernity and order, 'Mad Tom' strides out of the distant past as a palpably contemporary figure.

But to trace the roots of his bizarre career we must return to a time long before the first shocking news of violence and revolt reached the newspapers, before that news spread outwards across the Kent countryside, before young Henry Hadlow mounted his plough horse in the still of morning and went galloping up the hill towards Hernhill church; a time before the first shots were fired. Years before, in fact, to the city of Canterbury, in the fervid weeks before a tumultuous general election, when the man who called himself Sir William Courtenay first appeared to dazzle, bemuse, and outrage the people of England.

1. 'AN OUTRAGE UPON COMMON DECENCY'

The impostor arrived in the city as the summer of 1832 declined towards autumn. His appearance was enough to attract attention. He was a big man, six-feet tall, broad of shoulder and deep of chest, with the thews of a wrestler. His dark hair flowed to his shoulders from a central parting, and his beard was dense and full. The 1830s were a beardless age; even the brief fashion for military 'moustachioes' and side-whiskers had largely faded – the new king, William IV, had banned them in the army – and Englishmen on the whole were uniformly clean-shaven. One etiquette book of the period suggested that an 'unshorn chin has a degenerating aspect, and is only, if at all, excusable in the lowest laborer and mechanic.' Foreign to respectable grooming and notions of hygiene, the beard suggested cultural, racial and perhaps even moral difference. It suggested republicanism, religious eccentricity, and bohemian decadence. More particularly, it suggested the exotic, infidel world of the Turk, the Arab and the Jew.[1]

Perhaps the impostor was already dressed, on the day he arrived in Canterbury, in the 'gay and imposing costume' that he would later assume. Perhaps the beard alone was enough to mark him as undesirable. Either way, the landlord of the Fountain Hotel in St Margaret's Street promptly discovered that he had no beds available. Undeterred, the newcomer strode onward, 'with the velocity of a wild Arab', into the Parade and through the doors of the Rose Inn, where the host proved more open minded. He took the best room in the house, with a balcony above the main entrance. And that, for some time, was all that Canterbury saw of him.

The city in 1832 was in many ways still the sedate, provincial place that Dickens would evoke in *David Copperfield*, with its 'old houses and gateways, and the stately, grey Cathedral, with the rooks sailing round the towers.' The city had been left behind by the modern industries that had revolutionised much of the rest of England. Besides its breweries, Canterbury had no manufacturing to speak of, and the 13,649 inhabitants recorded in the census of the year before were still mostly lodged within the circuit of the medieval walls. It was a wealthy city nonetheless, with a rich agricultural hinterland of hop gardens, orchards, wheatfields and arable land. And in many ways the apparent calm was deceptive: the political and social storms of the reform era had swept through Kent just as fiercely as elsewhere. Behind its genteel façade, Canterbury was riven by political factionalism and primed for further conflict.[2]

News of the strange and secretive new guest at the Rose leaked out gradually over the following weeks, carried principally by the staff. The newcomer was named Count Moses Rostopchein Rothschild, they reported. He was fabulously rich, although currently required to live modestly to avoid attracting undue attention to himself. He had recently travelled to the east, spending much time in Palestine and Arabia, and his mission in England was somehow related to relieving 'the distressed Jews of the Holy Land' from oppression and hardship.

Beyond that, however, the Count remained a tantalising enigma. He emerged only in the mornings, walking the streets in silence, dressed sometimes in a suit and cape of Italian cut, at other times in fabulous garments of red velvet and satin, trimmed with gold lace, and with a 'Turkey cap' upon his head. Despite his name and purpose, he seemed at least to be a Christian, attending the non-conforming Union Chapel on Watling Street every Sunday, although some claimed he visited the local synagogue as well. His appearance went a long way to supporting his identity, as did his strange accent. Even his complexion appeared darkened by the eastern sun. Few would have guessed that he might not be what he pretended.[3]

They would be surprised, therefore, when several months after his arrival in Canterbury, the stranger threw off the husk of 'Count Moses Rothschild' and emerged in an entirely new and glitteringly original persona.

The spark for this transformation was the death, on 12 September 1832, of Sir John Courtenay Honywood, fifth baronet of Evington and former Sheriff of Kent, at the age of only forty-five. The baronet, heir to an old Kent family, had died on his estates a few miles south of Canterbury. His valet, a man named Collard, had somehow inherited his master's wardrobe and other personal possessions. Appearing in Canterbury a month or so later and advertising the items for sale, Collard quickly received an invitation to visit the reclusive Count Rothschild at his rooms in the Rose. The Count purchased a sword, a pair of heavy gold epaulettes, and other items of court apparel. He also purchased the services of Collard, who was otherwise unengaged. More importantly, he purchased a new identity. Soon afterwards, he would appear before the world as Sir William Percy Honeywood Courtenay, rightful heir to Powderham Castle and the Earldom of Devon.[4]

The name was an audacious stroke and cleverly judged. The recently deceased Sir John had been the nephew of the real Viscount William Courtenay. Notorious in his teens for his involvement in an affair with the dissolute aristocratic novelist William Beckford, Courtenay had been obliged to leave England back in 1811 for the more prosaic purpose of escaping his creditors. He had moved first to New York and later to Paris, where he remained. In March 1831, the House of Lords had agreed to revive Courtenay's long-dormant ancestral title of Earl of Devon, and his claim to Powderham Castle, but there was little possibility of the fugitive earl returning to take up either of them. The impostor could, it seemed, borrow his name and title with impunity.

With Collard at his side, the newly revealed knight made his first public appearances. 'Count Rothschild', it turned out, had been a mere ruse, a false identity assumed to elude nefarious enemies, but now Sir William Courtenay chose to step forth bravely, in his true guise at last. Very soon he had become the most celebrated of local celebrities, and the topic of 'universal conversation'. It is not hard to see why; where the Count had been a mysterious foreigner, parsimonious and reclusive, Sir William was every inch the patriotic Englishman, proudly and piously Christian, and ferociously gregarious. As autumn chilled into winter he was everywhere in Canterbury, talking to everyone, buying drinks for all – even if one of his new-found friends usually found himself picking up the tab. He retained the gaudy velvet and silk costumes of his Count Rothschild days, with the addition of gold epaulettes, a cavalry sabre, and often a small scimitar worn on a golden chain around his neck. He retained aspects of the Count's backstory as well, including his oriental adventures; it was in those 'distant and insalubrious climes', one reporter suggested, that 'he had acquired his duskiness of complexion, and his strength of feature, and his violence of gesture, and his profusion of beard.'[5]

Sir William was a talented and powerful orator, too, eloquent and charming to his friends, fearsome and bombastic to his foes. Onlookers were drawn to 'the brilliance of his eye, the melody of his voice, and the elasticity of his muscles and limbs'; the women of the city in particular, reports suggest, found him intoxicating. If he was often uncouth and crude in his manner, he had good reason: while travelling in the east, so the lawyer at his trial would later claim, 'he had slept in the tent of the Arab, he undauntedly met the scimitar of the Turk, he had visited the tomb of the prophet Mahomet, and bowed devoutly at the holy sepulchre at Jerusalem.' During these lengthy adventures, Sir William had 'thus acquired habits and manners not accordant with [the] rules of polished life.'[6]

Exploding onto the social scene like a garish rocket, Courtenay rapidly made himself so popular that he struggled to keep up with his social commitments, being obliged to run or ride from one engagement to the next. Undaunted, he was initiated into every city fraternity that would admit him: the No.1 Lodge of Odd Fellows, the Lodge of Ancient Druids, and even the Ancient Order of Prussian Hermits. To Viscount Courtenay's borrowed titles he added a few more of his own devising: besides being the last Knight of Malta, he was also King of Jerusalem, and King of the Gypsies, too. Such honours, it seemed, he had gleaned on his travels in eastern lands.

But why, some asked, was this wealthy and renowned nobleman living in reduced circumstances at a provincial hotel? Why did he spend his time consorting with local shopkeepers, artisans and agricultural suppliers, when he knew so much of the court, high society, and fabulous foreign lands? The first question at least could be satisfyingly answered: Sir William Courtenay was being persecuted by 'traitors' within his own family – up to and including the Duke of

Cumberland, the King's brother – who conspired to deny him his rightful inheritance, and the lands and honours that were his due. Not only had Powderham Castle been wrongfully snatched from him, the noble Knight had also been swindled out of Hales Place, the large manorial estate a few miles from Canterbury, currently unoccupied after the death of Sir Edward Hales without an heir.

Conspiracies, family feuds and stolen inheritances were the stuff of popular melodrama, then as now, and for many the spice of conflict and intrigue only added to Sir William's glamorous allure. They added to his credit as well: once his full inheritance was restored, the impostor claimed, he would gain enormous riches and would reward all who had believed in him handsomely. There were rumours, indeed, that he was already receiving money, from an unknown source: oyster barrels filled with gold sovereigns were being shipped secretly to Canterbury. For many, this imaginary fortune was all too tantalising.

The valet Collard had dropped from the picture – perhaps because he expected to be paid for his services? – but Sir William quickly attracted an entourage, or retinue, content to follow him merely for the lustre of his association and the potential for reward. The watchmaker Greenwood and a medical practitioner named Robinson feature among Courtenay's Canterbury supporters. A Jewish leather merchant called Elijah Lazarus, derided by Handley as a 'foolish, half-witted fellow', quickly took Collard's place as the impostor's uniformed valet, 'dressed in as fantastical a manner, although not so gay as his master.' John Waters Banks, a local writer of impassioned religious verse, was among them, too, and the Reverend James Crowther, a clergyman of the Church of England. Most prominent was George Denne, a farmer and landowner; the impostor's biographer 'Canterburiensis' rather snarkily refers to Denne as Courtenay's 'squire', and claims he lent his new master over £1,000 during the period of their association.[7]

Doubtless many of these followers were drawn by the promise of future riches and high position. Sir William seems to have offered them places in his household, and as stewards of his estates, once they were restored to him; 'I will give the keys to all my wealth,' he had told Collard, 'and make you a gentleman forever.' Some were no doubt seduced by the stranger's exoticism and glamour, and the sheer entertainment of his company. But a few at least clearly believed everything he told them. The watchmaker Greenwood was a Quaker, and supposedly a 'respectable' man in Canterbury, but he followed Sir William loyally. Many years later he would stand weeping over his corpse, a believer to the bitter end.[8]

But still there were persistent questions about Sir William Courtenay's credentials, his behaviour, and even his sanity. For all that the newcomer claimed that he possessed 'certain papers' authenticating his claims to various properties and titles, nobody seems ever to have seen them. And while he supported himself on relentless bravado, self-confidence, and the credulity and generosity of his closest followers, others found his persona less convincing.

The public of the eighteenth and nineteenth centuries were nervously fascinated by the idea of impostors. In a society in which wealth, power and prestige very often derived from birth and inheritance, from who you *were* rather than what you had achieved, imposture posed a disruptive threat to the social fabric. Seven more years were to pass before the first human likeness was captured by photography, and in the absence of anything resembling identity documents – even birth certificates were seldom recorded – a person's name, character and standing could only be legally established in the same way they had been since the Middle Ages: by the public testimony of trustworthy people. If sufficient testimony could be mustered as to someone's credentials, it could be held to stand. The real Viscount Courtenay had been living abroad for over twenty years and had probably never been seen in Kent. Nobody in Canterbury could realistically have recognised him or found anyone to attest to his true identity. On the other hand, 'Sir William Courtenay' had a wide range of people only too willing to vouch for him.

Surprisingly, there are relatively few known examples of imposture carried to a successful conclusion – perhaps because the truly successful were never detected. In 1817, Mary Baker, a 'young deluded fantasist', had pretended that she was in fact Princess Caraboo, from the island of 'Javasu'. Her persona fooled many, including a magistrate and his family in Bristol and a group of Oxford scholars, who spent some time trying to decipher the faux princess's concocted language. In that same year, Olivia Serres claimed to be the neglected daughter of the Duke of Cumberland, and attempted to defraud his brother, the Prince Regent, by claiming that she possessed secrets that could damage the royal family. But the greatest imposture of the century had to wait several decades more: Arthur Orton, a Wapping butcher's son who had spent many years in Australia, returned to England pretending to be Roger Titchborne, heir to a baronetcy and long suspected lost at sea. The missing man's mother claimed to recognise the impostor, and granted him generous support, to the disgust of her family and wider society. The case of the 'Titchborne Claimant' would become one of the great celebrity cases of the age. But none of these figures conducted their impostures so openly, and on so public a stage, as Sir William Courtenay. Suggestions that the man was a fraud, or worse, arose almost at once. One of the first to link his name with imposture, however, was the impostor himself.[9]

In October, while still using his Count Rothschild persona, he wrote a letter to the *Kent Herald*, warning the public of the activities of 'a puppy, calling himself Captain Czernowski, a Polander' and 'an impostor on that brave and much injured nation.' The mysterious Polish captain was, of course, never again mentioned, but the letter is proof of the newcomer's talent for self-publicity. The people of Canterbury could only have imagined what dramas might lie behind the quarrels of these exotically-named foreigners! In pointing at the entirely fictitious impostor Czernowski, 'Count Rothschild' might seem to be distracting attention from himself.[10]

Some of his wilder gestures around this time, though, suggest that he was actively goading those around him to challenge his identity, perhaps so he could more vigorously assert it. As the weeks passed, so his performance grew ever more showy, ever more transgressive.

The real Viscount Courtenay, somebody had pointed out fairly early on, was known to be a man of some considerable age; notorious in his teens in the previous century, and having fled the country in 1811, the exiled aristocrat must surely be in his sixties by now. The man so boldly claiming that name, however, appeared no older than forty at most. How could this be?

As if challenging his accusers to disbelieve their very eyes, the impostor next appeared with his hair and beard turned grey with powder, walking with a stick and dressed in the iron-grey garb of an older generation. This, he seemed to be suggesting, was his real appearance; he had previously masked it with a deliberate display of youthful vigour. It seems impossible that anyone could have fallen for so crude a charade, but apparently many did so. Perhaps, by widening the plausibility gap so greatly, the impostor had turned it into a leap of faith, and those who had invested so much of their reputation in his support had no choice but to follow him across it. Or perhaps, as Charles Handley, vicar of Hernhill, would later write, 'they wanted to be deluded, and so they were deluded.'

But by accepting Sir William's transformations, many people perhaps made themselves willing accomplices in what might have seemed a colossal practical joke. Simultaneously the mysterious foreigner Count Rothschild and the patriotic Englishman Sir William, both the exotic adventurer and the pillar of the aristocracy, the rich man and the pauper, the 'old gentleman' and the 'gay young cavalier'; the impostor became an actor playing more than one role in the same drama, stepping briefly from the stage only to emerge moments later in a new guise. By demanding the people of Canterbury accept the fluidity of his identity, he effectively challenged the boundaries of a society built on trust, on fixed hierarchy, and on the prestige of names and titles. For his followers, and for those entranced and drawn along by the lustrous cavalcade of his performance, Sir William Courtenay must have seemed a protean, almost phantasmagorical figure, heroic in his defiance of all constraint, and even of reality itself.

But what was this extraordinary figure doing in Canterbury, and what did he plan to do next? No doubt many wondered just that, whether in dismay or delight. Their curiosity would have been rewarded, at the beginning of December, when Sir William Courtenay, Knight of Malta, Earl of Devon, King of Jerusalem, announced that he would be standing as an independent candidate for parliament, for the Borough of Canterbury, in the forthcoming general election.

The election of December 1832 would be the third in as many years, and the culmination of a period of extraordinary turbulence in Britain. Since the death of King George IV in 1830, the country had been swept by waves of social and political dissent. Demands for parliamentary reform, for Catholic emancipation, for the abolition of slavery in Britain's colonies and of tithes in Britain's countryside, and for a more equitable and representative society, pitched the nation into a frenzy of agitation. This was an age of emotional and demonstrative politics and intense factionalism, of 'monster meetings' and impassioned radical speeches, and of no less heated and often violent conservative reaction.

When the second reading of the Whig government's proposed reform bill was rejected by a Tory-dominated House of Lords in October 1831, riots erupted in London, Nottingham and Derby. In Bristol, forty-eight hours of violence left large areas of the city centre destroyed by fire and scores of people dead, many of them cut down by the sabres of regular dragoons unleashed upon the crowd by the panicking mayor and military commanders. Once more the country seemed upon the brink of chaos. Queen Adelaide apparently believed that 'an English Revolution is rapidly approaching', and her fate would be 'that of Marie Antoinette.'[11]

In May of the following year, after another round of political deadlock, government resignation and opposition failure, Earl Grey managed to force his reform bill through both houses, and on 7 June it entered into law as the *Representation of the People Act, 1832*. Better known today as the Great Reform Act, the new ruling granted the vote to a greater number of the male population and redrew the electoral map to reduce corruption and increase the parliamentary representation of the new manufacturing and industrial districts. A fairly moderate development, we might think; nevertheless, conservatives reacted with anguish and despair. The Kent grandee Lord Winchelsea, who had given up an initial attempt at pretending to be a reformer, believed that the Act heralded 'the downfall of his country, the closure of the Lords, the end of the Monarchy, revolution no less.' The Duke of Wellington was pithier, writing simply that 'the government of England is destroyed.'[12]

In reality, the new legislation, born of such struggle and greeted by many people with such jubilation, was intended to quell further demands rather than to answer them. It may have ended some of the more egregious abuses, and somewhat extended the electoral franchise, but many in the months that followed felt that the Act had failed to deliver on the promise of genuine change. Few in Kent would have noticed much difference as they approached the first general election after the passage of the Act. While the new ruling had increased the electorate in the country by nearly 50 per cent, still only 18 per cent of the male population were entitled to vote; women, for the first time, were officially excluded.[13]

In Canterbury, the original electorate of 1,209 freemen of the borough were now joined by 302 newly-enfranchised '£10 householders' – or men who owned or rented property of that value. Only 1,511 names appeared on the new electoral register, officially compiled for the first time under the terms of the new Act, voting for a city population of 13,649. The borough still returned two members of parliament, as before. The county of Kent, which had previously returned another two members, was now divided into east and west, with two each. This at least gave the local Ultra-Tory grandee Sir Edward Knatchbull, forced by the liberal enthusiasm for reform to concede in Kent without a fight in 1831, a chance at recovering his lost seat.[14]

Like most of the rest of Britain, Canterbury had long been gripped by the passion for factional politics. 'There are few places in the country,' the *Times* declared, 'where party feeling runs higher than this city.' There was a Whig newspaper and a

Tory newspaper. There were Whig pubs and Tory pubs – rather more of the latter, with so much of the hop-growing and brewing industry leaning in that direction. The two factions had not yet gained the full party organisation that we know today and still resembled rough consortiums of powerful men and their supporters, familiar from the Georgian era. While the Tories drew much of their support from the Anglican Church and the 'agricultural interest' of the countryside, and the Whigs from the rising wealthy classes of the new manufacturing towns, both factions were resolutely aristocratic in their outlook, and in the candidates they put forward for parliament. Even so, their definitions were in flux, with many on the Tory side, bruised by their defeats over reform, advocating abandoning the term altogether in favour of 'the broad standard of Conservatism'. On the other side, many found Whiggism too restrictive a club, and began to describe themselves principally as liberals, and the Whigs as the 'Liberal Party'.[15]

Canterbury's hinterland was still in the grip of the Tory-dominated landowning gentry and their tenant farmers, but the city population was firmly in the reformist camp. In the election of April 1831, the two determinedly aristocratic Whig candidates, the Honourable Richard Watson and Viscount Fordwich, had been returned unopposed. By the following year, with the reform bill passed, Tory fortunes appeared grimmer still. In August, the Archbishop of Canterbury, notorious for his dislike of reform, was pelted with stones and dung by a liberal mob as he left a dinner given in his honour at the Guildhall. An attempt by the conservative borough council the following month to force the nomination of two of their own faction to be mayor had led to a mutiny by the liberal freemen of the city, who propelled their own favoured reformist alderman into the position instead.

On 4 September, shortly after the first arrival in the city of 'Count Rothschild', Canterbury hosted its own Reform Festival, under Whig patronage. It was, wrote the *Kent Herald*, 'one of the most triumphant days that the friends of Reform ever witnessed in this neighbourhood.' The streets were decked with banners and ribbons, while a crowd of around 3,000 assembled in a meadow opposite the Dane John monument, just outside the city's medieval walls. There a great open-air meal was laid on, featuring 'prime sirloin and rounds of beef, legs and shoulders of mutton' and 'excellent old English plumb puddings.' After a 21-gun salute, a 'beautiful fire balloon, of various coloured silks' was launched into the sky, although it ignited very soon afterwards. More than one commentator subsequently reported that it was this very event that first suggested to the impostor that he should involve himself in Canterbury politics. If so, the idea must have taken a long time to germinate.[16]

Few in the Tory ranks, though, had any enthusiasm for the general election that December. Two reckless young conservative aristocrats had put themselves forward as candidates, but after only a few days of desultory canvassing they withdrew, crestfallen. Canterbury, it appeared, was in the pocket of the liberals, and the Whig party was guaranteed another easy, and inexpensive, electoral triumph.

So the appearance of a new challenger, only ten days before nominations closed, was sudden and unexpected. Sir William Courtenay was a man of no declared faction, with no established network of support or patronage. While many still believed that he was a fraud, an impostor, a mountebank or a madman, he had, over the few scant months since his arrival, established himself as a powerful celebrity in the city. In an age of populist politics, when a demagogue could swing crowds to his will, such a magnetic and charismatic maverick could prove highly effective.

Immediately, of course, there were claims that the Tories had put Sir William up to it. The newcomer's candidacy might create, some suggested, 'a mutiny in the popular camp, and divert the public suffrage from one at least of the sitting candidates.' Not, of course, that the Tory faction hoped or expected that he would win. But he might just humiliate and embarrass their Whig rivals and put them to unwanted trouble and expense in defeating his insurgent campaign. Courtenay himself and his followers naturally denied any such notions; the idea of standing for parliament had come to him, he declared, unbidden, and was perhaps of divine inspiration.[17]

Electoral culture in the 1830s still retained much of the boisterous Hogarthian quality of the previous century. Despite the vote being restricted to a small minority of the population, elections were mass-participation events. The candidates would set up their election committees and go forth to win over the people – not just the voters – with demonstrations of patriotic sentiment, popular spirit and public largesse. There would be marching bands and flags, free food and drink, great throngs mustered to clap and cheer their own faction, and to jeer and boo their opponents. The rowdy 'chairing' of a successful candidate around the town by his supporters often depended on 'beering' them adequately during the canvassing period. After the uncontested Canterbury election of 1831, the Tory *Kentish Gazette* reported a 'spiritless' chairing of the victorious liberals, who had 'determined to discontinue the allowance of "heavy wet" to the disappointment of the freemen, being naturally thirsty souls.'[18]

While the days of the election campaigning resembled a vast street festival, at times they spilled over into something more like open warfare. Visiting French aristocrat Alexis de Tocqueville was unimpressed, describing 'shouting speakers, stones and fisticuffs, all the orgies ... of English liberty.' In one Kent polling station, the booths were guarded by squads of 'javelin men' to keep back the mob, with carpenters on hand to make running repairs, should the enthusiasm of the surrounding crowd turn destructive. Often the candidates' own electoral committees fully conspired in the violence, employing gangs of 'bludgeon men' to intimidate opposing voters. The Tories in Kent retained the services of local pugilist William Elliot, known as Boar Shields, who was notorious for wading into the throng with flying fists. The Whigs might have considered themselves more genteel, but were not above publishing 'black lists' of skilled labourers, newly enfranchised by liberal efforts, who had subsequently broken their promises and voted Tory; such men might find their reputations and even their livelihoods threatened.[19]

More obvious corruption was enabled by the open form of polling; there was no secret ballot, and everyone could see how everyone else voted. The men of Canterbury would step into the booths and make their choice under the scrutiny not only of the polling clerk but also the candidates' own clerks and inspectors, checking that all voted as they had promised or been compelled. While it was illegal for the candidates themselves openly to bribe voters, there was no legal constraint at the time on the activities of their agents and committees; some party agents claimed commission on buying up votes in bulk, while others arranged for voters to exchange 'refreshment tickets' for beer and gin at party-affiliated public houses. Another ruse allowed voters to nominate two friends who would receive ten shillings each for protecting the party flags, or 'colours', during the election ruckus. Identifying colours for parties were imprecise at the time and often varied between constituency. The Whigs had long used blue as their badge, to the extent that they were often called the 'Blue Party', or just the 'Blues' or

'True Blues'; the colour was associated with the liberal reform movement more generally. The Kent Tories preferred purple and orange, while both sides used white.[20]

In constituencies like Canterbury which returned two members to parliament, each voter was given two voting slips, or tickets. They could therefore choose to vote for only one candidate – to *plump*, as it was called – or to *split* their vote by using both tickets for different candidates. When there was a choice of two parties running, a voter could therefore neutralise their own vote by splitting it, thereby satisfying any promises made to either side without the risk of offence. But in situations like Canterbury's in 1832, where the two sitting candidates both belonged to the same party, the option of splitting votes gave an advantage to independent outsiders, and in particular to maverick figures like Sir William Courtenay.

'On Friday evening,' reported the Canterbury correspondent of the *Times* on 11 December, 'a long address was circulated, calling upon the citizens to support a third candidate, signing himself Sir William Percy Honeywood Courtenay, Knight of Malta, which, from its singular composition and open truths, was much sought after ...' This electoral address was printed as a broadsheet, copies of which later sold for between one and five shillings, and opened as follows:

TO THE FREEMEN AND INDEPENDENT ELECTORS OF THE ANCIENT AND HONOURABLE CITY OF CANTERBURY

Patriots and Brother Countrymen: the time is now arrived, when the true feelings of English blood must proclaim through the votes of your Members of Parliament, whether Englishmen will be free, or Englishmen will be in bondage. The present awful and alarming state of the British Constitution of King, Lords, and Commons, loudly calls forth every energy of her strength in protecting her Agriculture and Commerce, and bad is the blood of that Englishman who does not in her defence, boldly and manfully assert his birthright to Purity of Election ... [21]

Ironic as it may seem for an impostor to set out his stall on the promise of purity – truthfulness and lack of corruption – such a pitch was calculated to appeal to a public grown weary of political shenanigans. The historian Rohan McWilliam has suggested that the political writings of impostors in this period 'veered between romantic Toryism and radical Liberalism,' and Sir William Courtenay's initial address was composed of precisely those elements. It combined rambunctious and aggrieved patriotism (England was 'once the pride and glory of the world,' but 'if there be not unity at home, how is it possible that the voice of the British Lion can send forth his thunderbolts as the Lord of the Isles?') with familiar radical calls for reform – on tithes, for example ('The tithes of England are the property of the poor ... And the greatest abomination in the sight of God and man is that the poor of the land should be robbed of their right ...').[22]

It also issued some crowd-pleasing blasts against political factionalism, guaranteed to appeal to those who had endured years of reforming rhetoric and social strife, only to see the same band of smug aristocrats once more monopolising power ('What is man, if his mind is shackled to any party, whether it be in church or state? ... Any man who belongs to a party, whether Tory or Whig, cannot serve the public.').

But what might have distinguished Courtenay's address from those of his competitors was its strongly religious colouring. In places it reads more like a thunderous religious tract: 'No true wisdom, riches or honors [sic] are attainable by human means. All these gifts are the free election of God in Christ, for in him was the Godhead bodily.' A little later the writer pulls the two together, in what must have seemed an overly neat juxtaposition: 'Therefore, if Christ is made the object of our faith, sound politics as a statesman is the effect. How can two walk together unless they are agreed?'

While the Evangelical revival of preceding decades had lent far greater passion and energy to religious expression, few political speakers of the 1830s drew upon its language. There was quite enough rhetoric in the arguments of reform and reaction, and the familiar clashing discourses of party politics, without the need for spiritual reflections. Those that did reference their faith generally contented themselves with a conventional piety, perhaps wary of exhibiting an unseemly 'enthusiasm'. Sir William Courtenay lacked a party platform or an established political direction, but his radical evocations of faith would nevertheless have given his words an authority and a moral purpose that his listeners and readers would instantly have recognised, and perhaps respected.

'By the permission of Almighty God,' his broadsheet ends, 'and under his protection as my only friend, I will meet you at the hustings ... Suffice it, for the present to say, that I am the heir of that family which none in Europe can excel, neither in ancient pedigree or illustrious action ... SIR WILLIAM PERCY HONEYWOOD COURTENAY, Knight of Malta. Rose Inn, Canterbury, Dec. 5, 1832.'

By mid-afternoon the following Saturday, a crowd had gathered in the street outside the Rose, agitators among them calling for Sir William to make an appearance. Like many another populist demagogue to come, he chose to appear on high above his supporters, addressing them from the hotel balcony while dressed in his militaristic finery. At the culmination of his speech, the impostor threw handfuls of coins down into the assembled crowd below. A writer for the *Times* called it 'a scene bordering much on the ludicrous,' but did not see fit to record the content of his speech. 'The gentleman is supposed to be insane,' the report concluded.[23]

According to other witnesses, Sir William was a skilled and powerful orator, as several of his quoted pronouncements and exchanges suggest. He seems to have been able to think very quickly, responding to calls and ripostes from the crowd, his opponents, and from hecklers alike. One witness likened his style to that of Henry 'Orator' Hunt, a well-known radical reformist campaigner of the day; Hunt's address to a massive crowd in St Peter's Fields in Manchester in 1819 had been broken up by cavalry in the 'Peterloo' Massacre. The impostor Courtenay had very likely seen Hunt speaking in London in more recent years.

The tastes of the crowd in the 1830s street tended towards the melodramatic, the grotesque and the gaudy. They thrilled to celebrity gossip about actresses and aristocrats, and tales of conspiracy among the wealthy and powerful. This was an age of mountebanks, mesmerists and puppeteers, sideshow prestidigitators and quack doctors, when the boundaries between popular theatrics, preaching and politics were never as clearly defined as their practitioners might have liked. John Belchem, in his history of nineteenth century popular radicalism, describes 'a burlesque "counter theatre" which mocked and demystified the establishment and its public ceremonial,' a form of politics intended to 'ridicule establishment pageantry and to out-match it.' In this environment, Sir William Courtenay in his glittering tinsel and velvet, 'bedizened with gimcracks,' as a contemporary writer scoffed, was not so much of an aberration as he might have seemed. Instead, he was an emanation of the popular mood, a vastly enlarged phantasm of his age, boisterous and blustering, bringing the colour and flash and imagination of the stage to the political arena. And by all accounts, the crowd loved him for it.[24]

Courtenay may have lacked a proper election committee and later named the religious poet John Waters Banks as his sole agent, but over the days that followed he set about publicising his candidacy with heroic gusto. He had taken to riding a horse, a grey or white mare so spirited, he claimed, that only he could control it. The Reverend Charles Handley, himself a keen judge of horseflesh, called it a 'scraggy bit of blood', while another witness claimed the animal was a worn-out old thoroughbred, lately used as a coach-horse, and not worth forty shillings. Sir William also commissioned one or more local artists to produce paintings and etchings of him dressed in his finery; he never paid for them, although the impostor's later notoriety allowed at least one unfortunate painter to recoup his losses and make a considerable profit.[25]

On 10 December, nomination day, an extraordinary crowd thronged the Guildhall of Canterbury. On the hustings, the two Whig candidates, Richard Watson and Lord Viscount Fordwich, were duly proposed and seconded. Their speeches, however, were almost drowned out by the stamping, clapping, shouts and roaring laughter of the spectators. 'Courtenay, we want Courtenay!' the reporter of the *Kentish Observer* recorded them yelling.

Sir William, dressed in his gold-trimmed crimson velvet jacket and cape, was now proposed and seconded by Canterbury grocer Mr Southee and the watchmaker Greenwood. He commenced his own speech with theatrical bravado, leaping up onto the central table and turning to address the crowd. Beneath the portraits of civic worthies, the racks of arms and the ancient battle flags of the Kent regiments, Sir William struck a heroic stance, throwing his voice to the furthest extent of the chamber. To the applause of the multitude, he promised to 'reform the House of Commons ... take the burden of tax from the shoulders of the poor and industrious classes, and fix it on those of the rich.' Again mixing blazing reformist rhetoric with appeals to the lost greatness of the past, he proposed 'a return to the good old days of roast beef and mutton, and plenty of prime, nut brown ale.'[26]

Clearly he knew the tastes of his public. His speech was greeted with roars of acclaim. An initial vote was taken by show of hands – the old method, still used to decide elections that were in little doubt – and, to enormous popular glee, Lord Fordwich and Sir William Courtenay were declared winners. The Honourable Richard Watson, of course, refused to concede on such a basis, and a full poll of voters was announced for the following day.

Under the terms of the new Reform Act, voting could only extend for a maximum of two days – previously polls had run for as many as fifteen. After the first day's polling in the Guildhall, however, the count revealed that Sir William, despite the enthusiastic uproar of the nominations, had received only 177 votes, fewer than half that of either of the other candidates. One local journalist suggested that the impostor's antics, both at the nomination and during the polling that followed, had alienated as many as they had entertained: 'the wretched buffoonery of the man did then and there deter a considerable number ... from encouraging by their votes such an outrage on common decency.'[27]

Undeterred, Courtenay and his supporters urged the people of Canterbury to greater efforts, the printing press in an outhouse of the Rose Inn banging out further public addresses through the day and night. 'COURTENAY FOR EVER!' one declares, before pointing out that over a thousand freemen of the city had not yet taken the opportunity to vote:

> We have the opportunity now to do it, commence polling early, firmly, freely, and determinately. Elect the boast of Canterbury – the orator of modern times – the True Blue – and the friend of the people. Do not split your votes, but give *Plumpers*. Pay no attention to the trickery of time-serving and interested men. But have Courtenay, elect Courtenay, and proclaim Courtenay for ever.[28]

Interestingly, Courtenay here publicly declares himself a 'True Blue' – a reformer, that is, aligned with the liberals of the Whig Party. He may have originally been prompted to stand by the Tory faction, but he was now aiming to fight Fordwich and Watson on their own turf.

An address issued on the last day of polling provides more reasonable advice for undecided voters, or those constrained by promises to the other candidates: 'Split your votes to keep your word, but never turn out old Courtenay.' This one claims to issue from 'Powderham Castle, Devonshire', a harbinger of the impostor's later mystical ability to be in two places at once. Another published flyer advises 'those whose votes have been refused, in consequence of having received parochial relief' to apply to Sir William, who will insist on their behalf. Still another, probably issued at the same time, broadens Courtenay's reformist stance even further, to include universal male suffrage on the basis of national service: 'Every man who is willing to serve his country by the laws of England, from the age of eighteen to forty-five, is entitled to vote, openly, manly, and without fear. Sir William Courtenay will prove this fundamental principle, that Universal Suffrage and Annual Parliaments are the only just rights of true born Englishmen.'[29]

So great was the confusion on the first day's polling that the Sheriff ordered the construction of a third polling station in the Butter Market. There, 'the Knight of Malta was to be seen clad in velvet and gold, and flying from station to station as fast as a barouche and pair could convey him, haranguing the multitude, and performing a variety of manoeuvres ... not exactly in accordance with the important business of an electioneering contest.' By four o'clock, the polls were closed, and at the final count Sir William Courtenay was found to have received 375 votes. Watson and Fordwich, however, had gathered 834 and 802 votes respectively.[30]

With the electors and other spectators once more gathered in the Guildhall, the victorious members made their speeches; the Honourable Richard Watson was glad that the people of Canterbury had chosen moderate liberals as their representatives, rather than elect an Ultra [Tory] or Radical to the seat. Lord Fordwich, meanwhile, made a mocking reference to 'the noble knight of Malta in his gorgeous apparel,' and said that he expected Sir William Courtenay would now take up his rightful seat in the House of Lords. This time, luckily, there was a reporter willing to record Sir William's response, together with comic accents and flourishes, and the interjections of the crowd ('Applause' and 'Immense Applause'; and, with an eerie note of foreshadowing, 'Good, good ... I have been looking all my life for a man like him, and now he has dropp'd from the clouds!').[31]

Responding first to Mr Watson's address, Sir William told the assembly that he was glad to be neither Ultra nor Radical, but instead was 'the man who would defend the rights of the people, and is ready to spill his blood in defence of old England.' He than claimed, quite bizarrely and uniquely, to have 'fought and killed hundreds in Ethiopia, in Abyssinia, and all over the world.' Turning next to Lord Fordwich, he asked 'if a man such as myself, of illustrious blood and high *character*, has a right in this free country to wear what he pleases without asking his leave or anyone else's?'

So far, the crowd was with him, cheering his every word. The enthusiasm slackened as Sir William spoke of his care for 'the orphan, the fatherless and the widow', and asked his audience to 'go to the widow Lewin, who lives near the Cattle Market, and ask what I have done for her.' This, apparently, elicited a more negative reaction: whether the widowed Mrs Lewin was an unpopular figure, or the nature of her relations with Sir William were held to be disreputable, is sadly lost to the record.

He was on firmer ground with his closing points. Courtenay would, he declared, refuse to support either the Tories, who had 'robbed the poor man and the tradesman, the artisan and the labourer, of the sweat of their brow,' or the Whigs, whose 'show of reform' had 'held the cup to the people's lips but would not let them taste.' He closed with a renewed sense of purpose, and defiance: 'Lord Courtenay has offered you men of England plenty of sport at this election, and now by the Lord Harry he will offer himself for their choice tomorrow, *for the county*.'[32]

It could be that, as one local writer suggested, Sir William Courtenay's electoral campaign had always been intended as a joke, 'more a whim than of serious intention', and no doubt many in Canterbury took it that way. Sir William had certainly offered them 'plenty of sport'. He turned what could have been yet another one-sided and rather genteel borough election into a carnival that people would remember for decades to come.[33]

Years later, an elderly citizen of Canterbury would claim that Courtenay's support had come almost entirely from Tory partisans, 'and at least 300 respectable Conservatives voted for him in order to annoy the opposition party.' This may be true: the listing in the Canterbury Poll Book for the 1832 election shows that the majority of those who voted for Sir William chose him as their sole candidate – casting *plumpers* – rather than split their vote with another. Among them were doubtless many who would normally have voted Tory, if a candidate had been available. Of those who did split, most went for Fordwich as a second choice, with a lesser number opting for Watson.[34]

But there is also little doubt that a great many people took Sir William Courtenay rather more seriously. Took him, in fact, as a champion of sorts. That the majority of these supporters came from the poorer classes, and therefore lacked the vote under even the new reformed system, is unsurprising. More remarkable is the number of votes the impostor did poll, and the 'almost idolatrous devotion' he inspired among 'no small number of higher rank.'[35]

And even now, they had learned, Courtenay refused to concede defeat. The nominations for the East Kent county election would be held on 17 December, with polling due to commence a week after that. For the people of Canterbury, there was plenty more sport to come. A jubilant crowd – numbering in their thousands, according to the *Times* correspondent – conducted Sir William from the Guildhall, as if he had indeed been the victor. In traditional style, they took the horses from the traces of his carriage and drew him themselves up and down the High Street and St Dunstan's, roaring out *Rule Britannia* as a fife and drum played. Sir William 'thanked the assembled populace at every corner of the street, being dressed in his scarlet robes, and Turkey cap, and continually flourishing his scimitar to persons who opposed him.'[36]

At the Rose Inn, the champion appeared once more on his balcony above the street, scattering coins to the milling throng below him. Hoarse from speechmaking and bombast, he could make only the briefest address, but his subdued words were drowned out by the cheering and cries of the crowd.

None could know it, but this moment of popular acclaim on the balcony of the Rose Inn would perhaps be the high point of the impostor's career. After this, Sir William Courtenay's fortunes would plunge. He would have a long way to fall, before he could rise again in a new and far more terrifying guise.

2. 'TRUTH BEARS OFF THE VICTORY'

The rain was cold and the road was muddy as the long cavalcade straggled the six miles from Canterbury to the racecourse on Barham Downs, where the nominations would take place. Earlier that day the factions had assembled in the city with their drums and marching bands, under their colours. Sir Edward Knatchbull's Tories carried a huge orange and purple banner before them, presented by the conservative ladies of East Kent and reputed to have cost £500. It was rumoured that the radicals had promised to capture the banner and destroy it; one hundred farm labourers in clean white gabardine smocks escorted the flag on the journey to the hustings, promised as much food and as much beer as they could drink to defend it, each man armed with a stout bludgeon and wearing an orange hat-band emblazoned with the name KNATCHBULL.

Sir Edward himself, riding alongside his colour-guard, perhaps did not share their rowdy enthusiasm. He was a leading member of the Ultra Tory faction whose opposition to Catholic emancipation had helped bring down the Duke of Wellington's government back in 1830, thereby precipitating the political storms that had lately engulfed the country. He had subsequently opposed electoral reform, with no greater success. An MP since 1820, when he had taken over the East Kent seat from his father, the fifty-year-old baronet Knatchbull regarded political power and status as his birthright. He was fine example of a Tory country grandee, a man of principle, although 'not very bright by nature,' as the radical MP William Cobbett put it. A strong defender and advocate for the agricultural interest, according to his wife's biographer Knatchbull was 'at his best when speaking on subjects like cattle, seed, malt and apples.'[1]

In both the historical record and his own letters he comes across as a stolid, rather stubborn, cantankerous man, inclined to see in the slightest symptom of progress a sure sign that the sky is falling.* In recent years his mood had been further soured by the antics of his romantically-inclined son, aged twenty-four and more interested in German poetry than agriculture; Norton Knatchbull had returned from a Grand Tour of Italy and the Rhineland to announce his betrothal to a young woman of sixteen, whose flighty modern attitudes and spendthrift ways Sir Edward found deplorable. Young Norton accompanied his father to the hustings that bleak morning in December, along with his new wife Mary.[2]

Having lost his East Kent seat the year before, Knatchbull now intended to regain it. His principal adversary, however, was not the Whig Sir William Cosway, whose supporters marched beneath the 'true blue' banner of reform, but his former Tory colleague John Pemberton Plumptre, who had so passionately embraced the cause of reform that he was now presenting himself as 'liberal but anti-revolutionary.' The handsome, humourless

---

* He also had truly appalling handwriting, which is always liable to annoy researchers. As his daughter-in-law wrote: 'No one knows Sir E and no one understands him.'

Plumptre had once been the favoured suitor of Fanny Knight, niece of the novelist Jane Austen and now Sir Edward's wife. But it was the political betrayal that Edward detested, and he now regarded Plumptre as his personal enemy.[3]

How he might have regarded the fourth candidate presenting himself for nomination that day is less certain. Sir William Courtenay had last appeared only three days previously, at the Kent and Canterbury Cattle Fair. It was a grand occasion, concluding with a dinner held in the market room attended by Knatchbull and other local grandees. Sir William had cut an eccentric figure among them, attracting attention with 'many mad freaks,' as a local journalist put it, 'such as jumping upon the bare backs of some spirited colts, and trying their mettle as well as showing his own.' By these and other feats, the newcomer made 'such a display as fully to convince every person that he was insane.'[4]

Knatchbull would have observed the impostor's borough political campaigning from the sidelines, perhaps amused at the discomfiture of the Whig candidates. But he would not have regarded Courtenay as any sort of threat for the county seat. Out here in the agricultural heartland, where 'the Tory gentry rallied to the cause and the tenant farmers did their duty,' the gallivanting Sir William could not hope to summon the sort of popular mobs that had flocked to him in Canterbury.[5]

By eleven o'clock, the processions had reached the racecourse, where a horseshoe of big farm wagons was drawn up facing the grandstand. Between twelve and fifteen thousand people had braved the cold and wet to witness the nominations, hear the speeches, and enjoy the pageantry and the largesse of the candidates and their committees. The pugilist Boar Shields had accompanied Knatchbull's party and offered an open invitation to fight anyone from the radical faction who opposed him;

the radicals had taken to taunting Knatchbull's Tories with cries of 'Bullock's liver and barley bread!', after one Tory canvasser had suggested that the poor could be fed cheaply on such a diet.[6]

Sir Edward was proposed and seconded, followed by Sir William Cosway and J. P. Plumptre Esquire. The proposal of the fourth candidate, Sir William Percy Honeywood Courtenay, immediately ran into a hitch: his seconder, the Canterbury surgeon Robinson, was found to be ineligible as he was not a freeholder in the county district. After a brief delay, the baker Chapman stepped forward to support the nomination, explaining that Sir William owned more acreage in Kent than any other candidate, and (rather less encouragingly) that there could be no question of his identity.

Throughout the candidates' speeches that followed, the impostor continued to draw attention to himself, clapping and cheering in a mocking way long after everyone else had fallen silent. He had at first adopted his 'aged gentleman' guise, too, leaning on a stick, but soon resorted to his usual appearance. Rather than take his place on the grandstand with the other candidates, he had positioned himself in the enclosure directly in front of it, occupied by the journalists, perhaps so they could catch every word of his own address. 'His antics were approaching to buffoonery,' wrote the correspondent for the *Times*, 'and his dress, black velvet with silver epaulettes, red velvet cap with gold band, and his countenance almost enveloped in mustachios – in fact, a perfect Don Whiskerando, attracted considerable attention ... so full of *rhodomontade* were his speeches that the reporters closed their books, declining to take notes of such an outrage on common sense.'[7]

Luckily somebody at least was taking notes, and we can gain an idea of Sir William's latest platform. Alert to his public, he had abandoned most of the more overtly reformist rhetoric of his Canterbury speeches. Already, in a printed pamphlet of around this time, he had denounced the Reform Bill as 'a disgrace to children of four years old,' and 'only fit food for the king's tobacco pipe.' Instead, the impostor put himself forward in the agricultural interest, taking almost a traditional Tory stance, mustering his fury only in his opposition to the payment of tithes to the church. After accusing Cosway of self-interest and Plumptre of hypocrisy, he merely suggested that Sir Edward Knatchbull had been seen canvassing for votes on a Sunday with a local parson; Sir Edward did not deny it – he had committed no crime, had merely spoken to one prospective supporter, and refused to regard such activity as improper on the Sabbath – and the impostor gave ground with surprising grace.[8]

After this the gathering dispersed, the candidates with their bands and flags and supporters trudging back through the mire to Canterbury, where further parading and hot dinners awaited. Had Sir William Courtenay already guessed that he had overextended his reach, and was about to suffer a fall? As the clergyman Charles Handley of Hernhill, also present that day and shortly to cast his vote for Knatchbull, put it, the impostor 'soon found he had mistaken his powers & it was one thing to come before the mob at Canterbury, and a very different thing to offer himself to the gentry and freeholders on Barham Down.' His conduct that day, noted the *Kent Herald*, 'excited the merriment of some, and the pity of others.'[9]

Over the next three days, before the polls opened, Sir William attempted with great energy to spread his fame and reputation across the hinterland of East Kent. There would be polling booths in Canterbury and Ramsgate, Ashford and New Romney, and Sittingbourne, too, and Sir William would need to canvass the voters at every location. As in the borough

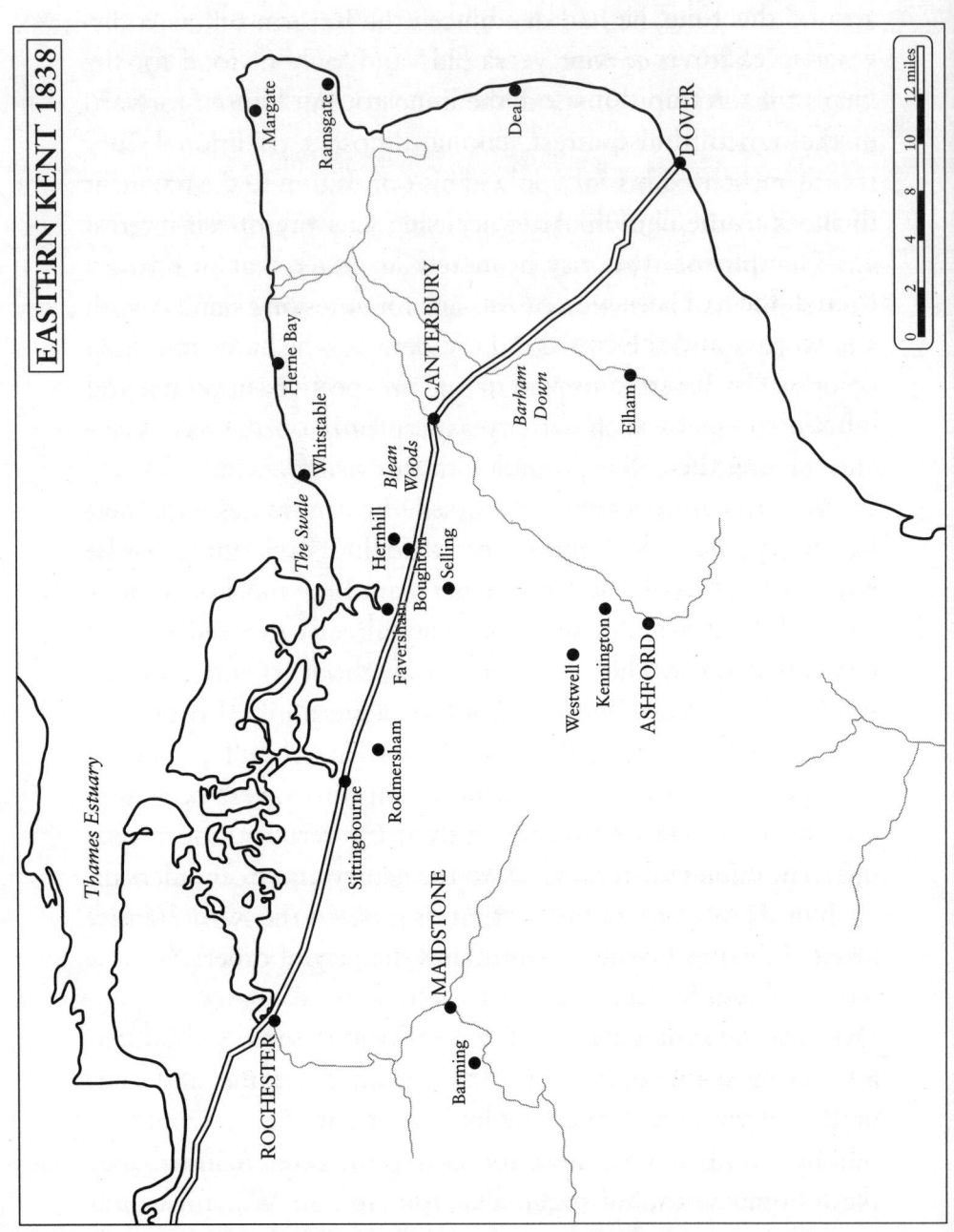

of Canterbury, the Reform Act had marginally increased the size of the Kent electorate. But the 7,026 registered voters were spread over a much greater area, and the vast majority were still the traditionally inclined tenant farmers who voted dutifully with the squire. The majority of newly enfranchised men were beholden to the party interests that had secured them their vote, and Sir William Courtenay meant nothing to them.

Nevertheless, the impostor and his little retinue gamely toured the constituency, riding the public coaches between Canterbury and the coastal towns, and up and down the long straight Roman road to Sittingbourne. Even decades later, the inhabitants of these places would remember his first appearance among them. 'He used to kiss all the children (me among the number) and seemed very fond of them,' one woman from Boughton said. 'He carried a lot of white peppermints about with him and distributed them among the youngsters.'

Another recalled a different reaction. As a child, she had heard that the Knight of Malta would be visiting her hometown of Whitstable by coach and was so terrified that she hid behind a door on news of his approach. Her mother told her that Sir William was 'going to do good,' and she should come and see him. 'He had an immense black beard down to his waist,' she remembered, 'and was a very fine man.'[10]

But all the peppermints in Kent could not swing the tide in Sir William's favour. In Sittingbourne, at the end of the first day's polling, he learned that he had secured no votes at all. Worse, as he rode back along the highway a small girl dashed into the road and was trampled by his horse. The child was not badly injured, but it seemed a bad omen.

Sure enough, when the votes were counted at the end of the following day, Sir William Courtenay still had no votes in Sittingbourne. He had no votes in Ashford or in Maidstone, none in New Romney. In fact, in the entire East Kent division he had polled only four in total. Two were from his proposer George Denne of Canterbury, and his seconder John Chapman of Westgate Holy Cross. A third was from a William Huxtep of Patrixborne, and the last came from a London man called Reynolds, who happened to own land in Ramsgate and thereby gained a freeholder vote.

Interestingly, three of the four – including Courtenay's ultra-loyal 'squire' Denne – had split their votes rather than *plumping* for him alone. All three had also voted for Sir Edward Knatchbull, the Tory candidate. Knatchbull was duly returned, although to his great displeasure he came second to his turncoat rival Plumptre. Sir William was not the only candidate nursing a grudge that evening.[11]

Courtenay's reaction came very quickly, in a handbill initially rejected by a Canterbury publisher for being potentially libellous, but later circulated in the city:

> O Yes! O Yes! O Yes! I, Lord Viscount William Courtenay, of Powderham Castle, Devon, do hereby proclaim Sir Thomas Tilden, Sir Brook Brydges, Sir Edward Knatchbull and Sir William Cosway, four cowards unfit to represent, or to assist in returning members of Parliament to serve the brave men of Kent ...
>
> Any gentleman desiring to know the reasons why Lord Courtenay so publicly exposes backbiters, any man of honor shall have satisfaction at his hands, and in a public way according to the laws of our land, trial by combat – when the Almighty God, the Lord of Hosts is his name, can decide the 'truth' whether it is a libel or not. I worship truth as my God, and will die for it – and upon this we will see who is the strongest, God or man.[12]

But the impostor's invitation to settle the matter by single combat went unheeded. On the last day of December, the *Kentish Gazette* reported that he had recently put to sea at Dover in an open boat, in the teeth of a winter gale, and sailed to Boulogne for some undisclosed purpose. Whether he ever landed in France, and what he did there, remains unclear, but he was back in England quickly enough, and once again attracting notice.

Sir William's brief experience of canvassing in the areas surrounding Canterbury had introduced him to a new set of associates, and new fields for his endeavours, and as the new year dawned, he began to spread his influence out into the countryside of Kent. He may have succeeded in gaining a rather wider circle of friends among the local gentry and landowners in these districts than was later apparent. Even the caustic Charles Handley, vicar of Hernhill, was somewhat equivocal about the newcomer, who 'had acquired such refined cunning and deep deceit as to render his graceful manner of familiar conversation irresistible, among the labouring classes and in many cases among persons of better condition.'[13]

Handley's statement almost suggests a personal knowledge of this 'irresistible conversation'. Could he too have been, perhaps briefly, impressed by the charismatic Knight of Malta? If Sir William was ever a visitor to Handley's parlour at Mount Ephraim, the clergyman is careful not to mention it.

Many of those who encountered him around this time refer to Sir William's deep religiosity. Since his first appearance in Canterbury he had exhibited a fervent piety, of course, but now it gained still greater force. Perhaps, with his route to political power temporarily blocked, he hoped like so many charlatans before and since to claim new authority as a lay preacher or religious advisor. Or perhaps he felt that God had decreed his electoral defeats as he intended a different calling, and his mission should now become a spiritual one. Either way, many were deeply impressed. George Francis, who owned Fairbrook farm less than a mile west of Hernhill, would later confess that he had 'never in his life enjoyed greater pleasure than in hearing [Sir William] explain the Scriptures.'

In his statement to the Parliamentary Select Committee, Francis says that he first met the man who called himself Sir William Courtenay in December 1832; this would have been at the time of his election canvassing, either in Canterbury or the surrounding districts. Francis was a good dozen years older than Courtenay, but clearly took him for a gentleman, and had no trouble accepting his claims of aristocracy and great wealth; he was 'captivated,' as Charles Handley puts it, 'by Sir William's fine dress and winning manner.' Like the impostor's other followers back in Canterbury, Francis rapidly developed an enormous respect and admiration for the younger man, verging on reverence. He invited the stranger to come and visit Fairbrook, whenever he might require lodgings outside of the city. Courtenay took him up on the offer, and made several stays with Francis and his family, of up to a fortnight at a time.[14]

Fairbrook appears much the same today as it did in the 1830s: a neat redbrick house with a tiled roof, just off a lane that runs north from the back road between Boughton and Faversham. The white-painted sash windows look out eastwards across a gentle valley to the wooded ridge beyond, where the tower of Hernhill church is just visible through the trees. The correspondent for the *Times* described it as 'a pretty little brick villa with a garden in front, and a very nice orchard in the rear,' although the row of fine trees that once shaded the lane have since gone, and the open fence that edged the garden has been replaced by a dense laurel hedge.[15]

The house was probably built by George Francis himself, or perhaps by his father, in the first decades of the nineteenth century. As a family home, it perhaps replaced the sixteenth-century timber-framed cottage down by the road junction, or the other old buildings further up the lane, subsequently used as labourers' accommodation. The red brick and tile, the sash windows and the front garden, all speak of a desire for rather more respectability, even gentility, than the family might previously have possessed. Francis farmed a few hundred acres of wheat, hops and orchards, and was a churchwarden of Boughton and a member of the Faversham Farmers' Club. He certainly had aspirations to a higher station, for his children if not for himself. Charles Handley, in a damning verdict which has since settled over Francis like a shroud, calls him 'a person of small understanding & little education, but of great pride and insatiable vanity.'[16]

This seems unjust, and Handley was probably just trying to shift any such accusations from himself. Francis may have been aspirational, overly earnest and rather prickly about status, and deeply gullible, too, but for all he was condemned subsequently by many in the area, nothing in the evidence he gave after the impostor's death suggests that he was unusually vain or stupid.

All the same, the yeoman farmer with aspirations to gentility, denying or distancing himself from the life of the soil that had sustained his forebears, was a familiar figure of the day, and commonly mocked and derided. In 1842, the journalist Alexander Somerville spoke to a Dorsetshire labourer who described just such a man, a farmer who has his daughter 'playing on the piano on a Saturday night to drown the noise of them brutes of labouring men what come to get their wages through a hole in the wall; what cannot be allowed to set foot within a farmer's house now-a-days ... lest they defile the house of a master what gets rich as they get poor.' Was the owner of Fairbrook perhaps a similar sort of character?[17]

George Francis may have wished Sir William to take a role in his household beyond honoured guest and religious advisor. Decades later, the nonagenarian George Packman, who lived nearby during this period, claimed that the impostor 'used to court a lady at Fairbrook, but in consequence of his getting a little fast with her they turned him adrift.' The lady in question was most likely his host's eldest daughter, seventeen-year-old Eliza Jane Francis. Her twin brother Robert was possibly away at school at this time; Francis's unusually named younger son Vinus, daughters Ellen and Jane, aged thirteen and eleven, and eight-year-old George Junior still lived at home. If George Francis at some point intended Courtenay to marry his daughter, Handley's comments on the man's 'great pride and insatiable vanity' might find their focus. But, as we will see, Miss Francis herself appears to have gained an exaggerated regard for her father's unusual house-guest, and may have been the guiding force behind the proposed match.[18]

There were also two other women at Fairbrook: Francis's wife Martha and his unmarried sister-in-law Mary Horne. Thirty-six years old, Mary wore glasses for her short-sightedness and carried an ear-trumpet for her partial deafness. She, too, developed very strong feelings for their guest, and together with her niece Eliza would continue to revere Sir William long after George Francis had abandoned the cause.

Many of the accounts of Courtenay's activities in Canterbury dwell on the strong attraction felt towards him by women. Old ladies, we are told, used to hug him, ply him with glasses of gin and bestow kisses upon him, while younger women waved handkerchiefs from their windows as he passed in the street. Now he was out in the countryside, and further from verifiable truth, the rumours and allegations grew warmer still. 'Respectable tradesmen's wives,' wrote the popular scandal-sheet *Penny Satirist* in June 1838, 'thought nothing of kissing either his hands or feet, and many a husband among the peasantry has been known to quit his bed, and leave Sir William to rest beside his wife.'[19]

This kind of scurrilous accusation has since become part of Courtenay's legend. It seems unlikely. The impostor was moving amid a tightly knit and often interrelated network of families and settlements, where privacy was a rare luxury and rumour travelled fast. For all their respect for the newcomer and his gentry or aristocratic status, few would have risked their reputation with any wife-swapping antics. The *Satirist*'s story sounds very much the sort of thing that the metropolitan elite believed of the benighted 'peasantry', and that people have always believed about mysterious charismatic leaders. The only possible evidence for Courtenay exercising a sort of *droit-de-seigneur* might be the case of Charles Kennett, whose cottage on Dunkirk Common was another of the impostor's temporary residences during this period. In October 1833, Kennett's wife gave birth to a son, baptised William Courtenay Kennett. The child would presumably have been conceived in mid-February, exactly the period when Sir William was in the area, and perhaps even living at the cottage. But it would be very unlikely for Charles Kennett to advertise any cuckoldry so openly. Other local friends and supporters of the impostor would name children in his honour, too. The Blaxland family of Graveney and the Ransoms of Boughton would give their children the middle name Courtenay, as would William Wills, the future mainstay of the impostor's local support. Like them, Kennett probably named his child in honour of a man he admired, and continued to respect, rather than in recognition of some secret paternity.[20]

Besides, this admiration and respect had quickly spread far beyond the labouring people and small farmers. As early as 7 January 1833, at Boughton church, Sir William Courtenay stood as sponsor at the baptism of the daughter of Commander James Gabriel Gordon of the Royal Navy. Gordon had served gallantly at sea during the Napoleonic War and had since overseen the naval dockyard at Sheerness. Known by courtesy as Captain Gordon, he had met the impostor the previous December and had quickly been impressed by 'his character for religion and morality,' later claiming that his 'religious habits are as strong as any man he knew.' Indisputably a gentleman, Captain Gordon RN was about as far from a common labourer or even a small farmer as one could get in the immediate environs of Boughton. If such a man believed in Sir William Courtenay's credentials, good character and stainless morality, who could gainsay it?[21]

Over the winter of 1832–33, the bare fields and muddy lanes around Boughton and Hernhill can have held few inducements to wander far from home. Nevertheless, Sir William Courtenay kept up his roaming and visiting, alone or accompanied by his faithful retinue, and word of his movements flew ahead of him. He frequented Sunday services at the local churches, spoke at meetings of his supporters in local pubs, and attended concerts performed under his patronage at Faversham and in Canterbury. In February he teamed up with a travelling entertainer, Mr Fitzgerald, who was touring the east coast towns with a satirical comedy lecture about the fashionable pseudo-sciences of Physiognomy and Phrenology. Courtenay and Fitzgerald formed a double bill, appearing to packed houses in Ramsgate, Margate and Deal. Sir William seems to have been the main draw; he was greeted by pealing church bells in Folkestone and in Hythe, and by 'deafening cheers and waving of hats and handkerchiefs.'[22]

But this nineteenth-century version of end-of-the-pier celebrity showmanship was only intended to stoke Sir William's local support; he had a greater and more serious cause to pursue in the meantime. Besides his pleasant hours of biblical explanation with Farmer Francis and family at Fairbrook, his time in the parlour with Miss Eliza, and his 'irresistible' conversation with gentlemen and ladies of the 'better classes', Courtenay was also associating during this period with the working people of the surrounding parishes. His ongoing spiritual mission had led him to become the 'friend of the poor cottager and the labouring man.' And, to the deep chagrin of George Francis, it was not just Charles Kennett that was the focus of his charity and friendship.

On the first day of March, Sir William was in Rochester attending the trial of some Whitstable men arrested for smuggling. They had been aboard the vessel *Admiral Hood* when it was waylaid by the Navy revenue cutter *Lively* off Goodwin Sands and were accused of throwing a number of tubs or casks containing contraband spirits into the sea before their capture. 'Attired in grotesque costume,' and with 'a small scymatar suspended from his neck by a massy gold chain,' Courtenay first put himself forward as legal counsel to one of the accused sailors. He then gave evidence for the defence: he had been at sea himself that day, he told the court, aboard the fishing boat *Active* of Deal, and had seen the tubs drifting on the tide from France, hours before the appearance of the *Admiral Hood* or the revenue cutter. His evidence did no good; the men were convicted anyway. Courtenay next drew his sword and declared that he would 'take the whole crew of the *Lively*, aye and double the crew, with the lawyer at the back,' in mortal combat, but they declined the offer. He ended his day by storming the stage of a nearby theatre, after a performance given in his honour, and leading the audience in a passionate rendition of *God Save the King*.[23]

The impostor seems to have been trying by this strange intervention to broaden his potential constituency even further. Kent had a strong maritime tradition, and smugglers were often regarded as local heroes rather than criminals. Courtenay admired the character of the accused men, he said, and thought them excellent seamen; if taxation were removed from the poor, he later claimed, then smuggling would cease. Clearly, he now intended to be the fisherman's and smuggler's friend, as well as the friend and protector of the poor cottager, the labourer, the widow and the orphan. It may have been this sort of activity which came to dismay George Francis, who clearly felt little connection with the lower and criminal classes, and wished to keep himself, his family and his guest from any closer association with them.

Luckily for Farmer Francis and his desires for upward mobility, Sir William was also engaged in a different project during this period, and one that would keep him far from the lives of the common folk. The impostor had always been a voracious reader, consuming books and tracts and newspapers – many of his known speeches and public statements are obviously drawing on current affairs and the ongoing controversies of the day. In the spring of 1833, having been denied the opportunity to speak at length from the benches of the House of Commons, he turned instead to print media, and there appeared in Canterbury the first edition of a new printed pamphlet or broadsheet.

Above the masthead image of Britannia seated in splendour with the nation's naval strength on one side and her agricultural bounty on the other, appears the bold motto:

THE BRITISH **LION** WILL BE FREE

Beneath it, flanked by thundering verses, the echoing slogan:

TRUTH BEARS OFF THE VICTORY

Successive editions follow the pattern of the first: two sheets folded to make eight double-columned pages. The first two editions, in fact, are largely devoted to introducing the themes of the paper, together with a vigorous appeal to the necessity of a free press as the foundation of liberty. Only in the second issue do we find the following statement of intent:

> Our weekly publication will be issued regularly on Saturdays, that the poor, especially, may have an opportunity to read on the Sunday, as it will ever contain that direction for the lower orders of society, so necessary in these eventful times. Agents will be appointed in all the neighbouring towns and villages, to deliver them at two pence each – and ... the overplus will, by a discreet hand, be given away to the distressed widow, orphan, and poor of the land.[24]

Succeeding issues of the paper bore an engraving of a sturdy lion on the title pages, garnished with bold slogans. Here at last we find the true voice of Sir William Courtenay, composed at his leisure, unfiltered by the partisan optics of the journalists who otherwise recorded fragments of his speeches. Much of the writing in the first three editions of the *Lion* is rather staid, however, and even conventional in its platitudes. There is little of the verbal flash and fizz of Sir William's public appearances. But neither are there any signs of madness; these are not the rantings of a fanatic or a maniac, as we might have expected by the author's reputation alone.

The targets for Sir William's ire in these early editions are largely conventional, too; the 'tyrant Buonaparte' stands as an adversary to English Liberty, as he had done for a generation by then. The 'infidel' Voltaire and the 'scorpion' Tom Paine are damned for their republicanism and atheism. Courtenay's political views might also seem quite uncontroversial today, although at the time they prowled the furthest margins of accepted radical doctrines. Throughout his ongoing issues, Sir William argues against political factionalism, and for lower, or at least fairer, taxation, an end to church tithes, higher wages and lower rents for the poor and better circulation of income, to the benefit of all classes:

> Whatever Whig or Tory may say – the present state of the country fully shews the truth of our argument, that unless the tithes are wholly given up, rents brought down to a standard value, taxation borne by those who have the property to pay it, England must go to a revolution, then Sir William Courtenay will in his relative value be credited – the people must be heard when justice demands it, and when were the wants of any people so great as the present?

The model for the new publication would seem to be papers like the *Political Register*, by the reformist campaigner and later MP William Cobbett, itself growing from a seedbed of popular political tracts, broadsheets and handbills dating back to the previous centuries. These were papers written for a popular readership, using popular language that channelled the rough humour of taverns and pubs and the combative two-fisted attitude of partisan politics. In 1819, following the 'Peterloo' Massacre, the last of the draconian Six Acts had imposed a fourpenny stamp tax on all news publications priced at less than sixpence. The intention was to make political newspapers prohibitively expensive for poorer readers. Cobbett's *Two-Penny Trash*, a pamphlet-sized paper of 1830 subtitled 'Politics for the Poor', evaded the tax by only publishing monthly. The *Poor Man's Guardian*, published by radical journalist Henry Hetherington, sold at only a penny in defiance of the new law, and bore the slogan 'Knowledge is Power' in place of a government stamp.[25]

Circulation of these cheap unstamped papers was forbidden by the regular post; instead, they were printed on the fly and distributed by hand, sold beneath the counter in shops, and passed around in pubs. Despite the restrictions, some had a print run in the tens of thousands; one magistrate in Gloucestershire claimed that Cobbett's work was read 'in every Country pothouse.' Even so, they were not ubiquitous; Frederick Liardet, investigating the homes of labourers around Dunkirk and Boughton, found 'not a Penny or Saturday Magazine, nor any one of the various cheap publications of the day… none of the cottagers examined had even heard of such things.'[26]

This, however, was the sort of readership that Sir William Courtenay was intending to reach with his new paper. In fact, a lot of the material in the early editions of the *Lion* resembles an awkward blend of religious homilies and undiluted Cobbett, whose writings are filled with paeans to an idealised rural England of the past, the 'land of roast beef' and 'plumb pudding', where Englishmen were truly free. The speeches of Sir William Courtenay also drew upon these themes. Courtenay adopted Cobbett's passionate reverence for the British monarchy, too, his often xenophobic patriotism and intense piety, his hatred of tithes, corrupt politicians and the established church. He even adopted his dislike of Methodists – extended in Courtenay's case to include Unitarians. Thankfully, he did not also adopt Cobbett's dislike of Jews. Instead, perhaps in reprise of his 'Count Rothschild' persona, he praises them: 'let Christians love Abraham's race; for Christ was also a Jew,' he writes and hopes that they 'will soon become a great nation again in their own land.'[27]

The third issue of the *Lion*, titled FAITH, is entirely devoted to religious matters – perhaps we find here a shade of the 'scriptural explanation' that so enraptured Farmer George Francis? – and its discussion of the human and divine nature of Christ might have seemed obscure to readers who were not paying attention to the religious debates of the day. Just over two weeks before the issue's publication, the celebrity preacher Edward Irving had been tried before the Presbytery of Annan, charged with heresy in 'maintaining the sinfulness of the Saviour in his human nature.' Courtenay respected Irving and was doubtless aware of the ongoing debate. In the *Lion*, he contents himself with a sensible middle course: 'Christ was God, perfect in his deity, and perfect in his humanity.'

Few people at the time, however, would have been attending to his opinions on religious matters; by the time of the third issue's publication, the author himself was locked in a jail cell.

The first indications of the impending doom of Sir William Courtenay, Knight of Malta and King of Jerusalem, came shortly after the conclusion of his election campaign in Canterbury. He was recognised in the street one day by a man from London named Smith, the owner of a boarding house in Pentonville. The man calling himself Courtenay, Mr Smith declared, had been his lodger for several months the previous summer, giving his name as the Honourable Sydney Percy, and had left suddenly while considerably behind on his rent.

The impostor neatly evaded these accusations by first denying them with great passion and then disappearing from public view. He had around this time moved out of his rooms at the Rose Inn in Canterbury and taken lodgings in the nearby Old Palace, part of the surviving precinct of St Augustine's Abbey. But on 18 March, while he was once again passing through the town, Courtenay was suddenly arrested and bundled off to Westgate Gaol, adjoining the twin towered fourteenth-century city gate. He was charged with committing perjury during the trial of the smugglers at Rochester, and it was only with difficulty, and after he had spent an uncomfortable night in the cells, that his supporters found two bondsmen willing to post the required bail, permitting his liberation until his scheduled appearance at the Kent Summer Assizes in July.[28]

His next peril, however, arose only nine days later. Thomas Stroud, a waiter at the Rose Inn, alleged to the Canterbury magistrates that Sir William Courtenay had swindled him out of a considerable sum of money, lent under false pretences. Stroud's suit was followed by a number of others on the same charge, including one brought by the former valet William Collard against 'Lord Courtenay' and his Jewish servant, Elijah Lazarus. The accusation was serious, and the mayor immediately granted a warrant for the arrest and detention of 'Moses Rothschein Rothschild, alias Lord Courtenay, of Powderham Castle, the County of Devon', on a charge of embezzlement.

After a riotous initial hearing at Canterbury's Guildhall the following day, the accused man was once again committed to Westgate Gaol to await trial.[29]

George Francis arrived from Fairbrook the next day and went to visit the prisoner in his cell. Although he judged the quarters unsuitable for the accommodation of a gentleman, he found Courtenay to be 'happy, and resigned to the will of heaven,' as the prisoner himself put it, 'persecuted as he is for the Poor's sakes,' and reduced to 'to a bed of straw, and bread, potatoes, and nine ounces of meat per week, and all this because he loves his king and country.'[30]

By now news of the arrest had spread through the city, and a substantial crowd was gathering around the Westgate. When the prisoner showed himself at a barred window, he was greeted with roars of acclaim and shouts of defiance. 'We will rescue you!' the crowd shouted. 'We will soon have you out!'

As the shops lowered the shutters over their windows, fearing a riot, the magistrates retreated to the Guildhall. Anonymous letters threatened that unless Sir William was released there would be a repeat of the 'Bristol affair', referring to the fatal rioting and arson in that city in 1831. Fifty years later, a Canterbury man who had witnessed the scene as a boy claimed that the crowd 'would have torn down the prison and fired the whole city.' As the evening deepened, Canterbury was 'entirely at the mercy of the mob.'[31]

There was no garrison in the city at that time, so Alderman Brown sent an express message to the nearest military unit, the depot companies of the Rifle Brigade, based fifteen miles away at Dover, asking for assistance in support of the civil power. From the jail window, meanwhile, Sir William continued to harangue his public; they should restrain themselves from violence, he told them. He too must suffer, as Christ had suffered before him.

Darkness had already fallen when the troops arrived from Dover, riding in the light carts known locally as fish vans. The green-jacketed riflemen were under the command of Captain John Gossett, a veteran of the Peninsular War and the Battle of New Orleans. As his men were forming up, he was hit on the head by a stone, apparently aimed at somebody else. Besides a few broken windows, that minor injury was the only violence of the night, and the presence of Gossett's troops occupying the Guildhall and the special constables patrolling the streets was enough to deter any wider conflagration. By dawn, order was restored once more in Canterbury, the shops reopened, and the storm appeared passed. The Lord Lieutenant of Kent later wrote to the mayor and corporation, praising 'their prompt, zealous and intrepid conduct in saving the city at the time of the alarming riots.' Others were less impressed: an editorial in the *Kentish Chronicle* commented that 'four old women, and one old man, with three birch-brooms, could have saved the city as effectively.'[32]

It was another nine days before Sir William Courtenay was released from Westgate Gaol, his more resourceful friends and supporters having managed to secure a writ of *Habeas Corpus* removing him to the Court of the King's Bench in London, where bail could be posted. As he left the prison, he was met once more by a cheering crowd, and people scrambled for the nuts and oranges that he threw among them, presents he had received from his many admirers while in his cell. He departed at once for London, where the judge Sir John Patteson of the King's Bench accepted the bail tendered by his wealthier supporters.[33]

On 12 April 1833, he returned to Canterbury in triumph. Sir William's impending return had been advertised beforehand by handbills posted throughout the city, and by the time his retinue was first glimpsed descending Harbleton Hill a vast crowd had gathered to receive him. An unattributed and highly satirical account, reprinted five years later by the Select Committee investigating the impostor's release from Barming Asylum, conjures a ludicrous array of lower-class characters, rosy-cheeked children and chattering women, all waiting to glimpse their champion. Their flags, ribbons and cockades are uniformly blue – the Whig colour – and the writer seems eager to tie the returning Knight of Malta to the Whig cause. They even throw in an absurdist counter-procession of bears, monkeys, and a camel, in case the reader is inclined to take any of it seriously.

Parading around the city behind flags bearing the slogans 'Truth bears off Victory' and 'The British Lion will be Free', haranguing the crowd at every corner, Sir William declared his 'determination to prosecute the mayor and corporation for sending him to gaol,' that he 'freely forgave Thomas Stroud, the waiter,' and that 'he defied any one to produce another living Lord Courtenay except himself.' At times, according to the satirist's account, he addressed the crowd while standing on the back on his horse in the manner of the famous circus performer Andrew Ducrow.[34]

After this triumphant circuit of the city, the impostor resumed his rented chambers in the Old Palace. Appearing at a window overlooking Monastery Street, he once again addressed the cheering throng. Not everyone in Canterbury, however, showed such enthusiasm for the Knight of Malta. That evening Courtenay attended a musical performance at the Apollonian Club, a venue at which he had previously been greeted with great reverence and respect. At his first appearance, the orchestra laid down their instruments and left the room, followed by the club's deputy president.

Several of the remaining gentlemen 'evinced their respect for Sir W. Courtenay by hissing as he bade them good night.' No doubt disturbed by this reception, the impostor chose to withdraw almost entirely from Canterbury to Fairbrook. A song printed in the *Lion* celebrates his safe return to the home parish of those who had supported him through his legal troubles and were now eager to 'welcome to Boughton this friend of the poor / Who are anxiously waiting to cheer him.'[35]

But in Boughton, too, Sir William's reputation had already suffered, and many were far from eager to welcome him, or anxious to cheer his presence among them. George Francis had been a member of the Faversham Farmers' Club since 1815, but when he hosted a dinner meeting of the club at Fairbrook back in March none of the other members had deigned to attend, perhaps fearing that they would be asked to share a table with the disreputable Courtenay. As news emerged of the impostor's ongoing ill-fame, the rebuff was followed by expulsion. 'The members declined dining with him,' the club-book entry reads, 'and he is declared to be no longer a member of the club.'[36]

Despite these minor disruptions, Sir William lived relatively quietly on bail for nearly twelve weeks. We hear of no meetings, no speeches during this period. The local press seemed only interested in whether he would appear for his embezzlement trial. Many were already placing bets on him failing to show up. He continued, however, with his literary efforts, and four further editions of the *Lion* appeared by early May.[37]

Perhaps because his recent experiences of trial and imprisonment had aggravated him, or because he was already facing charges of both swindling and perjury and felt less constrained by caution, these later editions of the *Lion* are more vividly expressive in style, and fiercer in their attacks. Issue Four opens with a plea to 'liberal patriots and friends to justice' to 'defend the noble-minded Courtenay, in his heroic career, for the liberties of his country, and the support of his king.' The impostor then gives his own third-person account of his time in London, his arrival in Canterbury, and his difficulties with the waiter Stroud, who 'seeing so much gold and other riches belonging to this illustrious stranger, formed an attachment to him, for a snack at the loaves and fishes, and ... stuck to him like cobler's wax.'

Successive issues go on to blast the corruption of Parliament, the emptiness of the Reform Act, and the defects of the current administration, 'those paltry men, who brought forward such a heap of trash, and inanimate matter, as never before offered a British nation.' His hottest fury, however, is roused by the recent imposition of martial law upon Ireland, as he writes in an eerily foreshadowing passage:

> Whatever could possess a reforming ministry or House of Commons to resort to such an extreme and bloody resource? Forsooth, because the people of Ireland felt themselves oppressed by tyrannical landlords, merciless middlemen, and oppressive tithe-mongers ... how long will it be ere the same 'Reforming Parliament' will apply the red coat puppy as a judge, and the sword wreaking fresh from the slaughter of our countrymen as the verdict for the British peasant, or working mechanic?

A page later, and Sir William becomes the advocate for the 'red coat puppy' as he inveighs against the practice of flogging in the army (a cause that Henry 'Orator' Hunt had also championed): 'There is not a body of finer men in the whole world than the army of the United Kingdom,' he says, 'but we are sorry to add, that many of the officers are not worth two-pence per dozen.'

In another issue, he breaks from a Good Friday homily on the nature of sin to attack the Corporation of Canterbury, those 'turtle-soup gentry and public wine-bibbers,' who 'use every unmanly and grovelling method to support their falling dynasty.' He rages, too, against the partisan local press, the Tory *Kentish Observer* and the Whig *Kent Herald*: 'Is it because the British Lion speaks the truth,' he asks, 'and supports the liberties of his country, that he is from week to week attacked by such cowardly dastards ... the one a supporter of bullock's liver for the poor; and the other to gull the people by infidel blasphemy and party spirit[?]'.

The penultimate issue ends with the lyrics of two songs, not an uncommon addition to political pamphlets and handbills of the day. Set to the tune of *The Conquering Hero*, the song entitled LIBERTY resounds like an anthem:

> Lo! deliverance is at hand;
> Courtenay's made a noble stand,
> He, the tyrants has arous'd,
> He has freedom's cause espous'd,
> CHORUS:
> Britons must be – will be free:
> Truth bears off the victory!

Courtenay's 'noble stand', however, was still to come, and those who had placed bets on him jumping bail would be disappointed.

Immense crowds surrounded the Canterbury Guildhall on the first morning in July, as the impostor arrived in an open post-chaise escorted by hundreds of his supporters, men and women alike. He entered the hall to stand trial before the mayor and recorder, a full bench of magistrates, and a grand jury pledged to 'banish from their minds everything they might have heard previously, and be guided solely by the evidence before them.' This would not be easy; Sir William's appearance was greeted with 'one burst of cheering,' and as the trial commenced the shouting of his supporters made it impossible for the prosecutor's counsel to make himself heard.

'The noise, confusion and tumult in the hall at this time,' the correspondent of the *Times* reported, 'beggared description: "Courtenay, Courtenay" resounded from all sides, intermingled with other exclamations, loud hootings, hallooing, whistling and screams.' Amid the chaos, the impostor calmly conducted his own trial, questioning those around him and asking that various witnesses be brought forward to attest to his identity. He hoped to live and die as Lord Courtenay, he said. Anything else was preposterous. 'They little knew whom they had before them; that he was the heir of Courtenay he could prove by 500 witnesses.'[38]

The small matter of the swindling charge, meanwhile, appears to have concerned him very little. He pleaded not guilty to 'obtaining by false pretences one promissory note for the payment of five pounds and thirteen promissory notes for the payment of ten pounds each.' In fact, he announced, it was Thomas Stroud who owed *him* money! Finally, in despair and finding themselves unable to proceed due to the violent tumult in the courtroom, the magistrates granted a writ of *certiorari*, removing the case altogether to the King's Bench. 'Never,' the *Kent Herald* stated, 'was a scene so completely disgraceful witnessed in any Court of Justice.'[39]

Once again, Sir William was free to leave on bail, 'amid the most deafening cries, which he in vain attempted to prevent.' On the Guildhall steps, he addressed the crowd, announcing his intention to abandon politics forever. He was neither a republican nor a democrat, he told them, but solely a royalist, 'and would spill his life's blood in defence of the throne.' Then, after once more expressing his determination to reclaim his lost rights and titles, he bade a grateful farewell to his public and boarded a waiting coach.[40]

He would return to Canterbury several times more, but without much fanfare, and only to visit friends. The majority of the people of the city, those who had been so dazzled and captivated by him over the preceding eight months, had seen the last of Sir William Courtenay.

3. 'SIR WILLIAM COURTENAY ... HAS BECOME INSANE'

The courtroom in Maidstone was packed, the heat overpowering. So many spectators crowded the public galleries that several ladies had to be seated on the judicial bench. All eyes were on the man who stood before the dock.

Those expecting Sir William to appear at the Kent Assize Court in his famously gaudy outfits and glittering accessories may have felt let down. He was dressed instead in a plain and sober frock coat with a velvet collar, and clutched what appeared to be a small Bible in his hands, which he consulted from time to time. His crowd-pleasing antics were restricted to taking frequent sharp inhalations from a small bottle of pungent liquid, and occasionally gripping hanks of his luxuriant black beard between his teeth.

At least the matter of his identity was not a question for the court. 'Whether he called himself Parker Warbeck, or Napoleon Buonaparte,' the prosecution had explained, they would try him by that name.[1]

The case itself was clear enough: Sir William Percy Honeywood Courtenay was accused of wilful and corrupt perjury in giving false evidence during the trial of the smugglers captured aboard the *Admiral Hood* back in February. Mr Serjeant Spankie, counsel for the Crown, laid out the particulars of the case for the jury, calling in the magistrates' clerk who had presided that day to confirm Sir William's claims given in evidence. He even called Lt Shambler, the officer commanding the revenue cutter, to repeat his own story.

Then he brought in his crucial witness. Thomas Wright, the eighty-three-year-old vicar of Boughton under Blean, testified that on Sunday, 17 February 1833, at the very moment that Sir William Courtenay claimed to have witnessed the capture of the *Admiral Hood* off Goodwin Sands, he had seen the man himself sitting in the pews of his church during afternoon service. Mr Wright clearly recalled seeing Courtenay that day, he said; it was Quinquagesima Sunday, and one of his congregants had asked whether his sermon had been directed at Sir William in particular.

The venerable vicar then went on to say that this was the first time that Courtenay had attended his church. To this the defendant gave an expressive reaction, as if, the court reporter gently suggested, he found these 'testimonies inconsistent with strict truth'. In fact, Sir William Courtenay had attended the christening of Commander Gordon's daughter at that same church back in January, but the Reverend Mr Wright, pressed on the issue, claimed that the christening had taken place after the 17th. The parish overseer of Boughton, however, could also testify that Courtenay had been in church that day; he had made a note of the appearance of such a widely famed figure in his memorandum book. At this, the defendant 'turned up his eyes and grinned with great complacency.'[2]

Mr Wells, counsel for the defendant, had been brought in by Sir William's wealthier friends to defend him during the riotous trial in Canterbury Guildhall, and he intended to do the same here. But the mood in the crowded, sweaty courtroom in Maidstone was quite different, and neither Wells nor his client could count on a supportive audience. The people of Canterbury had been coaxed and flattered by Sir William for months; to the Maidstone public he was a stranger, a fascinating curiosity, perhaps, but not a champion to inspire the passions of the mob. Mr Wells would have to work harder here. It did not help that Sir William kept seizing him by the lapels, at one point almost pulling off his feet, while trying to whisper suggestions to him.

The jury should not be swayed, Mr Wells told them, by things they may already have heard about the man in the dock. He went on to claim that Sir William's lengthy travels in exotic eastern lands had caused him to develop strange mannerisms that some might find uncouth, and a strange way of calculating time by the moon rather than the sun, which may at times cause him to determine dates differently to other men. But the case for the defence rested mainly on character witnesses. These Mr Wells produced one by one to attest to Sir William's fine qualities, and they read like a muster-roll of the impostor's most devoted followers.

Captain James Gordon, R.N. thought the defendant 'incapable of committing the crimes imputed to him,' while George Denne believed Sir William to be 'a man of most religious sentiments. The most religious one he ever knew.' John Morris Thomas of Canterbury believed him 'utterly incapable' of 'the diabolical charges' of which he was accused.

Mr George Francis of Fairbrook echoed the heartfelt praise of the impostor, who had entirely convinced him of his moral virtues and religiosity; Sir William Courtenay, he claimed, 'would rather die than sin against his God.' According to John Waters Banks, the writer of religious verses, Sir William's knowledge of the word of God quite surpassed that of the entire clergy of the established church of England.

Most passionate of all was the former surgeon George Robinson, who cast the defendant in a Christlike guise; since meeting Sir William he had forsaken the medical profession, he told the court: 'I have given up everything to follow him, and would follow him still.'[3]

The judge, Mr Justice James Parke of the King's Bench, appeared to give little value to these testimonials, and moved directly to his summing up of the case. At this point Sir William Courtenay, who had listened with satisfaction and occasional agreement to the words of his supporters, now spoke up suddenly. Was he, too, not allowed to speak in his own defence?

No, the judge told him; his counsel had already addressed the jury on his behalf, and the defendant had thereby forfeited his right to speak.

Sir William's blustering reaction suggests that this came as a shock to him. Surely, he must have assumed, he would now get the chance to work his spell of oratory on the Maidstone crowd and jury, animating them with his presence and winning them to his cause? As he sank back into his chair and listened to the judge's summing-up, Sir William Courtenay must have felt the situation slipping from his grasp. He had bargained everything on his chance to speak, to snatch another miraculous victory from the air, and it had been denied. Now his fate was in the hands of other men.

He lost, of course. It took the jury a mere twenty-one minutes of deliberation to reach their verdict: Sir William Courtenay was guilty of wilful and corrupt perjury, but recommended to mercy. For the first time, the impostor appeared to recognise the magnitude of his error, and the colossal odds stacked against him. He appeared, the court reporter says, *thunderstruck*. He 'stared wildly at the jury, then cast his eyes to heaven, and clasping his hands appeared resigned to his fate.'

Silently, he shook hands with his supporters, some of them already in tears. He had begun following the guards from the dock when the clerk of arraigns called him back, asking him if he wished to state why sentence should not be passed upon him. It was a mere formality, but Sir William snatched at it.

'*May* I then be allowed to speak?' he asked, with deliberate emphasis.

Only, the judge said, in addressing him in mitigation of punishment.

Now, finally, the impostor had the chance he had desired so much. But already it was too late. He had lost his case, and he had lost the crowd, too; they had come wanting a show, and he had failed them. Instead of the fantastically dressed performer they had heard so much about, the celebrity orator who had thrown Canterbury and the coastal towns into delirium, they got only this strange shabby figure, reduced throughout the trial to mute gurning and grimacing. Sir William began to speak with his usual vehemence and animation, but he was extemporising now, trying to drag back control when it had already escaped him. Instead of making his case with eloquence, turning the arguments of his accusers back upon themselves, winning his audience with his wit and irreverence, he found himself desperately denying everything. Addressing the jury and the public gallery as often as the judge, he began to explain that he had never claimed to be at sea on February the 17th – he had never claimed anything about any smuggled goods, any tubs or vessels ... All that he had done had been from a warm heart and a good cause, how could he be blamed for that? The oath he had been tricked into taking was 'contrary to my faith, and contrary to my conscience.'

All the while, the scurrying pencils of the court reporters from the *Maidstone Journal* and the *South Eastern Gazette* recorded his words, in flowing dramatic monologues cut through with the exasperated remarks of the judge. 'It is not of any use to address the jury now,' Justice James Parke told the defendant, 'or to pretend that you are not guilty.'

But still the speech went on. 'My God!' Sir William cried, turning once more to the public galleries. 'What if this were the justice of the whole country! Ah, did you know my heart, and the real wishes of Sir William Courtenay for you, you would not judge me. I would lay down my life for you. I would take all my prosecutors and my judges to my heart, for they *know not what they do.*'

He spoke in vain. 'No decided feeling of interest,' one court reporter dryly noted, 'appeared to be excited among the populace.' Instead of the roars of support, the cheering and enthusiastic laughter he might have wanted, and that he had come to expect from his appearances in Canterbury, he spoke into the dull silence of a packed and overheated courtroom, hearing only disinterest and growing contempt echoed back at him. 'The gross prevarication and contradictions of the prisoner,' another journalist suggests, 'had completely prevented his extraordinary address from producing that effect which he doubtless anticipated.'[4]

Still the impostor blustered onwards: he could not be condemned; he could be tried only by his peers in the House of Lords. In his despair, his entreaties became even more pathetic.

'Kent!' he cried, clasping his hands and gazing upwards. 'Your God will see me done justice to! If I have been convicted by mistake ...' ('No mistake at all,' the judge broke in.

'Nothing can be clearer.') '... I will say that I am innocent as a lamb. God knows I know nothing more about it than the man in the moon. As to popularity, I detest it. I hate politics ... I will never dabble in politics any more. They are a whirlpool of misery.'

Abruptly his words ceased. He paced, agitated, back and forth in the dock.

The judge asked: 'Have you done?'

Yes, he replied. Yes, he had done. It was over.

Nothing remained now but the sentence, and after all he had heard the judge saw no reason for any consideration of mercy. 'William Courtenay, otherwise called Sir William Courtenay,' he pronounced, had committed 'wilful and corrupt perjury, to the great displeasure of Almighty God, to the evil example of all other persons, and against the peace of our said Lord the King, his crown and dignity.' He would therefore face the full penalty for his crime: imprisonment for three months in Maidstone Jail, followed by transportation 'to such place beyond the seas as his majesty ... shall direct, for the term of seven years.'

In silence the guards led the condemned man from the courtroom. He appeared resigned, stunned by the judgement and the severity of the sentence. But he must submit. It was, he told his jailors, *the will of God*.[5]

It was barely more than a fortnight before the impostor's identity unravelled.

'SIR WILLIAM COURTENAY'S REAL CHARACTER DISCOVERED!' reads the blazing title of a handbill printed by the Canterbury newspaper editor Henry Ward. 'HIS LADY AND BROTHER-IN-LAW HAVE *POSITIVELY IDENTIFIED HIM*.'[6]

The full story spilled out in the days that followed, first in the local and then the national press. The man who had masqueraded as Sir William Courtenay, Knight of Malta and King of Jerusalem, was, it turned out, really named John Nicholls Tom. He was a maltster and spirit merchant from Truro in Cornwall, and his family had been searching for him since his mysterious disappearance over a year beforehand. It was perhaps one of their newspaper adverts, describing Mr Tom and asking for news of his whereabouts, that had alerted a sharp-eyed onlooker in Canterbury or Maidstone.[7]

The facts of the impostor's life were, naturally, considerably less exotic than many of his former supporters had been led to believe. John Nicholls Tom had been born in St Columb Major in 1799, the son of an innkeeper and farmer, and after spending a few years as articled clerk to a local solicitor he had taken employment with Lubbock & Co, wine and spirit merchants in Truro. He worked in the company's Pydar Street premises for seven years, and when the managing partner, Mr Turner, retired in 1827, he appointed John Nicholls Tom as his successor. The company prospered, and Tom added a malting operation to the wine and spirit business.[8]

He was a popular man, known for his Herculean strength; on several occasions he gave demonstrations of his physical prowess, once heaving a mighty keg onto the back of a wagon, when five other men could barely lift it. He was fond of sailing, and also a keen and capable cricketer, acclaimed as one of the best men at the wicket in all of Cornwall, or perhaps England. In 1821, he married a local woman, Catherine Fulpit, 'a lady of good fortune and respectable connections,' as the *Maidstone Gazette* later pointed out. Clearly, he did not lack for resources, or the hopes of further improvement.[9]

Things had begun to go wrong when John Tom's mother fell into a fit of mental derangement and was committed to the lunatic asylum in Bodmin, where she subsequently died. The following year, in June 1828, a fire destroyed his Truro warehouse and offices. John Nicholls Tom claimed a large insurance pay-out and rebuilt his business, but his fortunes never recovered, and he drifted first into depression and then deeper into mental illness.

By December 1831, he was under the care of two doctors brought in by his family. One wrote that Mr Tom had experienced 'a very violent fit of apoplexy' and suffered from 'conjestion of the Brain.' The other diagnosed *monomania*. This was a particularly nineteenth-century affliction, supposedly leading its sufferers to become morbidly obsessed with particular subjects or objects while remaining otherwise rational. In Tom's case, the morbid obsession appears to have taken a religious theme; one of his doctors noted that he made 'constant allusions to Scripture.' They prescribed an entirely shaven head and frequent bloodletting.[10]

To the relief of his wife and relatives, Tom's fit of insanity seemed to have passed by January 1832. In May, he took charge of a shipload of malt, sailing with it to market in Liverpool. The cargo was worth, according to later reports, £1,000. Having sold the malt, Tom was supposed to return home. His wife received a single letter from him, written in Liverpool, 'in haste, with bad materials,' confirming the sale. Then she heard nothing more.

We might imagine that the possession of a relatively large sum of cash, far from home and the steadying influence of his wife and relations, and only a few months after he had recovered from an attack of mental illness, may have provoked in John Nicholls Tom a sudden desire for a change of life. In a letter to the Parliamentary Select Committee written after his death, Susan Tom, John's stepmother, reveals that in mid-February 1832, 'after he had been proved insane,' he had drafted a new will that gave all of his property to his wife Catherine. He 'did not consider he had a parent.' This tiny detail suggests a much deeper family dispute, and a desire by John Tom to repudiate his father and stepmother.

Family breakdown and trauma – often associated with the death of a mother – feature in the backstory of several charismatic cult leaders and preachers. Tom's fit of madness – whether 'apoplexy', *monomania,* or epilepsy as his family later called it – may also have played a part in shattering his old sense of self and generating a psychological rebirth that liberated him from conventional morality and conformity. But perhaps his desire for change had a more mundane origin. Why return to the depressing confines of his old existence, when he could simply travel somewhere new, adopt a new name, a new face and a new fate?[11]

What happened next remains extremely hazy and clouded with much subsequent myth-making. The impostor's pseudo-biographer, 'Canterburiensis', dreams up an Orientalist fantasia of travels in eastern lands, with the reborn Sir William Courtenay journeying to Constantinople and Beirut, presenting himself at the Lebanese retreat of eccentric aristocrat Lady Hester Stanhope, and visiting the ancient monuments of Jerusalem and the Holy Land. The story may have been based on tales the impostor himself told to the public in his Canterbury days – it at least suggests something of their flavour – or simply concocted from novels and travellers' accounts of the period. In reality, John Tom's wanderings perhaps led him as far as Le Havre at best. His family later declared that 'to their knowledge, he has never left England.'[12]

Shortly afterwards, he turned up in London, now using the name and title of the Honourable Sydney Percy. Here, he took lodgings in the house of Mr Henry Smith in Rodney Street, Pentonville, where he remained for several months. He allowed his host to believe that he was an aristocrat and had recently been engaged by His Majesty's government in the colonies; for reasons of confidentiality, he did not wish any of his wealthy friends to know that he had returned. He nevertheless received a number of letters, addressed to him by name, which he read in private. It was only some time later that Mrs Smith – less credulous than her husband, perhaps – took the opportunity of steaming open one of these letters, to discover that it contained only a blank sheet of paper.

'The Honourable Sydney Percy' then made a sudden departure from Pentonville, leaving a note and a collection of books on political and economic themes, in lieu of outstanding rent. He next appeared at the Clarendon Hotel, under the name of Squire Thompson. Already by this point he had developed an interest, or obsession, in certain obscure branches of the British aristocracy, and particularly in dormant peerages; his adoption of various names and titles suggests that he must have spent a long time scrutinising the newspapers.[13]

He also appears to have been interested in politics. 'Canterburiensis' claims that Tom had long before joined the Society of Spencean Philanthropists, a London-based organisation dedicated to developing the principles of the late proto-socialist Thomas Spence. This appears framed in a longer and very detailed romantic tale about an elopement, probably largely fictional, but it may have some basis in reality. Spence had advocated common ownership of land, social equality and universal suffrage, rights for women and children, and the abolition of the aristocracy; he later developed his ideas into a plan for an emancipated utopia, called 'Spensonia'. He died in 1814, and the society formed in his name was suppressed under successive Seditious Meetings Acts, in 1817 and again in 1819 following the violence at 'Peterloo'.

But Spence's ideas still had great currency, and many of the impostor's later pronouncements and publications certainly echo them. The *Penny Satirist* of June 1838 claims that, during his time in London, John Nicholls Tom was attempting to find a London publisher for a very Spencean-sounding pamphlet, titled *A Plan for Division of Landed Property in Great Britain, without injury to the established holders*. Many years later, a plaque erected in Christ Church, Dunkirk, described Tom as 'an insane impostor associated with the revolutionary Spencean Society.'[14]

Thomas Spence himself, for all his radical views and revolutionary concepts, had remained always moderate and polite in his expression and action, a man of the eighteenth-century Enlightenment. Many of the followers who subsequently revered his name, however, were quite different men. While holding to the Spencean core beliefs in the redistribution of land and property – the land was 'the people's farm' and must be restored to common ownership – their methods and behaviour often struck a louder and brassier note. 'Burlesque, ribaldry and rhetorical bombast' were not beneath the members of the Society of Spencean Philanthropists, who drew on the anarchic energies of 'tavern radicalism' to amplify their appeal. The militant Arthur Thistlewood once challenged Lord Sidmouth to a duel, while Thomas Preston toured the northern counties dressed in an eye-catching multicoloured costume. John Tom, as we have seen, would later adopt just these kinds of showy, attention-grabbing antics. But political melodrama and overt populism were not uncommon features of the age.[15]

'Sir William Courtenay ... Has Become Insane'

The summer of 1832 saw the final passage of the Great Reform Bill through parliament. It was time of fervent debate and social tension, in particular following the violent 'Days of May', when revolution once more threatened England. Living in London during those months, John Nicholls Tom would have been exposed to a heady blend of political influences. Henry 'Orator' Hunt made public appearances in the city around this time, and Tom almost certainly witnessed his powerful, declamatory populist speeches. He later claimed to have joined the congregation of the celebrity preacher Edward Irving, whose impassioned sermonizing must have influenced him, too.

Not all of Tom's activities during this period were so virtuous. Besides researching the aristocracy and following political and religious affairs, he seems to have developed his talents as an outright fraudster, too. As usual, the truth is difficult to discern beneath the accretions of later myth, but it appears that Tom adopted his new guise of 'Count Rothschild' during this period and paid several visits to the Jewish communities of the East End. He claimed to be raising money to help distressed Jews living under Ottoman rule in Palestine. Another story has Tom arranging the sale of a non-existent educational establishment to a schoolmaster from Leicestershire, and then vanishing once the money had been paid. That claim finds some support in the *Morning Herald* of 2 June 1838, although the details are vague and insubstantial. But whatever Tom's con-artistry might actually have involved, he seems to have raised enough to support himself, pay his bills at the Clarendon, and lay in funds for the next stage of his operation. He asserts in the *Lion* that he made several trips to Kent during this period, too, visiting Ramsgate, Margate and Herne Bay to study 'the application of steam engines to agricultural purposes.'[16]

Several months later, as summer began to ebb, John Nicholls Tom left the Clarendon Hotel. Dressed in a fantastical costume that he had apparently ordered from a London tailor, he boarded one of the new Thames steam packets and travelled down the estuary to Herne Bay once more. From there, he moved on to Canterbury and stepped into the world new-born.

What did John Nicholls Tom intend when he made his journey from London? How did a man with little to no experience of public speaking emerge as such a powerful and charismatic orator? And how did a relatively unexceptional wine merchant and malt-dealer from Truro reinvent himself, in the space of barely four months, as a skilled and effective fraudster and an impresario impostor? It was not long before people were labelling him *insane*; but is it enough simply to assume that he was mad all along?

One answer to the first question might be that his visit to Canterbury was intended as an extension of his London scams. Having seen how easy it was to assume an identity, and to profit from the credulity of others, he merely chose a new location for his endeavours, one perhaps less cosmopolitan and self-aware than London, and once more set about his trade. This would be the most obvious explanation. But why did he keep up the charade, even attending trial at the Kent County Assizes under his assumed name, charged with a serious crime? It would have been easy, after all, for him to have slipped his bail and vanished, dropped his name and identity and taken another. If he had any great loyalty towards those who had paid his bond, he would not have led them into such humiliation.

So, perhaps his religious ideas were more passionate and sincere than we might tend to credit today? Could John Nicholls

Tom have believed, even as early as 1832, that he genuinely *was* an agent of God, on a divine mission? Maybe the 'constant allusions to scripture' noted by the doctor in Cornwall were not so fleeting after all. If John Tom believed that God had set him the task of redeeming the country, even of bringing the Millennium – the thousand-year rule of Christ and the Last Judgement – as he would later claim, then any subterfuge or deception in the furtherance of that cause would be forgiven. For a Holy Warrior, anything can be justified.

But there must be something more, some motivation beyond religious conviction, mental disturbance, or criminal intent. Tom was clearly a man of exceptional talent, capable of creating and maintaining an illusion of identity so compelling that it seems to have convinced hundreds and perhaps thousands of people. The massive willpower needed to sustain a charade of that sort, over months and in the full glare of public attention, must have been extraordinary. His writings in the *Lion*, while often garbled, show that he was aware of what was happening in the society around him, and wanted to engage with it. They are not the product of a deranged or deluded mind.

John Nicholls Tom, it seems, honestly and completely believed that he had turned himself into somebody new by a radical act of self-invention. Once he had proved that he could convince those around him by presenting himself with confidence and verve, anything became possible. He was intoxicated by the power of words, and the power of performance. Intoxicated, too, perhaps, by the effect of that performance: the cheers and acclaim of the Canterbury crowds, the heartfelt devotion of so many to his cause. Such devotion, in fact, as to appear close to adulation at times, or worship.

Again and again in his speeches and publications he mentions truth. This cannot be simple dissembling. For Tom, the truth was something hard won, it belonged to those with the willpower, confidence and oratory to seize it and hold it. *Truth bears off the Victory*, as his slogan had it. For him, truth *was* the victory, won in battle against reality itself. Truth, and the power to remake the world around him through words alone, was his ultimate prize. *Reimagine* is a term used perhaps too frequently in our own time, but it describes quite accurately what John Tom was doing. He was remaking himself, and by extension remaking the world, by the power of his own desire, his own imagination. He stood trial in Canterbury and then again in Maidstone because he had become convinced of his ability to bend reality to his will. He had only to speak, to summon the divine force of his creative eloquence, and every boundary would fall. Words could make him a new man; they could bring him wealth and influence; they could bring him freedom, renown, and glory. In the end, his willpower failed him at Maidstone. He was denied the chance to make his greatest speech yet, and blast the locks of the cage that bound him by the sheer explosive power of his words.

Ultimately, I believe, John Nicholls Tom became possessed by the fictional character he had imagined into being. *Sir William Courtenay* was far more powerful than he was; he was more popular, more colourful, more eloquent and more attractive; he amazed crowds and elicited fervent acclaim and idolisation. He was a man with a direct connection to God, and a mission to pursue. Having become this person, there was no way that the impostor could return to being the mere John Tom, Truro wine merchant. He would remain as Sir William against all odds, even if it took him into criminal conviction and imprisonment. Even if it took him across the furthest frontier of sanity itself.

Mrs Catherine Tom first visited Maidstone Prison in August, accompanied by her brother-in-law Mr Hugo. After some initial difficulties they were granted permission to visit the prisoner. They found him calm and apparently resigned to his situation. Strangely, he had not been shaved of his hair or his beard, or dressed in the coarse prison uniform like the other inmates. It almost seemed that the jailors still considered him a person of distinction, perhaps indeed the aristocrat he had claimed to be. He had been convicted and imprisoned, after all, under his assumed name of *Sir William Courtenay*.

John Nicholls Tom refused to recognise either his wife or Mr Hugo, or to deny that Sir William was his real name. According to an attending magistrate, Catherine Tom then 'went into fits, but certainly they were very curious fits.' The visitors persisted, returning repeatedly to the prison and urging the staff doctors to study the reports of the medical men who had treated Tom during his period of insanity in Cornwall. Surely, they could see a connection with his present state?

The prisoner, however, would have none of it. When Mr and Mrs Francis of Fairbrook visited the prison soon afterwards, their friend introduced them to 'the person who called herself his wife' by the name 'Miss Perfect of Hammersmith.' On another occasion at Maidstone, in company with the naval officer James Gordon, Mr Francis met another man who claimed to have known John Tom in Cornwall, and who was keen to stress his genteel background; Mr Tom 'used to keep his curricle and a pair of horses,' Mr Francis was told, 'and a footman [and] he was one of the best cricketers and the most active man that could possibly be.' Nevertheless, the prisoner still refused to acknowledge his visitors, and when one of them offered him money to admit his true identity he flew into 'a violent passion', shouting 'I wish I had six inches of steel, [then] you should know what Courtenay's blood was made of.'[17]

George Francis continued in his belief that his friend Sir William was 'a persecuted man,' and the visitors from Cornwall were impostors. After this point, however, we hear little more about Captain James Gordon. It seems he may have begun to suspect the truth after all, and in later years wrote at least once to Mrs Catherine Tom. The prison doctors were also won over, although it took nearly two months – and a petition signed by Mrs Tom and 54 worthy inhabitants of Canterbury – to persuade them to examine the prisoner for signs of insanity. An act passed under King George IV stated that 'if any person while imprisoned ... shall become insane, and it shall be duly certified by two physicians or surgeons that such person is insane,' they could lawfully be removed to a lunatic asylum, 'or other proper receptacle for insane persons ...'

After making their examination, the two doctors at Maidstone were able to certify that 'William Courtenay, *alias* Sir William Courtenay ... now confined in the gaol at Maidstone,' had indeed 'become insane.' On 26 October 1833, the Home Secretary issued a warrant authorising that the madman 'be removed from the said gaol, to the lunatic asylum for the said county, there to remain until further order shall be made herein.'[18]

Kent County Asylum at Barming, just to the west of Maidstone, had been opened on the first day of January that year. It was a huge severe-looking building of grey Kentish ragstone, resembling a cross between an aristocratic country house and a prison – the same architect had worked on Maidstone Gaol – and was initially capable of accommodating 168 patients. Like others built elsewhere around this same time, the new asylum was a product of the improving and reforming spirit of the age. Madness, to the medical reformers, was no longer viewed as an absolute state but rather as an illness, an affliction that could be treated, and perhaps even cured. The *mad* were no longer to be regarded as objects of disgrace, embarrassment, or ridicule. The 1808 *Act for the Better Care and Maintenance of Lunatics* decreed that those so afflicted were to be properly accommodated in purpose-built facilities, clean, secure and well ventilated, with medical staff to care for them and treatment available for those who would accept it.[19]

We have a description of the Kent County Lunatic Asylum, by a later superintendent, James Huxley. He was writing in 1854, after the asylum had been considerably enlarged, but much of his account relates to the earlier section, as it was first established. The main building had four storeys, with three-storey wings to either side.* The lower floors housed 'the paralytic and otherwise feeble, the violent and noisy, and those who are habitually dirty.' There were also four padded chambers, to secure those 'reckless, or insensible to self-injury.'

The upper floors of the asylum, however, housed those inmates of 'better class', with 'cleanly habits, absence of much noise, violence, and mischief.' Some of these more tractable patients were even given private bedrooms, opening off long galleries used as communal spaces for meals and recreation. These bedrooms were clean, spartan chambers with slate-tiled floors, and iron-framed doors with inspection holes and handles only on the outside. The three-foot-square windows were seven feet from the floor and covered by wire mesh. It was in a

---

* You can still find the old asylum on modern maps and satellite views of Barming, just west of Maidstone; nowadays it has been converted into a deluxe apartment complex.

room of this sort, we can assume, that John Nicholls Tom was accommodated.[20]

In these well-ventilated wards and chambers – often overly cold in winter and hot in summer – the inmates would be kept as calm and tranquil as possible. They were fed on a regular diet of the blandest foods, calculated not to excite their senses; a standard asylum menu might feature boiled meat perhaps four times a week, otherwise oatmeal porridge, vegetable broth, and suet pudding or rice pudding.[21]

Superintendent George Poynder was very experienced in the new methods of asylum management, having worked at one of the prototype institutions at Gloucester in the 1820s. He was, it seems, rather strict in the application of these methods, and would subsequently be accused of being overly fond of the use of physical restraints in particular. In this he was not uncommon; most asylums still made use of the 'strait waistcoat' and 'coercive chair', besides employing cold showers and freezing plunge baths to treat 'mania' and depression. Some superintendents even 'galvanized' their inmates with an 'electrifying machine'. But it seems that John Nicholls Tom required no such restraint.[22]

'There is reason to believe that his mind has not been quite sound for many years,' Poynder wrote in the asylum's admissions register, when Tom was first committed to his care in October 1833. The register notes the patient's names, both real and assumed, and occupation – 'a Maltster by trade' – and then describes his habits and behaviour: '[Tom] would pursue some amusement for a time with great ardency then suddenly give it up without any assignable cause. This was attributed, by his friends, to eccentricity, but by whatever name it may be called, such conduct betrays an unsound state of mind.'[23]

Poynder found no reason to alter this initial assessment. In a letter of the following year, replying to an enquiry by George

Francis, he states that 'Sir William Courtenay ... has conducted himself in a peaceable manner, and conformed to the rules of this Institution, ever since his admission.' He goes on:

> As respects the state of his mind, at the time of his committing the act of perjury for which he was committed, I am of the opinion, so far as I am capable of forming a judgement on the subject, that it was decidedly unsound.
>
> On the subject of your last enquiry, whether I consider him 'harmless', 'provided his friends are willing to take him' I can only say that though I believe he himself would harm no-one, I cannot answer for the conduct of others, who might be excited by his unsound and extravagant opinions.[24]

Poynder's notes mention that his patient fell ill at one point, appeared to be starving himself, and refused to take medicine, although he does not mention what sort of medicine it might have been and whether it was a specific treatment or one applied more regularly. Drugs were administered in asylums at this time for a range of mental and physical ailments; opiates, aether and cannabis were used to sedate those with 'mania', or to treat melancholia. Otherwise, purgatives and emetics were common, and frequent bloodletting and blistering of the head or neck were considered to benefit the delusional. It is not clear from Poynder's notes what, if any, specific treatments were used in the case of John Nicholls Tom. However, while most asylum inmates were dressed in uniform clothing, and regularly shaved bald, Tom was permitted to retain his own clothes, and his long hair and beard, too. He received visitors on occasion – George Francis kept up his regular appearances. The superintendent's continuing use of his assumed name in correspondence suggests that he may have considered him to be of higher status than the majority of his inmates, and worthy of particular consideration.[25]

In fact, Poynder seems to have treated the impostor as an interesting subject of study. Superintendents had a duty to inspect their patients daily, but in Tom's case Poynder must have spent long periods of time either questioning him or (more likely) simply listening to his lengthy monologues. At one point early in 1834 he noted down in his casebook a selection of Tom's statements and beliefs, which he subsequently transcribed for the benefit of the magistrates:

'William Courtenay states his belief that the Saviour never slept as the Holy Ghost would not let him sleep ... He states his belief that some Jews never sleep. He condemns the Earth as deceitful because it is an object & mutable ...'

'He acknowledges himself to be a dangerous character, & that if he had been returned for Canterbury he should have been sent to the Tower ... A Conspiracy wd have been formed against him which might have cost him his life & which he considers may have been saved by his being sent to the Asylum. He thinks no man can stand against his talents as a speaker, though he considers himself as nothing in himself. My dear child, he says, I am in myself a non-entity ...'

'Every thing depends upon <u>self</u>, & <u>selfish</u> implies Lucifer ... No minister in his opinion understood divinity. He has heard Mr Irving several times and considers him a prophet ... A Pig is the most selfish animal in existence & a sheep the least, hence pork is the most indigestible Meat, & Mutton the most digestible.

He maintained that Pork required strong faith to digest it ... He spoke of himself as possessing more faith than any man in existence. His life was a very mysterious one which time must elucidate as it was incommunicable ...'

'He represents himself as not being under the influence of his senses & says he has no smell, but that he lives entirely by faith ... He considers a Tory an Alkali & a Whig an Acid. He regards Locke & Sir I Newton as two of the greatest fools that ever lived.'[26]

None of this would have seemed particular or unusual to Poynder. Asylum records from this period detail a range of extraordinary delusions, and notions of grandeur and prestige: one former workhouse inmate believed she was the rightful owner of the estates of Sir William Pilkington, while a coachman maintained that he was the wealthy 'Lord Clifton'; a serving woman from Preston claimed to be Lady Stanley, wife of a magnate, while a former teacher from Worcester announced that he was the Archbishop of Canterbury. Others suffered from religious mania: a schoolteacher from Tetbury proclaimed in 1828 that she was the Virgin Mary and 'Judge of the World', while a suicidal mother of seven believed she was immortal and already living in hell.[27]

So, can we determine anything about John Nicholls Tom in particular from the strange monologues that Poynder recorded? The historian Barry Reay identifies the possible influence of William Blake in the closing note about Locke and Newton. Some of these statements sound almost deliberately zany, though, exactly the sort of thing *a mad person might say*. Could John Nicholls Tom have been faking it, for the superintendent's benefit? Certainly, remaining in the asylum kept him out of jail, and prevented his being transported to Australia.

And if madness was indeed curable, he could perhaps after a few years reveal himself to be sane once more ... It is a possibility, perhaps, but it would depend on a high degree of self-awareness and calculation on Tom's part. If he were that clever, he might never have risked being convicted of perjury in the first place.[28]

Alternatively, he could have been genuinely delusional at this point, if not before, and perhaps suffering from some kind of paranoid psychosis or bipolar disorder. While Poynder's notes make his statements sound quite calm and deliberate, they could be the record of a speaker in the grip of a manic episode, or a psychotic one. Trying to develop a more comprehensive picture of his mental state would be impossible with the limited evidence we possess. In 1936, Ronald Matthews, in his book *English Messiahs*, suggested that Tom's delusions of divinity and excessive self-importance pitched him 'halfway between the paranoiac attitude of infantile tyranny and ... dementia praecox [i.e. schizophrenia]. Such a state ... has been classified as paraphrenia.' Few others since have been so boldly comprehensive in their diagnoses. Indeed, there is little more here than the confident declarations of 'monomania' and 'conjestion of the brain' by the doctors back in Cornwall.[29]

Otherwise, the mind of John Nicholls Tom is as closed to us now as the gates of the Kent County Asylum were to the man himself, and only imagination – ours as well as his own – provides a key. We might picture him, alone and pacing in his sealed slate-floored chamber, perhaps awaiting his next session with Mr Poynder. A strong man, he could easily have pulled himself up to the high sill of the window and hung suspended by his fingertips, gazing out through the mesh screen at the broad Kentish sky outside. Weeks passed, and then months, and then years. How did his mind develop over that long period of confinement? Did he become more confident in his assumed identity, or did that identity steadily change, transforming into something entirely new?

It would take only a couple of years for the world outside the asylum gates to forget about Sir William Courtenay. Initially, his celebrity endured, in Canterbury at least: a flurry of cheap publications in 1833–34 contained reprints of his election address and publicity pamphlets, and issues of his broadsheet the *Lion*, together with transcripts of his trial at Maidstone and some very colourful supporting essays and satirical verses. In 1835, news of the forthcoming elections to the new city council of Canterbury spurred John Tom, from within the asylum walls, to propose his own selection of candidates – another little detail that suggests he received special treatment at Barming. The men listed were mostly his original supporters in the city; loyally they responded with a heartfelt plea of their own for the release of Sir William Courtenay, who by his advocacy had proved that he was clearly not insane. Their petition was refused by the authorities.[30]

Courtenay's abiding fame, for the next few years, was sealed in April 1834 with the publication of William Harrison Ainsworth's historical romance *Rookwood*. Ainsworth would become one of the most popular novelists of his day – his books sold far more copies at the time than those of Charles Dickens – and *Rookwood* was a sensation. A cumbersome gothic melodrama of creaking crypts, stolen inheritances, lusty gypsies and dashing highwaymen, the novel also features a variety of anachronistic supporting characters. One of these is Sir William Courtenay, Knight of Malta, who at the time of publication was still an inmate of Kent County Asylum. Ainsworth's tale transforms him into a figure of folk mythology, picturing him among a gang of 'merry beggars' encountered by the highwayman Dick Turpin: 'To his side was girted a long and doughty sword, which he termed, in his knightly phrase, Excalibur; and upon his profuse hair rested a hat as broad in the brim as a Spanish sombrero.'

This extraordinary figure then tells his tale in the form of a song – which appears to be lifted directly from a twopenny publication of the year before mentioned in the *Kent Herald*. The chorus runs:

> *With my coal-black beard, and purple cloak,*
> *Jack-boots and broad-brimmed castor,*
> *Hey-ho! for the Knight of Malta!*

Together with the novel's very extensive footnotes, the song provides all that the majority of contemporary readers would know about Sir William Courtenay. So popular was *Rookwood*, in fact, that many at the time may have assumed that Ainsworth had simply invented the man. Fiction supplanted reality, and the farcical 'Knight of Malta', adrift in history, composed of equal parts poorly remembered fact and outright fantasy, became for many people the true story.[31]

Meanwhile, the country outside the asylum was changing. By the time John Nicholls Tom once more stepped forth as a free man, life in the rural districts around Canterbury would have become quite different. It would be a harsher world altogether that he would discover on his return.

4. 'LOW PERSONS OF SUSPICIOUS CHARACTER'

On 2 July 1836, Emily Jane Burford (also known as Emma) presented herself before General Gerard Gosselin, Justice of the Peace, at his office in Faversham, and laid a charge of domestic violence against her husband. The meeting was duly recorded by the office clerk:

> Emma, the wife of Willm Burford ([not] present) being sworn sayd On 30th June last my s'd Husbnd in consequence of my having corrected [one of my Children] beat me very much & kicked me – he is continually threatening to beat me and I am in danger.[1]

Emily Burford was twenty-three years old, and lived in the settlement of Dunkirk Ville, four miles east of Faversham. Church records show that she and William only had one child, a boy aged three at the time; unless the clerk was mistaken and simply assumed the couple had more children, or my reading of his handwriting is faulty, there may have been a second, unrecorded, child who did not survive infancy. 'Correction' in this case probably refers to physical punishment, but it was quite normal for the day. Was William Burford perhaps angry that his wife had hit the child without his permission? Did he believe that he held a monopoly on household violence?

He is constantly threatening to beat me and I am in danger. These few scant sentences provide a glimpse through a grimy window, into a domestic life distorted by suffering and fear. They tell us nothing about Emily's mental or emotional state at the time she brought the charge. They tell us nothing either about the sequence of events that may have led to that point; did Emily attend the meeting alone and of her own free will, or was she summoned by the magistrate or a constable, or persuaded to attend by a friend or relative? But they testify nonetheless to a certain determination, a certain courage in making that journey in defiance of her abuser and stepping forward before the magistrate. This was not the first time that Emily had been assaulted by her husband. But she intended that it should be the last.[2]

William Burford was clearly bad news. According to the lawyer Frederick Liardet, he was a 'decidedly bad character, a reputed sheep-stealer, and suspected to be concerned in several depredations.' On this occasion, General Gosselin ordered that Burford should be bound over to keep the peace, and required him to find two sureties who would promise £10 each against his good behaviour until the next Quarter Sessions. It was perhaps the best immediate outcome for Emily; with her husband the main breadwinner for the family, either a monetary fine or a spell in prison could have proved ruinous. Now at least she had some small measure of legal protection.[3]

Little less than two years later, Burford would become one of the most devoted disciples of the maverick messiah he knew as Sir William Courtenay. In the woods of Bossenden, he would be shot through the back of the skull with a 1.14oz lead musket ball. Emily Jane Burford would be there, too, in the fog of gunsmoke and the fury of combat, trying in vain to save the life of the husband who had once so terrorised her.

Walking the four miles back to her cottage after her visit to the magistrate's office, Emily would have passed through what would become the heartland of Courtenay's abortive uprising. The old Roman road still runs today as it did then, scored straight across the rolling countryside of Kent. This was the road that Chaucer's pilgrims followed on their journey to the shrine of Thomas Beckett. In the 1830s, it was the London road, used by the Canterbury and Dover mail coaches – the *Union* and the celebrated *Tally Ho!*

It was full summer, and England was in the middle of a heatwave. The haymaking had ended, the meadows cropped with the scythe and the hay raked and stacked into cocks, but the heavy work of reaping and the hop picking was yet to come. This was a fertile country, the soil a rich deep loam ideal for mixed agriculture. Liardet thought the tightly furrowed landscape, sown with small fields, orchards and hop gardens 'peculiarly English.' He found the people of the district less picturesque: 'What a pity that the moral condition of the inhabitants of so fair a spot should stand ... in such mournful contrast with its order and beauty!'[4]

Nearing Boughton, Emily would have passed the gates of Nash Court, the great mansion empty and neglected in this era while the inheritors squabbled in the Courts of Chancery. A lane split northward from the main road here, skirting the Nash estate towards George Francis's farm at Fairbrook. To the right of the road, the parish of Boughton under Blean stretched away across the countryside towards the little church of St Peter and St Paul, where Emily had been baptised, where

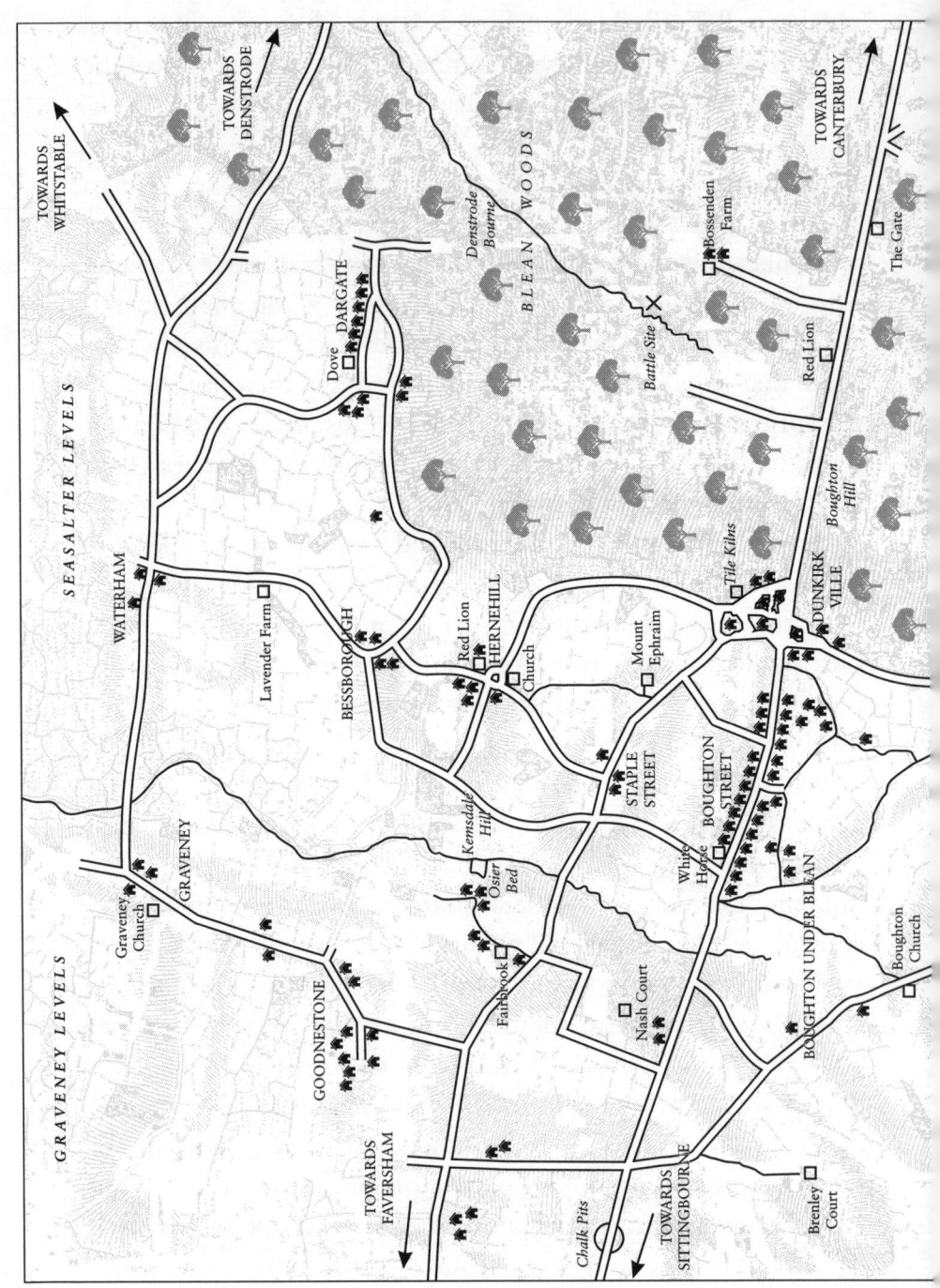

she and William had been wed, and where her father and four of her siblings were buried. The nucleus of the settlement – Boughton Street, as it was called – ran for a mile along the London road, the brick and timber houses and shops pinching the broad highway to a narrower thoroughfare. Today, the bypass carries the heavier traffic clear of it, but you can walk along the street and still see many of the same brick and weatherboarded cottages that Emily Burford would have passed in the high summer of 1836.

To the left, on the higher ground, three windmills raised their sails. Beyond them lay the undulating country of Hernhill parish. On the next ridge stood the big house, Mount Ephraim, home of the Reverend Mr Charles Handley. Beyond Mount Ephraim was Hernhill itself with its square church tower, and the Red Lion pub on the green. Dargate lay over to the east, on the fringes of the Blean woodlands. North of Hernhill, past the hamlets of Bessborough and Waterham, the land flattened out towards the sheep pastures of the Seasalter levels, before fading into the mudflats along the shore of the Swale estuary and the Thames beyond.

As the last houses of Boughton Street fell away, Emily would have passed the invisible eastern boundary of the parish, and entered Dunkirk Ville, a straggling settlement of cottages, small garden plots and fields cut from the skirts of the woodland. Ahead of her, the highway kept straight on up the slope, carrying the traffic of mail coaches, carriers' carts and fish vans on towards Canterbury and Dover. The trees were cut back from either side; the stretch across Boughton and Harbledown Hill had once been the haunt of highwaymen.

The Blean was a royal hunting forest back in the Middle Ages, and wild boar roamed there as late as the fifteenth century. It still remained for the most part scrub woodland and waste, cut into here and there by small fields and plots of farmland, demarcated by fences and streams and little wandering tracks that threaded between the coppice plantations. It was only in the late eighteenth century that the squatter settlement of Dunkirk had first emerged at the ragged edges of the woodland. Nobody seemed to know quite when it had appeared, or how it came to be named. Hasted's *History and Topographical Survey of the County of Kent*, published in 1798 but still considered sufficiently authoritative for the *Times* to quote forty years later, claims that Dunkirk was 'a place exempt from the jurisdiction of either hundred or parish, as in a free port, which receives all who enter it without distinction,' and had thereby gained its name. Others have assumed a link with the smuggling trade to the Flemish coast or suggested that the name was adopted from a prominent house in the vicinity.[5]

In later years, the centre of Dunkirk migrated up the hill to the east, nearer the church built in 1841 to 'civilise' the district. But in the 1830s, the heart of the original settlement lay immediately beyond the Boughton parish boundary, at the foot of the hill, around an approximately triangular scrap of hollow ground bordering the highway, called Dunkirk Common. It was a rough and rambling place, boasting nothing grander than cottages of timber and clay-cob, with roofs of thatch. It was inhabited, Hasted says, 'by low persons of suspicious character, who sheltered themselves there.' By his day, the 'free port' of Dunkirk had been gathered into the jurisdiction of the Lathe of Scray and the Hundred of Westgate, and made an extra-parochial settlement. Now it was officially the Ville of Dunkirk; most of the inhabitants stepped freely across the parish boundaries into Boughton or Hernhill for their baptisms, marriages and burials.[6]

Even so, the ill fame of the place endured. The correspondent of the *Times* wrote that Dunkirk 'labours under a most disgraceful reputation. The men are said to be most of them poachers, and of the women it is enough to say, that they had their reasons for making Courtenay their favourite.' Charles Handley, writing to the Archbishop of Canterbury of his efforts to educate the inhabitants, explained that Dunkirk housed between 600 and 700 people, 'almost exclusively consisting of small occupiers, many of them freeholders & labourers & has been from time immemorial notorious for characters of the worst description to be found among our rural population.'[7]

In 1836, this was Emily's home. She had been born Emily Jane Packman, daughter of a labourer from Boughton under Blean. As with most families in the district, the Packmans were widely spread; Emily had relations in Hernhill and Denstrode, and in Faversham, too. Church records give witness to a steady pulse of childhood tragedy and loss. Only three years after Emily's birth in 1813, a younger brother died in infancy. Next, she lost her elder sister Caroline. In the summer of 1821, her father Thomas died, and her sister Margaret as well. The following year, her sister Louisa perished. By the age of nine, Emily had lost a parent and four siblings. No cause of death is recorded for any of them; the most recent typhus epidemic had faded by the time Caroline died, and cholera did not reach Kent until 1832. Hasted claimed that the district north of Boughton Street was 'a most unpleasant and unhealthy country'; malaria spread from the marshes along the Swale in summer. The historian Barry Reay has estimated that the seasonal mortality figures for Hernhill and Dunkirk do not suggest a malarial zone. But there may have been a host of other reasons for these spikes in deaths within individual families. Accidents and infections were frequent, food was often scarce, and the diseases of poverty and poor living were endemic.[8]

In 1827, the Commissioners of Woods, Forests and Land Revenues ordered a survey of the Ville of Dunkirk. The resulting map still exists, kept in the National Archives at Kew. It is enormous, almost ten feet by seven, the sheets of intricately drawn paper glued to a canvas backing; to view it you have to unroll it like a carpet on the big map table in the reading room. The level of detail is extraordinary. Every house is drawn to scale, every path tracked, every stile plotted. The woodlands are sewn with tiny, illustrated trees. An associated reference book, or *terrier*, provides a key to the map and lists all the owners of houses, fields and orchards, and the tenants where applicable. Several of the names listed would feature, decades later, in the inquests on the Courtenay uprising: Kennett and Packman, Branchett, Culver and Mears.[9]

Down a lane that branched from the highway, facing Dunkirk Common, stood an isolated cottage tenanted by Thomas Kennett. Kennett's wife Sarah was Emily Jane Packman's aunt. Their son William, about twenty at the time the map was surveyed, would marry into the neighbouring James family. Five years after the surveyors had passed through Dunkirk with their measuring rods and notebooks, William Kennett would become one of the first local supporters of the impostor Sir William Courtenay. Further across the common was a cottage listed as being owned by Mrs Packman (spelled 'Peckman') and tenanted by John Packman. Either may have been related to Emily's family, although her own widowed mother still lived in Boughton at this time.

In all directions, a tracery of pathways stretched into the deeper woodland. Only the London road kept to its straight route, directly up the incline of Boughton Hill and across the flat plateau at the top. Half a mile further on, past an isolated roadside pub called the Red Lion (a confusingly common name), a track strikes off to the left between the trees, heading for a clutch of buildings surrounded by fields in a clearing of the woodland. The 1827 map shows the track and the fences, the tight knot of barns and the L-shaped dwelling house, all of it owned by Mr George Gipps Esq, and tenanted by William Culver. And away to the north-west of the farm perimeter, spreading to the winding stream called Denstrode Bourne, was Bossenden Wood.

At the time the map was drawn, nothing marked this place as exceptional. Just over a decade later, it would be a scene of bloodshed.

One freezing foggy Sunday, back in November 1829, two men had entered the property of John Browning, Hernhill farmer and poor law overseer for the Ville of Dunkirk. Breaking into a building behind the farmhouse, they stole two tame rabbits worth three shillings from the hutches. One of the men was named John Packman. The second was William Burford. The two men were swiftly caught, detained, and stood trial before Sir Edward Knatchbull MP at the Epiphany Sessions in Canterbury in January. They were both found guilty of feloniously breaking and entering Mr Browning's property, and of theft, and sentenced to twelve months' imprisonment in St Augustine's jail.

After the men had spent only half a year in the cells, however, the magistrates examined them once more and decided to accept a plea for their early release. The grounds established for clemency were that Packman and Burford had exhibited good conduct in jail, they were penitent, and 'likely to conduct themselves honestly.' In the case of William Burford, that expectation would prove rather wishful.[10]

While Burford himself is easy to identify, his partner in crime is not. There were at least six men of that name living in the district. The 1830 Indictment Roll states that both Packman and Burford were labourers, and 'late of the parish of Hernhill.' There was indeed a John Packman from Hernhill, aged twenty-two at the time; his brother Adman lived in Dunkirk, and John was perhaps the tenant of the cottage on Dunkirk Common owned by Mrs 'Peckman'. But William Burford was from Boughton, not Hernhill; it is at least possible his accomplice was also in reality from that parish, in which case we might identify him as Emily Packman's older brother John, aged eighteen.

Bearing in mind William Burford's later reputation, the rabbit-theft may have been his idea. Like Emily, he was the child of a Boughton labouring family. He was born in May 1805, and was twenty-five years old when he emerged from St Augustine's. A year and three months later, just after the harvest, he and eighteen-year-old Emily were married by the Reverend Thomas Wright at the church of St Peter and St Paul in Boughton. In the church register, the bride is recorded first as 'Emma', then crossed out and corrected to 'Emily Jane'. Neither she nor her new husband could write their own name: both just left a rather irresolute X as their mark. A list of the men who followed Courtenay in 1838, possibly compiled by Charles Handley, states that William Burford could 'read imperfectly.' A similar list kept with the Knatchbull papers classes him as 'supposedly illiterate.' Frederick Liardet, investigating the backgrounds of the men who were killed, found that he 'could not ascertain whether [Burford] had received any education,' but noted that his cottage contained 'a Testament, and one or two other books of a religious nature.' Bibles, testaments and hymn or prayer books were often the only printed matter available to the people of the district. Even so, it is unusual that Burford possessed them and seemed to value them. It seems unlikely that Emily could write, but girls from working families at the time often spent longer in school than boys, and were more often able to read; might the books have belonged to her?[11]

William was a labourer, but he lacked regular employment. Only the live-in farm servants had yearly contracts. Instead, like the majority of other rural labouring men in early nineteenth-century England, Emily's husband would have to find casual work whenever and wherever he could. The harvests required many hands – haycutting with the scythe in June, reaping the wheat and barley with the sickle in August and September, picking the hops and fruit in September and October. The skilled spring and autumn labour of ploughing and seed-drilling would usually be carried out by the contracted farm servants, but farmers might bring in casual workers to do the harrowing and weeding, the manuring and the ditching. Emily would have worked alongside her husband during the harvest, gathering and binding the sheaves. She would have laboured in the hop gardens, tying and pruning the hops, while whole families helped with the picking. There was hard toil for women in the winter months too, pulling turnips and mangolds from the half-frozen soil.[12]

Otherwise, there were long fallow spells with no work, and no income. Some might find employment in the woods of the Blean: cutting and shaving hop poles, coppicing and clearing undergrowth. Evidence taken after the clash in Bossenden Wood refers to some particular skills, lost to us now: *flawing*, or stripping and treating the bark from felled trees, and *broom dashing*, or cutting poles from young wood, often left to itinerants on the margins of legality. But winters could be long and hard, and underemployed labouring families were compelled to turn to the parish overseers of the poor – men like farmer John Browning – for support. For all the risks, it is not difficult to see the attractions of theft, and of poaching; William Burford later gained a reputation as a sheep stealer, but he was not alone in that. The stolen sheep, and the rabbits he and John Packman lifted from Browning's hutches, were more likely sold to buy bread than eaten. Stealing wood was another possibility, either to sell or to burn as winter fuel.[13]

Like most other labouring families in the district, the newly wed Burfords would have rented a cottage for a shilling or two a week. These were mainly timber-framed constructions, walled with laths and cob, two rooms downstairs with floors of beaten clay and one or two bedrooms upstairs beneath the roof beams, with low windows peering out through the thatch. Compared to the more substantial brick cottages that replaced them later in the nineteenth century – often built on the same foundations – they could be dark and uncomfortable places, filled with the scents of close-packed bodies and the smeech of tallow candles. Two decades after the Burfords were married, the Earl of Shaftesbury inspected some labourers' cottages on his estate and found them 'filthy, close, indecent, unwholesome,' the inhabitants 'stuffed like figs in a drum.' Quite possibly the Burfords had to share a cottage with family members or other people; whole families might occupy a single room, all of them sleeping in the same bed. The *terrier* to the 1827 map of Dunkirk lists several buildings with multiple tenancy.[14]

Bread was their staple diet, eaten for every meal with cheese or onion, or simply dipped in water. Meat was an expensive luxury. A lucky family might keep a flitch of bacon smoking in the chimney breast or buy a bullock's heart or a calf's foot for the children at Christmas. Often their only animal protein was pig's lard. Few would eat hot food more than once a week: traditional old Kent recipes include 'kettlebender' – salted toast and dripping soaked in hot water – and 'shackells', a broth of bones and meat scraps boiled with vegetables. In an age before refrigeration or pasteurisation, fresh milk was hard to come by; most was churned into butter or used to make cheese. Labouring people drank their tea black, and often mixed it with strawberry leaves, mint and rue. Beer was the most common drink for everyone and considered a vital support for the labouring life.[15]

The radical journalist and essayist Alexander Somerville had been an agricultural worker in his youth and provides an unusually sympathetic and nuanced portrait of the rural labourers of southern England in his 'Notes from the Farming Districts'. A Hampshire furrow-cutter he interviewed in 1843 gave a frank appraisal of the domestic economy common to labouring families of the era:

> 'Yes, we pay a shillin' a-week of rent for house and little bit of garden; the garden grows some vegetables – not enough – but still it is a help to us ... Nettles, when in season, be good vegetable eating. We have a bit of lard or butter an we can; an cannot, why then salt must do – that be cheap, thank God; and if we have bread to eat to such a dish, why it ben't to be complained on. The worst is that we be as ready for another bellyful next morning and ha'nt got none.'[16]

The people of Boughton, Dunkirk and Hernhill, like many of those interviewed by Somerville a decade later, would have been all too aware that their lives had been getting harder in recent years, and were set to get harder still. They had been labourers for generations in most cases but were not blind to the inequalities of their situation, or to the harshness of the lives they had to endure. All the same, we should not regard them as passive victims of oppression, just as we should not see them as all alike, one faceless earth-coloured throng motivated only by shared and simple desires.

Emily and William Burford were distinct people, as individual as us, although most of what gave them individuality and agency is lost to us now. The patterns of their life have vanished, too, just like the houses they once occupied, erased by a later and more materially prosperous age. The deep-vowelled, hard-burred speech of the people of those villages has long been swamped by the linguistic tides spreading out from London and the estuary of the Thames, and is captured only by crackly old field recordings from the early twentieth century. Some of their distinctive words and expressions were noted down in the later Victorian and Edwardian period, and probably date from much earlier. People of the district spoke of their *moder* and *fader*, became *swelked* in the heat and *huvvery* in the cold, and referred to anyone from outside Kent as a 'foreigner' from the *Sheeres*.[17]

That little scrap of a deposition to the magistrate is all we have of Emily Burford's words, and even that was taken down by a clerk. All the recorded speech of the ordinary people of Boughton, Dunkirk and Hernhill is like that; all of them, whatever they say, are talking 'up', to magistrates and clergymen, and importuning journalists trying to fathom the depths of their ignorance. How might they have spoken to each other? How might Emily have protested to her husband of his treatment of her, and how might he (perhaps) have tried either to apologise or to excuse it? What songs did Emily sing to her infant child? What did she imagine her life might hold, in those first years of her marriage? All of this has vanished now, into the twilight of the deep past.

We have no idea what Emily looked like either, of course. For her husband, there is at least a small picture available, though it could hardly be called a portrait. William Burford's corpse appears in a sketch by the *Weekly Chronicle* illustrator, laid on the straw in the stable of the Red Lion pub, with the dead Sir William Courtenay and five more of his fallen disciples. Burford lies on the righthand end of the line. He appears to be wearing a knee-length labourer's smock, and a round narrow-brimmed hat is set beside his head. Three of his dead comrades are dressed almost identically. He might also have a chinstrap beard – maybe he was growing his whiskers in emulation of Sir William, as some supporters in Canterbury were said to have done? – but it could just be a crude sort of shading.[18]

Another view of the same scene, reproduced in the book by 'Canterburiensis', shows the body at the end of the row as clean-shaven, and with a rather gaunt, raw-boned look. But we cannot know if the bodies are arranged in the same way as in the other picture, or whether the faces are accurately depicted. Burford was the only one of the slain to have died from a head wound; his body could have been the one described by the reporter from the *Globe*, with the features still distorted by death's agony: '[the] eyes were staring open, the nostrils dilated, and the hair starting from the head, and still stiffened with the clotted blood, which had flowed from his wounds.'[19]

So all that remains of William Burford might be a name on a grave notice, a few lines in official documents, and a vague and generic approximation of a labouring man, on smudged old newsprint.

In the late summer of 1830, only a month or two after Burford was released from jail, the countryside near Canterbury ignited into violence. Gangs of labouring men roamed the villages of the Elham valley, south of the city just below Barham Down, setting upon and destroying the machines that local farmers had hired to thresh grain after the harvest. By the end of September, the uprising had spread from Canterbury to Ashford, Dover and the coastal districts. From machine-breaking, the gangs turned to arson, burning hayricks, barns and machine sheds. An observer standing on the Dane John mound in Canterbury at nightfall reported seeing fires flaring on the horizon in as many as five different places. All Kent, it seemed, was roused to fury. Soon the rest of southern England would follow.[20]

There was nothing particularly new about agricultural machines; they had been in widespread use since the beginning of the century. The sudden eruption of machine-breaking in the late summer and autumn of 1830 was just the latest and fiercest manifestation of an undeclared guerrilla war that had gone on for over a decade in the English countryside. Since the end of the Napoleonic War in 1815, and the 'peace without prosperity' that followed, working people in the agricultural areas had seen wages fall and regular patterns of employment torn apart. A wet summer, a poor crop, could bring whole communities to the brink of hunger and destitution. Migrant Irish labourers arriving for the harvests, many believed, were undercutting the wages of local men. But it was the use of machinery on farms, usually hired for the season by farmers eager to trim away still further expense, that came to symbolise the shrinking horizons of labouring people. A single horse-powered threshing or winnowing machine could do the work of many men, for a fraction of the cost. Worse still, the machines could be operated by women, who were paid only a fraction of a male labourer's wage.[21]

Threshing with the flail was one of the hardest and most physically demanding jobs of the farming year. It was a man's job, and a lot of masculine pride was bound up in it.

The historian Carl Griffin has suggested that the threshing machine in particular was as much an affront to traditional gender dominance in village life as to traditional patterns of labour; the labouring man was being emasculated, just as he was being robbed of his employment. Much of the violence that followed had a distinctly gendered aspect too: the 'killing' of the machine was an act of male retribution.[22]

As violence pulsed and flared across the fields and along the village lanes, farmers and gentry began to receive letters from the mysterious 'Captain Swing', promising that dire and terrible vengeance would fall upon them if they did not raise the wages of their workers, lower rents and tithes, and cease using machines. By then, the breaking gangs had reached Ospringe and Sittingbourne, beyond Boughton. A band of men marched from Stockbury towards Detling carrying the black flag of revolution. Their leader, a Maidstone shoemaker, told a witness that 'it is your dandy houses and your dandy habits and your sinecure places that have brought the Country to this state ... Now we have righted this Parish we are to go thro' every other Village and Parish and do the same thing.' Another man told the High Sheriff of Kent that 'we will destroy the corn stacks and thrashing machines this year. Next year we will have a turn with the Parsons, and the third we will make war upon the Statesmen.'[23]

At the East Kent Quarter Sessions in Canterbury in October, seven men accused of machine-breaking were tried before Sir Edward Knatchbull, the same MP that had presided over the trial of William Burford earlier that year. Knatchbull found the men guilty but sentenced them to a paltry four days in jail. As a staunchly Tory traditionalist, he may have been quietly sympathetic of their hatred for rural change. More importantly, he seemed determined to downplay the severity of the offence, and to draw a clear distinction between it and the tide of arson and general rebellion sweeping his county.[24]

Still the fires burned. 'The whole of East Kent,' the *Times* reported, was 'thrown into a state of indescribable anxiety and terror.' By then, the uprising had spread to Sussex, Buckinghamshire and Dorset; it would soon reach East Anglia. Across the country, the Yeomanry, volunteer cavalry raised from landowners and their tenants, mobilised to confront the rioters. Regular troops marched into the country districts, too, and gangs of special constables guarded villages and farms. Steadily force began to prevail where legal temporizing had failed. On 20 November, in one of the last flickers of arson in Kent, two brothers from Denstrode burned a barn belonging to farmer William Wraight of Hernhill. The young men were named Henry and William Packman; Denstrode lies on the borders of Dunkirk and the parish of Blean, and they may have been distant relatives of Emily Burford. On Christmas Eve, before a huge crowd on Penenden Heath just outside Maidstone, the Packman brothers were hanged on the scaffold.[25]

The 'Swing riots', as they became known, had been the boiling-point reaction of a countryside long heating towards violence. In some ways, they were a success; the farmers of Kent initially gave up using machinery on their land. But the alarm that the violence had caused to the authorities, and to a government soon locked in the wild tumult of the reform era, would take longer to dissipate.

One of the first acts of the newly elected reforming government of 1832 was to set up a royal commission to investigate abuses of the laws regulating support for the poor. These dated back to 1601 and had developed over the centuries in a series of ad-hoc amendments and adjustments that never quite satisfied anybody. Under the terms of the laws, each parish was required to provide support, or 'relief', for the poor, sick and destitute of its own jurisdiction. Funding was drawn from the poor rates, paid by each ratepayer, and relief was allocated on a sliding scale based on the current price of bread. This system had endured for centuries but came under particular stress towards the end of the eighteenth century, when falling wages and changing patterns of employment put increasing numbers of people 'on the parish' for some or all of the year. Parish officials were now using the poor rates to supplement low wages or to fill gaps in casual employment or giving 'outdoor' relief (outside the workhouse, that is) either in cash or in kind.[26]

Over 1833 and into 1834, the Poor Law Commissioners – headed by Nassau Senior and Edwin Chadwick – assembled their findings and drew up their report. The old poor laws, they had found, were a shambles. Funds intended for the sick and needy were being used to support entire families of able-bodied labouring folk in idleness and poverty. Poverty itself, of course, was not the problem – it was merely part of the natural order. The real danger was *pauperism*, a degraded and 'demoralised' state in which the incentive to seek work is leached away and honest labourers became dependant beggars, living passively off parish handouts, unable or unwilling to better themselves. The growth of idle *pauperism*, the commissioners suggested, lay in part behind the outbreaks of violence across the country in 1830. Accustomed to receiving a livelihood for nothing, the poor had become demanding and insolent and no longer wanted to work for their bread. 'Can we wonder,' the report of the commissioners asked, 'if the uneducated are seduced by a system which offers marriage to the young, security to the anxious, ease to the lazy, and impunity to the profligate?'[27]

By subsidising the idle poor with benefits, the report advised, the parishes were rewarding indolence and suppressing the desire of individuals to better themselves through honest toil. Instead, new legislation should incentivise the poor to find work, by making the consequences of unemployment and poverty as dire as possible. From July 1835, 'outdoor relief' in England should be abolished for the able-bodied. If the poor wanted relief, they would have to work for it – and that work, commissioner Nassau Senior wrote, should be 'as hard as it can be made.' Those who would not or could not work and remained in poverty would be forced to enter the workhouse for their support. The old parishes would be grouped together into new Poor Law Unions, each with a monstrous new workhouse, built on the lines of a prison, to accommodate the feckless poor who refused to work for a living. And each new workhouse, Senior went on, would be 'as disagreeable as it can be made.' The culture of dependency would be smashed, they believed, once the idle poor came to fear the state more than they feared hard labour and exertion: 'the moral evil of pauperism' would be countered by the threat of retribution.[28]

Surprisingly, this effort to 'restore rustic discipline' by terrorising the poor into moral rectitude met with very little political opposition. The New Poor Law Amendment Act, based on the report of the commissioners, passed into law on its second reading in parliament. The legislation was enacted by a Whig government, and the new workhouses would be called 'Whig bastilles', but it had broad support from both conservatives and liberals alike. A mere twenty MPs opposed it, a mixture of traditionalist Ultra-Tories, radicals, and a handful of Irish members who doubtless glimpsed in the Act's harsh rulings what was coming down the road for their own communities.[29]

Before long, dire rumours of the new law were percolating through the rural districts that would be hit hardest by it. The old poor laws had been humiliating enough, but they had at least offered a safety net in hard times. The threat of the terrible new all-consuming workhouses was far worse. Families would be split up in these establishments, wives and husbands and even children sent to separate quarters and forbidden contact. Some feared that the corpses of the workhouse dead would be used to make pies, or to fertilise the fields. Under the 1832 Anatomy Act, unclaimed bodies 'in public care' would be donated to the medical schools for dissection; would that be their fate? Others claimed that the work of mortality would be hastened along by the issuing of poisoned bread. 'Some of the paupers actually believed,' a Devon commissioner would write, 'that if they touched the bread they would drop down dead.'[30]

Some of this at least was close to the truth. Life in the workhouse was intended to be harder and more unpleasant – 'less eligible', in the phrase of the day – than even the meanest subsistence that could be gained outside it. Inmates were stripped, scrubbed, shaved and deloused, then clad in rough and uncomfortable prison-like uniforms. They were indeed separated by age and sex, and forbidden under threat of corporal punishment to leave without permission. Fed on the cheapest and most repellent food, and little of it, they were kept cold and hungry in winter, and made to labour at hard, repetitive and degrading work – breaking stones, picking oakum from old rope, or grinding bones for fertiliser. All of it was intended to crush the spirit and deaden the soul.[31]

Effectively terrorised even before the new laws came into operation, the rural poor of England were close to despair. The problem was that there was insufficient year-round work available for labouring people. The casualisation of farm employment meant that rural families were often obliged at intervals to rely on parish welfare for their support, particularly during the winter months when work grew scarce. Now even this imperfect system was to be abolished, and the jobless poor herded into huge forbidding workhouses to be treated like criminals, or slaves.

As with the 'Swing' riots five years before, Kent was the first English county to explode. At the end of April 1835, the old parish poor law overseers were replaced by the relieving officers of the new Unions. Outdoor relief in cash, they announced, would now be replaced by a system of tickets, which could be exchanged for necessary goods. The allocations for children would be reduced as well. Many suspected, quite correctly, this was the first step to outright abolition of 'outdoor' relief. At the village of Bapchild, on the London road between Faversham and Sittingbourne, a crowd of local people set upon the new relieving officer and destroyed his books and papers.[32]

On 4 May, an angry crowd gathered in the parish of Doddington. Armed with 'sticks, stones and other offensive weapons' they began 'making a great riot, rout, tumult and disturbance.' They assaulted the churchwarden, the relieving officer and the newly elected guardian of the Faversham Poor Law Union, then imprisoned them in the church for two hours. Another band gathered that same day in Upchurch, on the far side of Sittingbourne. Again, they attacked the officials of the parish and new poor law, 'in the due and lawful performance of their respective duties.'[33]

The following day, the revolt reached Charles Handley's parish of Hernhill. A mob of fifty or more 'evil-disposed persons' – women as well as men – marched through the district behind a flag mounted on a hop pole. 'Riotously and routously' they overturned a cartload of bread intended for relief-in-kind, and assaulted Edmund Foreman and two other poor law officials. Among Foreman's attackers were George Packman of Staple Street, Hernhill, and two men from nearby Dunkirk, John James and James Glover; Glover had a cottage on Dunkirk Common, across the lane from Kennett's house. Another man, a young labourer named Thomas Tyler Mears, fled the village after the attack. Constable John Mears of Boughton, his cousin, spent the next four days hunting him down and bringing him to justice.[34]

That same day violence flared in Linsted, and on 6 May in Throwley. In adjacent parishes gangs of men gathered with clubs and stones, 'forcing the peaceable labourers to quit their work, menacing the civil authorities, extorting money, and committing violent assaults on parties who refuse to comply with their violent demands.' On the 7th, a mob surrounded the church in Rodmersham where the poor law officials were allocating tickets under the new system. Some of the men had blackened their faces. One carried a club inscribed with the phrase *Plenty or This*. The rioters snatched the tickets from those who had accepted them, bundling them back into the church to insist on the traditional cash payments instead. When the harassed officials tried to remonstrate with them, insisting that they were merely doing their duty under the law, the seething mob drove them back inside the church and blocked the doors, holding them captive for four hours and then pelting them with stones when they finally broke free.[35]

At Sittingbourne, the Reverend Dr John Poore of Murston, magistrate and Justice of the Peace, was meeting with his colleague General Gosselin at the Rose Inn to examine the men arrested in the preceding days' violence. They were interrupted by an invasion of local labourers, who threatened to 'wreak their vengeance' upon the magistrates unless the accused were released. Poore and Gosselin were then 'grossly insulted and locked up by paupers' for several hours in their own justice chamber.

Later that day, a detachment of the 28th (North Gloucestershire) Regiment of Foot arrived in Sittingbourne, summoned from their quarters in Chatham. After moving his troops into position in small groups to take the rioters by surprise, the officer commanding the detachment ordered them to fix bayonets and load with ball ammunition. He then told Dr Poore that he awaited his order to fire into the mob.[36]

Three years later, John Poore would find himself in a very similar situation in Bossenden Wood, confronting John Nicholls Tom and his band. On that occasion, the troops themselves would forestall his order to fire. In Sittingbourne, he did not need to give it; the assembled people had only to see the steely gleam of the bayonets and hear the ramrods rattling in the musket barrels to scatter in all directions. Twenty men were subsequently arrested for their 'violent and outrageous conduct,' and taken to Canterbury in carts escorted by special constables and a troop of Yeomanry cavalry with swords drawn. As the convoy passed through the streets, the people of the city groaned and hissed, hurling abuse at the escorting troopers. Some hurled stones as well. The brief uprising in the villages against the new laws had lasted only a week, but the ferocious outrage and lingering dread remained.[37]

In January, the massive new workhouse at Faversham, built close to the Oare gunpowder mills, accepted its first inmates. By 1837, the New Poor Law was in operation across the country. Not everything had gone the way of the reformers: the Union officials had found it impossible to abolish or even greatly to reduce outdoor relief payments for the poor, especially over the winter season. And, despite the enthusiastic calculations of the Poor Law Commissioners, the new system was to prove even more expensive than the old one had been. But the misery of the workhouses, and the mood of draconian moralising and tight-fisted austerity that had created them, endured. Already by the following winter they were claiming their first victims.

Shortly after they were married, William and Emily Burford had moved ten miles south of Boughton to the parish of Westwell, close to Ashford. William had relatives in the surrounding hamlets – there were at least four other Burford households in the district – and quite possibly he moved to find work, perhaps as a farm servant on a yearly contract. The couple's first child, Edward, was born at Westwell in 1833. They would have been far from Boughton and Dunkirk during the period that the impostor Sir William Courtenay made his first appearances there. But two years later, the Burfords had migrated once more.

In February 1835, William was apprehended by John Mears, parish constable of Boughton, for assaulting his wife, Emily. The note in Mears's day book states that Burford was living in Dunkirk at the time. Why they had decided to move there rather than returning to Boughton is unclear. Perhaps William was for some reason unwelcome in his native parish? Or perhaps it was just cheaper; residents of the extra-parochial district of Dunkirk were not liable for rates or tithes, so owners of cottages could feasibly charge lower rents on their properties. It was, in any case, a highly independent community, out of the immediate purview of state or parish authorities. Burford and his wife and infant son likely inhabited one of the cottages around Dunkirk Common, close to

William Kennett's house and the Woodman's Hall beershop. Emily was at least living close to her surviving family, her old friends and the places familiar to her from her childhood. But life in Dunkirk, in a cramped cottage with her small child and her vicious husband, cannot have been pleasant.

Constable John Mears, a plumber by trade, doubtless knew Dunkirk and its denizens very well. Both he and his brother Nicholas had plots of land in the same neighbourhood. Nicholas Mears lived a stone's throw from Kennett's cottage, just across the parish border into Boughton. Like Burford he was a man of violence, and had once been fined for assault; apparently, he also treated his wife 'like a dog' but was never arrested by his brother or brought before the magistrates for it.[38]

Mears's surviving day book notes a string of arrests and investigations in the district around this same time. In January 1835, he searched the Dunkirk cottage of William Packman for stolen property. He arrested George Branchett in May of 1835, and the same month searched the house and premises of Edward Wraight the Younger in Hernhill for property stolen from local farmer Edward Curling. Phineas Harvey (later described by the lawyer Frederick Liardet as a 'quiet, well-conducted man' who 'usually attended church') was fined costs in a charge of assault in September 1835. William Price also had his house searched by the constable in November, and James Wraight of Dunkirk was arrested that same month.[39]

Liardet would later claim that William Burford was the only one of John Nicholls Tom's followers to have had a poor reputation. This was clearly not true; all of those listed in the last paragraph would later fight for the impostor. The magistrate Norton Knatchbull claimed that several of his band 'were of notorious bad character'. But William does seem to have been a repeat offender. He was unlikely to have been involved with the 'Swing' disturbances back in 1830 – he had only just got out of jail at the time and perhaps would not have wanted to risk his liberty again so soon. But he was back in Dunkirk at the time of the anti-Poor Law riots. Might he have been one of the fifty or more 'evil-disposed persons' who gathered in the adjacent parish of Hernhill? Several of his new Dunkirk neighbours were among them.

In late September of 1836, nearly three months after Emily had given her testimony before the magistrate in Faversham, William was back in court, at the Michaelmas Quarter Sessions in Canterbury, to be tried for the assault charge she had brought against him. The result is recorded as 'no prosecution': William Burford had sufficiently mended his ways since the summer to be let off, for now at least.[40]

So what would transform William Burford, in the space of barely eighteen months, from a violent petty criminal and domestic abuser into the committed disciple of the new messiah Sir William Courtenay? What new resolution would lead him to take up arms in the cause of his master, and to fight and to die for him in Bossenden Wood? And why would his wife Emily risk her life in that same wood, throwing herself into the heart of the conflict to try and drag her husband to safety? The Burfords kept 'books of religious nature' in their cottage, but do not seem to have been regular churchgoers. Perhaps one or both of them held strong Christian beliefs nonetheless, although their piety would not have been recognised as such by the likes of Frederick Liardet or the Reverend Charles Handley.

Like many others in Dunkirk and the parishes of Boughton and Hernhill, the Burfords were still living in the immediate aftermath of the waves of violent revolt and state repression that had swept through rural England in the 1830s. Whether they had been directly involved in the Swing disturbances and the Poor Law rioting or not, they would doubtless have heard about it and felt the effects. Those disturbances had been put down, ultimately, by force. The grim strictures of the new legislation, with its doctrine of 'less eligibility', threatened the regular patterns of support in times that were already growing harder. It must have seemed that nothing the people of the villages could do would prevent their slide into misery and deprivation.

But those previous uprisings had lacked clear leadership and definite direction. Men like the Maidstone shoemaker Robert Price, who shouted about 'righting' the parishes, were only the local figureheads of the wider 'Swing' riots. In 1835, there had been no real leaders at all, or none that the magistrates could subsequently identify. Soon, though, a leader would indeed appear among the labouring people of the villages west of the Blean. A man not only of huge charisma and gentlemanly education, but of overwhelming religious and spiritual magnetism, too. A man who spoke in the words of the Bible, the holy truth that all had been taught to regard as the ultimate authority. This man would promise not only to better the condition of the labouring people, but also to make them better people. He would forge the downtrodden, demoralised, criminalised inhabitants of Dunkirk and Hernhill into an army of justice and turn their fists and boots and cudgels into holy weapons, directed in the cause of righteousness against all those who had oppressed them, judged them, imprisoned them and humiliated them for so long. He would place the sword of divine retribution in their hands and lead them to the Apocalypse.

At that moment, the man who would promise all this was still sitting placidly in a locked room in Kent County Lunatic Asylum.

But soon enough he would be free.

5. 'FROM THE BONDS OF SATANN'

One morning in the summer of 1837, almost a year after Emily Jane Burford had testified to the magistrate about her husband's domestic violence, another young woman awoke to the news that her uncle was dead, and she was now the Queen of England.

Many hoped that things would change for the better under the reign of the young Victoria. Among them were the family of John Nicholls Tom, who was still in the asylum at Barming after nearly four years. At end of August, shortly after being returned as liberal MP for East Cornwall in the first elections after the accession, Sir Hussey Vivian received a letter from Mrs Susan Tom, the convicted perjurer's stepmother. The letter had been forwarded by Edmund Turner, the Tom family's local MP in Truro; Vivian was by far the better connected of the two politicians.

'The young man in question,' Mrs Tom wrote, 'and for whose liberty I now solicit your benign influence with our august and lovely young Queen ... was convicted of perjury, and sentenced to transportation, before any of his friends, who were offering large rewards for discovering him, knew where he was ... and he was confined in an asylum in Kent. He is now much better, and wishes his liberty ... I feel assured, if you will condescend to undertake it, her tender and philanthropic heart will listen to you, for he has been guilty of no crime.'[1]

Vivian had already received a letter from Tom's wife Catherine, also forwarded by Turner, and had spoken to his father during his recent election canvassing at Bodmin. Now he duly sent the request for pardon up the chain to his friend Lord John Russell, reappointed Home Secretary in the Whig government of Lord Melbourne. Russell then wrote to the magistrates at Maidstone, requesting an assessment of the current mental state of John Nicholls Tom, also known as William Courtenay. On 8 September, Superintendent George Poynder submitted his report to the magistrates, who returned it to Lord Russell:

> William Courtenay, alias Sir William Courtenay, is in good bodily health, but of unsound mind [and] labours under delusions respecting his person and property. His wife has been to see him since his admission into this asylum, who informed me that his real name is John Nicholls Thom, and that he lived formerly at Truro, in Cornwall. Two or three persons who knew him while residing in Truro, have also visited the asylum, and identified his person as John Nicholls Thom, whilst he disclaimed all knowledge of them.
>
> He also fancies himself to be a knight of Malta, and heir to the Honeywood estate, as well as Powderham Castle.[2]

Despite the superintendent's caution, and clear evidence that Tom's delusionary condition had not altered in the slightest, Lord Russell apparently did not find anything in this report to militate against pardoning the subject. Surely the local celebrity of 'Sir William Courtenay' had quite dissipated by that point, and a patient recently released from an asylum was unlikely to command any great following? Besides, the man's fame, such as it was, nowadays rested in his cameo appearance in a popular historical novel. What could go wrong if he were freed? Russell could do a favour for Vivian, who could in turn do a favour for his colleague Mr Turner, and for Turner's constituents in Truro, the Toms. Less than a month after Poynder wrote his report, Lord Russell issued in the name of Queen Victoria a free pardon to 'William Courtenay' (the name under which he had originally been convicted), and an order for his discharge from the asylum.[3]

A problem quickly arose; the patient was unwilling to be discharged into the care of his family, and still refused to recognise them or any connection they might have with him. Catherine Tom paid more than one visit to the asylum, and managed at least one private conversation with her husband, but to no avail. Exasperated, Mr William Tom finally gave his permission for George Francis to deputise for him in removing his son from Barming, 'he having refused to leave his confinement with any other person.' Over the last four years, Mr Francis had maintained his regular visits to the friend he still called Sir William, considering him oppressed and persecuted, and unjustly confined. 'I declare before my God,' he would later claim, 'the only motive I had was kindness to a stranger.'

On a chilly day at the end of October, with a sharp frost in the air that hinted at the savage winter to come, Francis arrived at Barming asylum to liberate his friend. After consulting with the magistrates, George Poynder met Francis, who was with the patient and the matron of the asylum ('a very clever woman', Francis reported, who 'never saw anything insane, in any respect' in Tom's conduct). 'Mr Francis,' Poynder said, 'I feel great pleasure in delivering up your friend, Sir William Courtenay, into your hands; I wish him health and happiness!'[4]

Was the superintendent humouring his visitor, or did he still believe that in some way John Nicholls Tom *was* Sir William Courtenay? Perhaps in his lengthy sessions with the patient he had come to consider that both identities might be held simultaneously. We have the same difficulty today: should we call the man by his real name, John Nicholls Tom – an identity he had repudiated – or the name by which his supporters knew him, and many official documents referred to him? Calling him *Sir William Courtenay* seems almost to support the imposture. Perhaps, like George Poynder, we must accept that the two identities were not mutually exclusive: John Nicholls Tom – or *Thom*, to use the persistent contemporary misspelling – was merely the corporeal vehicle for the imaginary character Courtenay. Sir William and Mad Tom were two people inhabiting the same body, the same space. Which one of them was the impostor? From this point on, we must indulge the same dual perspective.

Before leaving the asylum, George Francis later claimed, Sir William – as he still addressed him – promised that he would have nothing more to do with politics and would never associate with poor people or address mobs. Instead, he would devote himself solely to proving the claims he had made about his identity and recovering the inheritance that was his due. Reassured by these words, Francis left Barming immediately with his friend seated beside him in the chaise and drove for Fairbrook. Back at the farm, he was able to return to Sir William the trunks of clothes and possessions that he had kept safe for him over the last four years. He presented him with his old grey horse as well, the 'scraggy bit of blood' that had so impressed the people of Canterbury, and which he had been keeping in hay and oats in his own stable for all this time, presumably at his own expense.

There had been a few changes since Sir William's last stay. The Faversham Farmers' Club had not readmitted Mr Francis to their society. His oldest son Robert now had a house of his own in Boughton Street and was hoping to gain his apothecary's certificate. But his second son Vinus had died the year before, at the age of nineteen – the pain of that loss is silent in the record of subsequent events, but it must have been acute and could have had a profound effect on what followed. The other children Ellen, Jane and George Jr were most likely still living in the house. His eldest daughter Eliza Jane Francis, meanwhile, had just turned twenty-two, and was still unwed.

Eliza and her aunt Mary Horne were not the only unmarried women in the area later to fall under suspicion for their involvement with John Nicholls Tom. We should not discount a possible misogyny in their presentation in our sources; unmarried 'spinsters', popular prejudice might suggest, were prone to strange urges. But if we can believe the reports of their extraordinary later behaviour, both women appear to have found Sir William Courtenay utterly hypnotic, and sexually compelling, too. Quite possibly he was the most exciting man they had ever met. Whatever genteel pleasures Mr Francis's aspirations might have provided for them – churchgoing, piano-playing, reading, or just staring out of the tall sash windows – must have paled before the glory of his return to Fairbrook.

Sir William, for his part, conducted himself towards the Francis family in 'the most gentlemanly manner.' In his conversation, he appeared humble and recondite. One must obey those in authority, he told Francis, even if they were of lesser status, for such was the law of the land. He spoke in respectful terms of the law now, which should always be supported and obeyed, and warmly of his country and his faith. 'He would go on in that strain,' Francis later recalled, in his stumbling and bewildered testimony to the Select Committee, 'only in far better language; he used very superior language in respect of his religion; and really I considered he has done me quite as much good as any clergyman that I ever heard ... I was fascinated with him,' he admitted.[5]

It is hard not to feel sorry for George Francis, for all his preposterous gullibility. Harder still not to feel sorry for poor Eliza Francis and her partially deaf, short-sighted aunt, Mary. They had maintained their faith in Sir William Courtenay in trying times, maintained their belief in his word, his identity and his intentions, and hoped that he might one day reward that faith and belief by proving them right.

They were to be cruelly and horribly disappointed.

Before the end of the year, it became apparent to Francis that his guest was making no effort to establish proofs of his name or deeds to his lands and titles. Instead, despite his solemn promise back at the asylum, he was most certainly associating with poor people. In particular, John Nicholls Tom was associating with one of Francis's own tenants, a small farmer in 'distressed' circumstances named William Wills who lived in one of the cottages adjacent to Fairbrook.

Once a prosperous smallholder, Wills's 'drunken and dissolute' lifestyle had left him, at the age of forty-five, living like a common labourer. Quite possibly he had known John Tom when he first stayed at Fairbrook, before he was sent to the asylum. The impostor may have given him money; according to the correspondent of the *Times*, his hold over Wills 'may be traced to some little services he rendered ... and to the relief he afforded him at times of distress.' Very soon, Tom was spending much of his time at the cottage, and William Wills would become one of his most committed supporters. According to a reporter at his later trial, Wills had always been 'fanatically inclined.' The reporter also provides a thumbnail sketch of him: 'His countenance is at once dull and melancholy. He is a tall, thin and rather ill-formed man. His dress and bearing showed that he was in a somewhat better class of life ...'[6]

Wills shared his cottage with his wife Lucy, more than two decades his junior and now heavily pregnant, and another labourer, Edward Newman. Both soon joined Sir William's circle of admirers. But John Tom must have been consorting with greater numbers than merely the inhabitants of Wills's home. His presence may have drawn others to Fairbrook, the curious or the courageous or those eager to profit from his famous largesse. He was probably touring the surrounding country too, revisiting his old friends: William Kennett, for example, in his cottage down on Dunkirk Common. William Burford may first have encountered him around this same time. Perhaps he was already 'addressing mobs'.[7]

All this was highly embarrassing to George Francis, who seems very quickly to have lost track of his old friend altogether. Tom's discharge from the asylum, and his residence at Fairbrook, had been reported in the *Kentish Observer* at the beginning of November. But when Norton Knatchbull, son of the MP Sir Edward Knatchbull, encountered Mr Francis a month later and asked him about Sir William, Francis was unable to tell him anything of his guest's whereabouts. When he returned at last to Fairbrook, the impostor discovered that Francis 'very much disliked his conduct' in doing nothing to prove his claims, and in 'going among the lower class.' Displeasure led to argument, and finally to confrontation.

'I had certainly a very severe dispute with him,' Francis later related. 'I wonder he did not shoot me, or knock me down, for he was a very great man.'[8]

Despite this, he continued to claim that his guest never showed any disposition to violence. Perhaps he remained as besotted as ever.

But before long, even Mr Francis reached the limits of his hospitality. Early in January, he discovered that his guest was keeping a pair of pistols in the house and demanded that he immediately remove them from the premises. On the 10th, he finally 'desired him to quit his house.'

John Nicholls Tom did not have far to go. From that point he seems to have taken up residence in Wills's cottage. George Francis would probably have been able to see him quite clearly from his front door, as he passed up and down the lane. Eliza may have visited him there, as her aunt Mary would later do. Tom brought his firearms with him too: Lucy Wills later informed the vicar Charles Handley that 'Courtenay' had brought two pistols to the house from Mr Francis's – 'he took one to Canterbury to get it repaired and then brought it back.' He left his horse in the Fairbrook stable, though; feed and grooming were expensive, and he would let his former host cover the cost.[9]

Snow was already falling by the time John Nicholls Tom departed Fairbrook. The year had begun with thick wet fog, but before the second week of January the temperature had plummeted below freezing and a hard frost set in. The snow continued, almost unabated, for weeks. The Willses and their new guest would soon be snowed into their cottage, just as the Francis family were snowed into Fairbrook. Snow choked the lanes and the frozen streams, filled the air, and obscured the horizon in all

Above left: John Nicholls Tom as 'Sir William Courtenay'. Frontispiece of *The Life and Extraordinary Adventures of Sir William Courtenay: Knight of Malta, alias John Nichols Tom …* by 'Canterburiensis' (Canterbury, 1838).

Above right: Sir William giving a speech in the Guildhall, Canterbury, December 1832, 'during the nomination of Candidates for the representation of this city in Parliament'. (Contemporary print, Dawes collection, Mount Ephraim)

Tom's lion banner of painted silk. Preserved today in the Dawes collection, Mount Ephraim. (Photograph by the author)

Mount Ephraim today. The current structure was rebuilt c.1880, on the site of the older house occupied by the Reverend Charles Handley in 1838. (Photograph by the author)

Bossenden House, viewed from the west and showing the surviving original rear elevation. The water tank is a modern feature. The Mears brothers would have crossed this scene from right to left, and Nicholas Mears was murdered at the front corner of the house, where the conifer tree now stands. (Photograph by the author)

'Courtenay with his Troops leaving Bosenden Farm, Culver's Residence': image from the *Weekly Chronicle*, 10 June 1838. The sketch shows the appearance of the original front elevation of the house, and the gap in the fence to the right where Mears was killed. At the lower righthand corner of the sketch is the spring where Sarah Culver gathered water, and the path into Bossenden Wood.

John Nicholls Tom 'as he appeared at the Affray, near Canterbury', from a contemporary print. (Image courtesy of Harvard Law School Library, Historical & Special Collections)

Above: 'Soldiers entering Bossenden Wood', from *The Life and Extraordinary Adventures of Sir William Courtenay...* (Canterbury, 1838).

Left: The track leading into Bossenden Wood today. (Photograph by the author)

John Tom in the act of shooting Lieutenant Bennett. 'A Correct Representation of the Scene of the Action', from *The Life and Extraordinary Adventures of Sir William Courtenay...* (Canterbury, 1838). In reality, Tom was much closer to the lieutenant when the fatal shot was fired.

Dramatic portrayal of the battle, from a contemporary print, showing 'Sir William Courtenay alias John Thom, The Pretended Messiah and his credulous followers'. The artist has compressed the space between the opposing parties, and shown the troops wearing white breeches, but otherwise the picture gives an accurate impression of the appearance of both groups. (Image courtesy of the National Army Museum, London)

Eyewitness watercolour sketch of the 'Affray in Bossenden Wood', by 'Capt M' (probably Captain George Minter, 45th Foot). The attached caption reads: 'The tall man with a Beard, club in one hand and murderous Pistol in the other, is Courtenay; Officer falling dead Lt Bennett.' Bennett's soldiers are shown advancing from the left, with Major Armstrong's firing line in the foreground. Armstrong himself is already riding into the melee. The 'Magistrates on horseback' shown at lower left are probably the Handley brothers and, facing away from the viewer, Dr Poore. (Image courtesy of Mary Evans Picture Library)

The Red Lion pub, Dunkirk, in 2018. (Photograph by the author)

The Red Lion in 1838, from *The Life and Extraordinary Adventures of Sir William Courtenay …* (Canterbury, 1838).

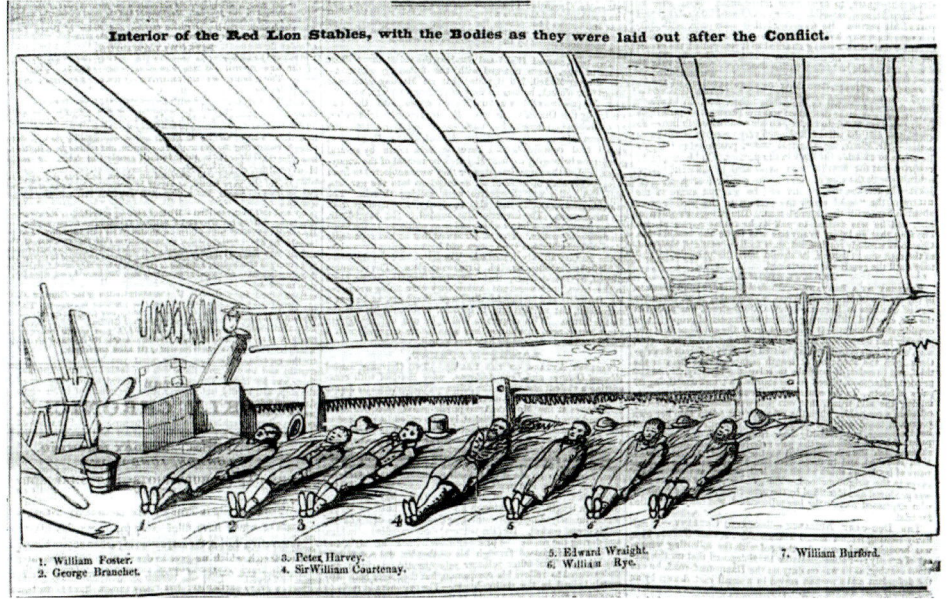

The bodies in the stable of the Red Lion, image from the *Weekly Chronicle*, 10 June 1838. 'Sir William Courtenay' is shown in the centre, with William Burford's body at the righthand end.

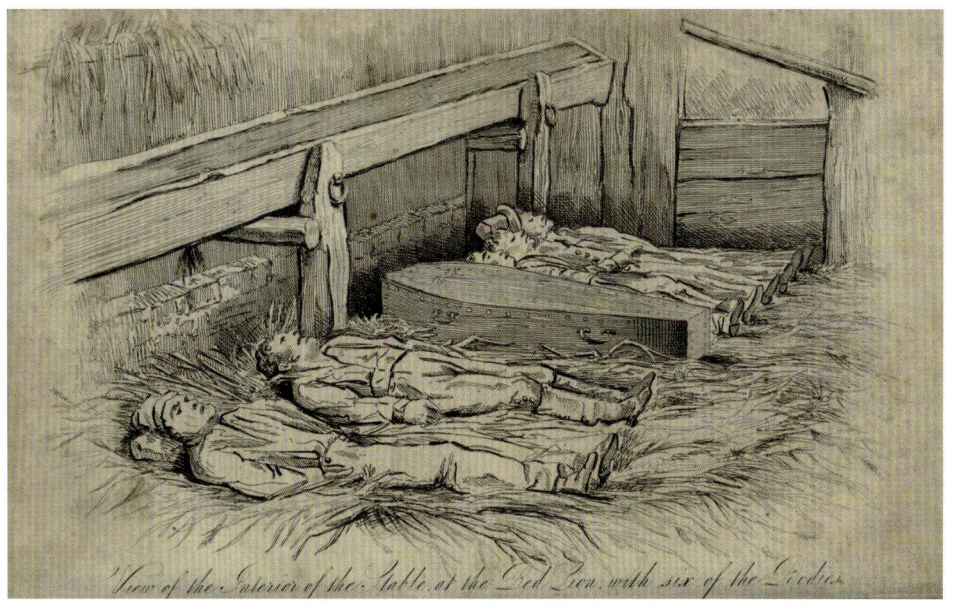

'View of the Interior of the Stable, at the Red Lion, with Six of the Bodies', from *The Life and Extraordinary Adventures of Sir William Courtenay* ... (Canterbury, 1838). John Tom's body, in the middle, has already been sealed inside his coffin.

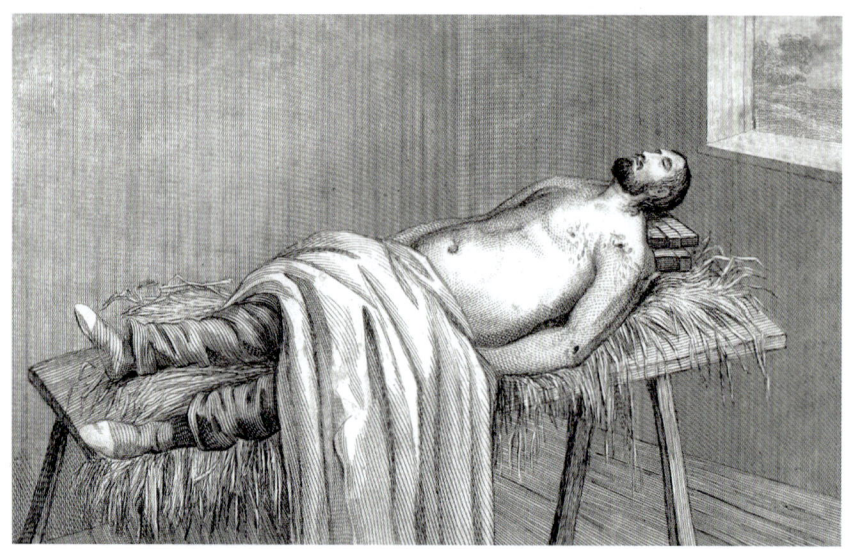

John Tom's corpse laid out for medical examination in an upper room of the Red Lion pub, from *The Life and Extraordinary Adventures of Sir William Courtenay ...* (Canterbury, 1838).

Commemorative plaque in the churchyard of St Michael's, Hernhill, close to the burial sites of John Tom and his followers. (Photograph by the author)

directions. The Thames and the Medway were a jumbled mass of ice. Nothing moved. Birds fell dead from the frozen sky.

There had been ferocious winters within living memory, but the cold spell that set in during January of 1838 – 'Murphy's Frost', as it became known, after the author of a new weather almanac – was worse than any could recall. It lasted in Kent until late February, and in northern parts of England until Easter. Once the thaw finally came it was replaced by weeks of cold driving rain that burst the riverbanks, turned the lanes to slick mud and flooded the crops in the fields. For the farmers, and for the labouring families who replied on seasonal employment, the bad weather had been particularly dismal. All agricultural work had come to an end for over two months. With the new Poor Law officials trying to restrict the issuing of 'outdoor' relief, whole families had been forced into the workhouses to avoid starvation and cold.[10]

George Branchett's family were among them. A mature man in his late forties with a wife and seven children, Branchett had served as a private in the East Kent Militia during the war against Napoleon, but by 1837 he was an out-of-work labourer living in the Ville of Dunkirk. In November, his wife Sarah died, and George and his children were compelled to enter the Faversham Union Workhouse even before the freezing weather set in. The deliberately 'less eligible' conditions soon took their toll. In January, his son William died. In March, his son Henry died. By April, George had escaped the workhouse, but in that month his son James and daughter Adelaide also died. With his three surviving children, he returned to his cold empty cottage in Dunkirk. In only six months, his wife and four of his children were gone, their lives pinched out one by one.[11]

Meanwhile, as the snow melted and the drenching rains of early spring finally eased, John Nicholls Tom had emerged from William Wills's cottage and began once more to tour the surrounding area. He had long ago, it seems, put aside the gorgeous and glittering outfits he had favoured in his Canterbury days. Now, he preferred to dress in more sober clothing, appropriate for the countryside: a dark blue coat and breeches, or a black velvet jacket with plaid trousers and broad-brimmed hat, or even a countryman's smock.

In early March, he had 'thrust himself' back into George Francis's house for a single night; Francis somehow avoided speaking to him, except to request that Tom remove his horse from the stables. The impostor did not comply with the request until 5 May, when he once again turned up uninvited at Fairbrook and took tea, presumably with his admirers Miss Eliza Francis and her Aunt Mary. The unfortunate Mr Francis on that occasion seems to have fled his own house to avoid the embarrassment of further interaction with his former friend – we might imagine him scuttling out through the back door as John Tom was greeted at the front – and went to have tea at his son's house in Boughton instead.[12]

Back at the neighbouring cottage, Lucy Wills had given birth to a daughter in February, just before the thaw. The parents had named the child Helen Courtenay Wills: a token of the respect they must have gained for their winter guest. Tom's connection with William Wills would introduce him to a new social network, and a circuit of potential new supporters. Fairbrook lay in a northerly spur of Boughton parish, but it was much closer to Hernhill, just across the valley to the east. Wills had been born in Hernhill, and he still played the flute and sang in the 'rustic choir' of Hernhill church. His sister Lydia Hadlow lived there with her husband and family, and she ran a day school for the local children.

The education that Lydia and her brother had received marked them out among their neighbours, who according to Liardet regarded them as 'prodigies of learning'; 'among these simple people, the capacity to read, and to converse with any degree of fluency upon the subjects treated of, is an infallible proof of superior talents.' Lucy Wills was probably literate, too, and may have taught at the Sunday school run by Charles Handley's wife. Their education and literacy gave all three a level of authority which would soon prove crucial in their promotion of the newcomer Sir William Courtenay, in the parish of Hernhill in particular.[13]

Hernhill was a rather different place to Dunkirk or Boughton. At its highest point, then as now, stands the flint-built medieval church of St Michael. Beside it is the village green, ringed by cottages, with the Red Lion pub on the far side. Beyond this nucleus, the parish comprises a collection of small hamlets and isolated farms and cottages, tucked into the green folds of the land and reached by burrowing high-hedged lanes. When Liardet investigated these settlements, he found that accommodation in Hernhill was on the whole far pleasanter than in Dunkirk. Probing the cottage interiors with notebook in hand, he was impressed to discover 'a sufficiency of wellmade chairs,' an abundance of 'crockery and culinary utensils,' and even in the odd corner 'a respectable-looking clock.' The neatness and cleanliness of the housing suggested to him an elevation in the morals of the inhabitants too. One would hardly have imagined that this same well-scrubbed parish had been the scene of desperate rioting and disorder only a few years beforehand. Or that it would provide the majority of John Nicholls Tom's most fervent armed support.[14]

The Reverend Charles Richard Handley was the social and spiritual head of Hernhill, both squire and parson combined; according to Liardet he was 'the only gentleman resident in the parish.' The rectory next to the church was old and dilapidated, and used now as a venue for one of the two day schools. Instead, since becoming vicar in 1817, Handley had made his home at Mount Ephraim, the large mansion on the hill between Hernhill church and the Boughton parish boundary. The house belonged to the Dawes family, as it does still, but the heir to the Dawes estates was at that time a clergyman himself, with a wealthy benefice in Staffordshire, and he had leased his Kent mansion to his brother cleric. The house that stands today was built in the later nineteenth century; the older structure that the Handleys inhabited was only a little less grand, an irregular red-brick pile with a multitude of windows and gables, chimneys and ornamental pergolas, surrounded by wide lawns and orchards.

Charles came from a Newark family of brewers and bankers. Two of his brothers and a cousin were MPs, of the liberal and radical factions, but Charles himself was a stolid conservative, and voted loyally for the Tory Sir Edward Knatchbull. He was keen on horses, and rode with the hunt. An oil on canvas portrait of him kept in Mount Ephraim, painted around 1820, shows a handsome, chubby-faced man with a prominent dimpled chin and a thick white cravat. By the time the impostor Courtenay reappeared in his parish Handley was over fifty, and no doubt content in his life of rural ease, the model of the early nineteenth century 'squarson'. He earned £300 per annum for his incumbency; no great sum of money, but his wife Cassandra came from wealth, and he could rely on her fortune.[15]

Cassandra was also patroness of the Sunday school that the Handleys had operated from their own home for over twenty years. Between sixty and ninety children from both Hernhill and the Ville of Dunkirk, Charles explained years later, were enrolled in the school at a time, and came to Mount Ephraim every Sunday for instruction in reading, writing and the gospel. The effectiveness of the education they provided is unclear – Liardet found most of the local children 'idle, mischievous, and vicious' – and the attendance seems to have varied, but maintaining the school in his own home must have introduced Handley to a great many of the younger generation in the district. Several of those who would follow the maverick messiah Courtenay were known to him personally. Hernhill, for all its scattered and rather secretive appearance, was a tightly knotted place.[16]

Of those in the parish who would fall under the impostor's spell, many were in better circumstances than those in Dunkirk. Edward Wraight the Elder, a small farmer aged sixty, owned twenty acres of land in his own name and rented thirty more. He was a notoriously curmudgeonly man, highly religious while no friend of the church: according to Liardet, he never attended, as 'he would not go to hear a man who robbed him every day of his life by taking tithe.' His son, also named Edward Wraight, seems to have been more genial. He and his wife Sarah – a relative of Emily Burford's mother – lived in Bessborough hamlet with their five children. Edward was described during his trial as a handsome, muscular man of athletic build, whose face was 'expressive of no other quality than that of extreme mildness.' He farmed his own plot, laboured on the land of others, and also operated as a 'higgler', or small trader, with his own horse and cart. Wraight the Elder's brother-in-law, Noah Miles, was also a landowner, and the publican of the Noah's Ark beershop in Fostall. He had six daughters 'all of marriageable age,' and was the only ratepayer in Hernhill to have voted for the Whig candidate at the last election.[17]

Another smallholder, Alexander Foad, farmed a few acres of hops and arable around the hamlet of Dargate. Foad had once been a gentleman's servant, and according to Handley had 'some education and knowledge of the world.' Even Thomas Mears Tyler, the young man arrested and sentenced to eighteen months' imprisonment with hard labour for his part in assaulting a poor law official back in 1835, owned a cottage and his own small patch of land.

What did these men, most of them relatively secure, many with families to support, see in the peculiar newcomer who called himself Sir William Courtenay? Unlike Burford and Branchett over in Dunkirk, they were not living in desperate poverty, or on the edge of the law. Whatever John Nicholls Tom said to them, as he rode about the muddy lanes on his grey horse, sat at their cottage hearths and drank their tea and their beer, was enough to impress not only avid 'enthusiasts' like Wills and his sister, but cantankerous old men like Edward Wraight the Elder, and polite, abstemious smallholders like Alexander Foad.

Charles Handley, eager to dismiss claims that the violent rebellion of his parishioners had been the result either of poor education or of religious ignorance, instead blamed it on a 'wicked conspiracy.' By going about the cottages of the poor and talking of social inequality, he claimed, Tom had stirred up 'those bad passions which belong to human nature – discontent with their station, envy of their superiors, the desire of possessing house & land and the absurdity, or delusion, call it what you will, that John Nicholls Thom was a great & powerful champion to lead them to the attainment of these desired objects.'

Tom's anarchistic revolutionary project, according to Handley, was 'the creation of his own imagination,' and was driven by 'fierce resentment against every person & every thing that stood in the way of his wishes. He represented the rich as the tyrants & oppressors of the poor, the two houses of Parliament worse than useless, the clergy of the Church as well as the ministers of dissenting congregations, as the false prophets who led the people astray.' But even Handley could not deny that religious ideas had also played their part in the impostor's appeal. Around the beginning of May 1838, he learned that the so-called Sir William Courtenay was once more 'becoming troublesome,' and 'intended to come forward as the preacher of a new doctrine, giving out that he was sent for that especial purpose.'[18]

In the England of the 1830s, many mainstream Christians held the return of Christ to be imminent, and an Apocalyptic sensibility coloured the works and thought of relatively sober churchmen, statesmen and artists. Both Lord Morpeth, a Whig peer, and the Anglican Ultra-Tory Sir Edward Knatchbull fully believed in the nearing approach of Christ. Many thought it by no means improbable that the Millennium – as it was called – would happen in their lifetimes. Events ranging from the economic crash of 1825 to Catholic Emancipation and the French Revolution of 1830 were enlisted as harbingers of the End Times. The Book of Revelations in particular was held to contain a checklist for the impending doom of the world, for those pious enough to understand its cryptic messages: they alone might hope to become 'priests of God and of Christ,' at the Millennium, and 'reign with him a thousand years,' until 'Satan shall be loosed out of his prison.'[19]

There was a big difference, however, in the timing of the End Times. Some – known as post-Millenarians – believed that Christ would only return to earth once everything had been set in place for his arrival. This usually involved an upsurge of popular morality and spiritual purity, fed by fervent missionary work, and in particular the mass conversion of the Jews to Christianity. Others – the pre-Millenarians – believed conversely that things would have to become as bad as possible for Christ to make his reappearance. Only once the world and suffering, sinful humanity had reached their lowest ebb would Jesus, like King Arthur, return to save the day, in 'the light of a morning which is to know no night ...' For both parties, the Millennium itself was nothing to be feared, but rather to be avidly awaited and embraced. Some, like radicals Thomas Spence and William Benbow, connected it to the *Jubilee*, an Old Testament term that they interpreted as a great day of gladness and celebration, when 'servants and masters knew no distinction,' and the land would be restored to the ownership of those who tilled and worked it. The post-Millenarian Thomas Spence, in particular, promoted the *jubilee* as a revolution, the 'End of Oppression, or the commencement of the political MILENNIUM, when there shall be neither Lords nor Landlords, but God and Man will be all in all.'[20]

Some pre-Millenarians, however, looked forward to more than just redemption and social justice. Their expected *jubilee* was also a day of Retribution. A leader among them was, or had been until his recent expulsion from the Kirk for his blasphemous notions of Christ's sinful nature, the Reverend Edward Irving, the superstar hellfire preacher of Hatton Garden. According to Irving, the Lord was 'coming visibly to confound his enemies and vindicate his people.' At the height of his popularity Irving – who John Nicholls Tom considered a 'prophet' – had preached to the wealthy elite and the greatest statesmen in the land, but he was building on ground raised by others before him, many of them far from the establishment. Apocalyptic ideas ran in a rich red vein through English history.[21]

The pseudo-biographer 'Canterburiensis' claims that even in childhood the mind of John Nicholls Tom was 'inflamed' by religious fanaticism. At the age of twelve, supposedly, he had boasted that 'Richard Brothers was one of the most celebrated characters of modern times [and among] the most inspired men which this country has produced.' Brothers, a former Royal Navy lieutenant, had risen to fame in the 1790s as a visionary doom-monger with a 'direct commission from heaven.' He declared that he would lead the Israelites back to the Promised Land, but when he later demanded that King George III renounce his throne he was tried for treason and ended his days in a lunatic asylum. Tom would certainly have been aware of Brothers later in his life, and may have read some of his books, bestselling publications filled with thunder and lightning, angels crying aloud, passages dictated by the Holy Ghost and terrifying glimpses of Satan strolling casually about London. Quite possibly he adopted his interest in Judaism and Zionism from Brothers too, although it was a common theme in Millenarian belief.[22]

While Edward Irving was the only leading Millenarian that we know John Nicholls Tom experienced at first hand, he would have been aware of several other leading practitioners too, and their ideas suffused the intellectual world that he inhabited. Joanna Southcott, aka Mother Southcott, the Bride of the Lamb and the Woman Clothed in the Sun, had succeeded Brothers in the prophesying business. Her sixty-five books of prophecies were supposed to forecast major world events, leading to the end of Satan's reign and the advent of the Kingdom of Heaven. She left further prophecies sealed inside a box, only to be opened at the moment of the world's greatest crisis. Southcott's chief inheritors were John 'Zion' Ward, whose 'spellbinding harangues' enthralled audiences from

London to Leeds, and John Wroe. The latter prophet gained a large following with his mystical blend of visionary evangelism and Judaism: in 1824 he ordered the disciples of 'Christian Israelism' to grow beards, while six years later God apparently commanded Wroe to take seven virgins to 'cherish and comfort him.' This sort of thing led to him being driven out of Ashton-under-Lyne for impropriety, and he ended his days in Australia.[23]

Wroe, in particular, was at the height of his notoriety in 1830–31, just before Tom left Cornwall; he may have inspired his famous beard, and perhaps his 'Count Rothschild' Jewish persona as well. The doctors who treated Tom during his first bout of mental illness in Cornwall mentioned his 'constant allusions to Scripture,' so religious enthusiasm already coloured his thinking at an early stage, whatever its source might have been. In his speeches in Canterbury during the 1832 election campaigns, and in several issues of the *Lion*, Tom makes frequent reference to religion, to Christianity and to controversies of religious interpretation (the human and divine nature of Christ, for example). Poynder's notes taken in the asylum also contain several odd statements of a strongly religious hue: '*the Saviour never slept as the Holy Ghost would not let him sleep ... He spoke of himself as possessing more faith than any man in existence ... he lives entirely by faith ...*'

Prior to his confinement in the asylum, John Nicholls Tom presented himself as a strongly religious man, a pious Christian, even at times as a prophet of sorts. But he had never claimed to be anything more than that. He had never claimed to be anything more than *human*. For all their relentless prophesising and grandiose posturing, their direct commissions and orders from God, none of the visionaries and Millenarian preachers mentioned above ever claimed to be a supernatural being.

None of them ever claimed, at least in public, to be Christ Himself. At some point during his years in Kent County Lunatic Asylum, however, or perhaps in the months that followed his release, John Nicholls Tom developed the notion that he was indeed the Saviour, Jesus Christ, returned to earth to bring the Millennium and herald the end of time.

William Wills and his sister Lydia Hadlow appear to have been the first and most active of his disciples. Lydia became convinced that Jesus had selected Sir William as the vehicle of his second coming, that 'Christ dwelt in his heart; and that his body was the temple of the Holy Ghost.' Her brother was more fervent still: just as the farmer George Denne had served as the impostor's 'squire' in his Canterbury days, so William Wills now acted for his newly developed incarnation. 'Nothing could exceed the infatuation of Wills on the subject of Tom's divinity,' said the writer for the *Times*. William and Lydia 'availed themselves of the power of reading the Scriptures to distort tenets, not very clear in themselves, into proofs that Thom was the promised Messiah. Better that they had not been taught to read at all,' he goes on, 'than to read so unwisely and for such dangerous and fanatical purposes!'[24]

The reporter follows this with an anecdote about Wills trying to convince some of the patrons of a local beershop to follow the new messiah. Finding it impossible to win them over, Wills stood abruptly to leave. 'I dare stay no longer,' he told them. 'Sir William will be angry: though a mile off, he knows what we are saying, and will be able to repeat every word to me.'

Others were less impressed than Wills by the idea of the newcomer's 'supernatural qualities'; his own family was divided by a violent feud on the subject. His brother-in-law John Foreman, the local carpenter and undertaker, scoffed at any mention of 'Courtenay', and considered him 'an impostor or a maniac.' Wills gravely told him that 'if he would go about the country thus, resisting the will of the Saviour, he ought to prepare his own coffin, instead of making those of his neighbours.'

Some in the parish, meanwhile, found the stranger more alarming than inspiring. 'We were all afraid of him,' said Elizabeth Arnold, wife of a Hernhill waggoner, 'because he had such an imposing manner with him.' Interviewed in old age, she clearly remembered Sir William's visit to her cottage one Sunday:

> 'Mrs Hadlow, who made such a great fuss of Sir William, brought him to my place, and I was never more afraid of anyone. I was glad to see the back of him. While I was taking the tea my hands shook, and Sir William exclaimed in his deep voice, "Mrs Arnold seems afraid". When my husband returned home he said "wasn't you glad to see the back of him?" and I said I was only too pleased when he left.'[25]

Around this time, Tom began suggesting that he had 'come down from a cloud' – an interesting echo of a comment by a spectator at Canterbury's Guildhall during his election speech in 1832. The comment had been printed in the papers at the time, which suggests that he had been reading his own press. The impostor also, several later reports claimed, drew scriptural parallels to underline his divine origin and magical powers. He was fond of pointing to his horse and making a connection with the second verse of Revelation 6: *'And I saw, and behold a white horse; and he that sat upon him had a bow; and a crown was given unto him; and he went forth conquering, and to conquer.'*[26]

But Tom and his disciples sometimes fell back on means of persuasion more suggestive of a fairground sideshow than a religious mission. On perhaps more than one occasion he fired his pistols into the night sky, claiming that he had the power to shoot the stars from their spheres; the pistols were loaded with a charge of wadded tow, oil and iron filings, which flashed and sparkled as they fell. This apparently impressed onlookers greatly, and once again there was a passage from Revelation to explain it: '*And the stars of heaven fell unto the earth, even as a fig tree casteth her untimely figs when she is shaken of a mighty wind.*' The wife of one of Tom's followers claimed that she heard 'strains of the most divine harmony' as the stars fell; a journalist slyly suggested that she might in fact have heard William Wills breathing a celestial air upon his flute.[27]

It was Wills himself, and those immediately recruited by him, who seemed to have played the strongest role in drawing together support for Tom's mission, in Hernhill at least. One Friday in late May he called at the cottage of Edward Wraight the Younger and his wife Sarah. As they drank their ale he asked them if they had heard of the great news, and of what was about to happen; 'No,' they replied, 'William Wills, what be it?'

The great Day of Judgement was close at hand, Wills told them. The Saviour had returned, and they must all follow him. And opening his Bible he showed them the passage in Revelations about the conqueror upon the white horse. They might not have been able to read the words, but he could tell them what it said. The following day, returning through the lanes in their cart from the Saturday market in Faversham, Edward and Sarah Wraight met Thomas Tyler Mears leading a horse – *Sir William's white horse*, he told them. That was sign enough for them.

'He told us that all the country would be up,' Sarah Wraight would later explain to Liardet. 'For the great jubilee was to come, and we must be with 'em. And so, sir, you see, next day poor Edward certainly did go to join 'em, little thinking what was to happen.'[28]

Since leaving the asylum, John Nicholls Tom had been on a journey. In part it was a journey of identity and definition; possibly he had already fixed upon his new role as Saviour while still confined in his chamber at Barming, but it had grown to consume him over the weeks and months since his liberation. It was also a physical journey, from the asylum to Fairbrook, then to Wills's cottage and the cottages of other supporters in Hernhill and Dunkirk. Sometime in the late spring of 1838, he had relocated once more. Perhaps because of local opposition, or because Hernhill was just too public an arena in which to develop what might still have been a mission in embryo, John Nicholls Tom decided that he must find a new base of operations.

Bossenden, in the middle of the Blean woodlands a mile east of the Hernhill parish boundary, provided that base. Here, Tom could reside undetected by his enemies, assemble his followers and gather his strength until the time came to reveal himself to the world and begin the work of revolution. Quite possibly he had visited the farm before, during his previous tour of the area in 1833. The house was old, probably dating back 200 years or more; the northern range was later demolished and rebuilt as a neat mid-nineteenth-century farmhouse, but illustrations of the period show the original building with its multi-paned slot windows, hipped roof and tall brick chimney stacks. According to the correspondent of the *Times*, Bossenden was 'formerly the mansion of a country gentleman, but of late years had been suffered to decay and has fallen into a very dilapidated condition.'²⁹

The house was tenanted by William Culver, an old farmer of gentlemanly appearance and evident wealth, who acted as bailiff for the owner Mr Gipps. Culver himself is described as a 'bitter opponent of Tom's principles,' but he was entirely dominated by his wife Mary and daughter Sarah, who were differently inclined. Mrs Culver, who had long been almost crippled by pains in her back, became convinced of Tom's divine powers when she sat down on a chair he had recently vacated and was instantly and miraculously cured.³⁰

Sarah Culver, meanwhile, is by far the most fascinating of John Tom's disciples. She was unmarried, and middle aged – two facts which made her instantly suspicious to the prejudices of the day, and to subsequent writers as well. P. G. Rogers, in his 1962 *Battle in Bossenden Wood*, describes her as 'forty years of age – a dangerous age! ... This lonely, frustrated woman, doomed to spinsterhood, leading a monotonous life in an isolated place, starved of affection, craving someone on whom to lavish all the pent-up affection within her, fell an easy and willing victim to Sir William's wiles.'³¹

In reality, Sarah Culver had just turned forty-five in May 1838. She was literate, apparently creative, and had clearly received an education in her youth. According to the *Times*, 'when younger [she] must have been a woman of some personal attractions ... Her nose is aquiline, eyes blue, and mouth rather large.' A reporter at the inquest that followed the clash in Bossenden Wood gives us a vivid image of her appearance: she was 'a strong, dark, heavy featured, masculine looking woman,' and 'attired as one belonging to the middle classes; she wore a black bonnet, a large dark shawl with a splendid border, dark muslin gown, neat leather gloves, and summer shoes.'

Her 'masculine' appearance may have been partly due to hirsutism, or perhaps polycystic ovary syndrome: 'strange to say,' the *Times* correspondent adds, 'she has a considerable beard.'[32]

Both reports testify to her 'extraordinary composure' at the inquest, where she appeared among the accused; 'as if she considered that all around her was a mere dream, or if a reality, that it was one from which, by some miracle, she might be released.' Her brother – who was not living at Bossenden at the time – later testified that Sarah had not been 'in her senses' for the last two years. She seems to have been even more convinced than her mother of Tom's supernatural powers. Not only was she one of the first to refer to him as the *Saviour*, but she claimed that he could change his shape at will; on one single evening she had witnessed him do this three times, while she watched.[33]

Perhaps because of the compelling air of contradiction in the descriptions of Sarah herself – that *splendidly bordered* shawl, those *neat leather gloves*, juxtaposed with her hirsute 'masculine' appearance – many have speculated about the nature of her relations with John Nicholls Tom. Was it merely a spiritual attraction? P. G. Rogers had no doubt that it was 'sexual in basis, though she herself was probably unconscious of this,' but saw 'no evidence whatsoever of an illicit relationship.' One contemporary reporter calls Sarah Tom's 'handmaiden', while the elderly Mrs Price claimed decades later that Sarah was 'sweet on Courtenay,' presumably based on local rumour. Others in more recent years have been less demure; Barry Reay refers to Sarah simply as Tom's 'lover'.[34]

As we have seen, 'Sir William' was supposed to hold exceptional charms for women of all classes, particularly older and unmarried ones. Of course, charismatic religious figures have often been accorded excessive qualities of sexual attraction and command. We might recall the prophet John Wroe, as people at the time would surely have done, and the seven virgins who 'cherished and comforted' him. In the case of John Nicholls Tom, the glamour and attraction seem to have been largely performance; there is no evidence that he actually formed any sort of physical bond with anyone after running away from his wife and his parents in 1833.

But as the anthropologist Kenelm Burridge suggests in his 1969 *New Heaven, New Earth*, the attraction of prophets was not merely sexual; membership of a religious group or cult – especially the privileged membership of the inner circle of true believers – might grant women a new authority and agency in an otherwise restrictive and patriarchal society. In particular, we might imagine that a woman like Sarah Culver – intelligent, educated, but long neglected or even mistrusted due to her appearance – could find meaning and focus in her devotion to Sir William Courtenay, and exceptional status too. If her role was to be that of Tom's Mary Magdalene, we can hardly fault her for it.[35]

After the impostor's death in Bossenden Wood, the investigating magistrates found a slip of paper in his breast pocket, stained with blood and perforated by a musket ball, with a poem supposedly written 'in a female hand.' The verse, with its idiosyncratic spelling and echoes of scripture, was subsequently reprinted in several of the press reports. Their implication is that Sarah Culver wrote it. If so, hers was less a religious conception of her Saviour than a romantic one. John Nicholls Tom, in Sarah's fantastical imagination, is transformed into a Byronic hero:

> *Is it a delusion? No, its peace I hear*
> *As yet welcome sweet guest*
> *A passing spiriet softly wispers*
> *Him safe from harm – and when*

The loud clash of War's alarm atacks
Him and boasts the tyrants proudly
Round him still his manly heart
Shall know no fear –
Then sink not oh my soul nor
Yeald to sad despair, the cause is
Great that calls thy Lord away
A sinking spiriet and a silint
Tear but ill becomes the child
Who from the bonds of Satann
May go free.[36]

Might Sarah have placed the poem in her hero's pocket, next to his heart, perhaps as a talismanic form of protection? Or did John Nicholls Tom himself treasure the verses? Either way, it is interesting that the first line denies that any of this is caused by 'delusion' – the belittling and almost ubiquitous term used by journalists, politicians and local farmers alike in describing the revolt. Sarah Culver must have been well aware of what certain people thought of her 'sweet guest'. But she would not hide what she thought of him; on the evening of Saturday 26 May, a caller at Bossenden found John Nicholls Tom asleep by the fire. As he began to speak to 'Old Culver', Sarah stopped him with a finger to her lips.[37]

'Hush,' she said gently. 'Hush, the Saviour is sleeping, you must not wake him!'

6. 'THE EARTH SHALL RISE UP'

The message appeared in the early hours of Sunday, 27 May, written in bold letters on the side of the old parsonage barn in Hernhill. To the left of the door the message read:

> *If you new ho was on earth your harts Wod turn*
> *But dont Wate to late*
> *They how R*

And to the right:

> *O that great day of gudgement is close at hand*
> *it now peps in the dor every man according to his*
> *woks*
> *Our rites and liberties We Will have*[1]

The handwriting, somebody suggested, was that of William Wills. If so, the claims about his great learning and education were perhaps exaggerated. To whom was the message directed? Most likely the unbelievers of the parish – the publican Edward Butcher, whose Red Lion stood just across the green, the undertaker John Foreman, or the farmer and poor law guardian Edward Curling. Most prominently, of course, the Reverend Charles Richard Handley, and his loyal flock.

Handley does not mention the writing on the parsonage barn in his own account of Tom's uprising, but it would be hard to imagine that he did not see it. Perhaps its exhortations about the *great day of judgement* did not fit with his argument that the violence was inspired by political conspiracy rather than religious conviction? Then again, the closing remarks might draw on radical politics: *Our rights and liberties* was a familiar cry at many a rally of the reforming era. But the phrase also echoed more traditional assertions of the rights of the freeborn Englishman, and a spirit of stubborn rural rebellion that dated back to the days of Wat Tyler.

As his parishioner stared in puzzlement at the message written on the barn – those who could read perhaps decoding it for those who could not – Charles Handley himself was preparing for his Sunday service. Hernhill and Boughton churches were so close together that the two vicars commonly alternated services between morning and evening, with many of their congregants attending both. That Sunday it was Hernhill's turn for the morning service. The weather had been cold and windy for days, with little sign of the approach of summer. Some would remember the seasons being altogether out of alignment at that time, and the leaves not yet on the trees even six weeks after Easter.[2]

The little flint-built church of St Michael's would have been crowded with its double congregation. Looking down from his three-decked pulpit, Handley would have gazed across a jumbled accumulation of box pews that dated back two centuries – stripped out in the later nineteenth century, like the pulpit itself – where the gentry and the wealthier local farming families would be seated in comfort during the service.

The labouring poor would be standing in the clear space at the back of the nave and around the walls, the men in clean white smocks or Sunday jackets, their heads bared, the women in best shawls and bonnets. Church services of the 1830s could last two hours, with most of that duration taken up with lengthy readings from scripture and recitation of creeds, with only the sermon offering some variety. The familiar hymns of today were mostly composed in the later nineteenth century, and congregations of the 1830s would instead have stood to a variety of chants, psalms, and 'anthems' now largely forgotten; Dr William Boyce's *Charity* was a favourite of the day.[3]

There was no church organ, and no piano either. Instead, the music was provided by the church band, and 'rustic choir' of male singers. In St Michael's, the band and choir were situated in a raised gallery inside the tower at the far end of the nave. Looking up from his pulpit, Handley would have seen them there, framed in a stone arch. He would have seen William Wills, the band leader and flautist. Would he have guessed already that Wills had written the strange message on the parsonage barn outside? Would he already have known that Wills – and the entirety of the church choir, too – and very probably a large proportion of the labouring men watching him from the back of the nave, were now among the confirmed disciples of the maverick Sir William Courtenay, who had declared himself to be the Messiah?

If so, he may have summoned to mind those verses of Matthew 24: '*For there shall arise false Christs, and false prophets, and shall shew great signs and wonders; insomuch that, if it were possible, they shall deceive the very elect …*'

Another man who might have been present among the congregation that morning – probably sitting comfortably close to the pulpit, rather than peering from the back – may have had a different reaction to the message on the wall of the barn. Major Benjamin Handley was the vicar's older brother; he and their nephew John Handley were guests at Mount Ephraim by the end of that week and could well have arrived by the Sunday morning. While Charles was a conservative Tory of the traditionalist, paternalistic type, Benjamin was quite the opposite in his politics. He had served in the army, fighting in the Peninsular war and the expedition to Buenos Aires as a lieutenant and then captain of the 9th Light Dragoons. Following the peace, he had purchased a major's commission in the 53rd Foot and settled down to the life of a country squire on reserved half pay. Standing as a Radical in the election of 1832 – at the same time as Sir William Courtenay was standing in Canterbury – the major had been elected as one of the two MPs for Boston in Lincolnshire. He had lost the seat again two years later, after an undistinguished term, but maintained his political convictions: ultra-liberal, even libertarian, arguing forcefully and often angrily for political reform, economy in government, and the repeal of taxes, duties and tithes.[4]

By the late 1830s, Benjamin was most passionately devoted to the Anti-Slavery cause. While slavery had been officially abolished in Britain's colonies in 1833, rather than gaining full emancipation many of the former enslaved had been compelled to continue labouring for their former masters, at the same work and on the same plantations, under the guise of being 'apprentices'. To men like Major Handley this was an obscene hypocrisy, and a betrayal of the cause of abolition itself; he had just attended a meeting of Anti-Slavery delegates held at Exeter Hall in London the previous Friday.[5]

The major was a short-tempered man, abrasive and sarcastic, and fiercely litigious. Not one to back down easily, either. He had seen battle, at Arroyo dos Molinos and Ciudad

Rodrigo. He had held his ground on the hustings at Boston in 1832 for four hours, in the teeth of a brawling, hostile Tory mob. In some ways, he might have seen common cause with John Nicholls Tom, at least in the political guise he had adopted when he first stood in Canterbury. *Rights and liberties* were principles he could respect. However, he was a man of his time and his class, and no revolutionary; during the 'Swing' disturbances of 1830 he had led the Folkingham Yeomanry in Lincolnshire and equipped them with 'sycimitar' swords from the Royal Ordnance Store at Hull. Luckily, their blades had not been required. But Major Benjamin Handley would be one of the few men brave enough to try and face down John Nicholls Tom open handed and place himself in the line of fire to try and reason with his followers in order to bring an end to the violence.[6]

The lines scribed on the side of the parsonage barn were not the only message circulated at this time. William Kay, the Scottish bailiff who managed Osborn Snoulton's property at Dargate, received a letter supposedly from Courtenay himself, warning him to 'make his peace with God, as he was shortly coming to settle his account.' Kay responded that he was armed and ready to defend himself if required. A local gentleman also got a letter, informing him that he would be shot dead if he did not follow 'Jesus Christ', in the earthly form of John Tom. George Francis too seems to have been the recipient of some sort of threatening communication, although the substance of it is not recorded. Some days later, Lucy Wills, William's young wife, reportedly said that Francis wanted to know who *wrote some papers*; 'he will know, but shall not live long to tell the tale.' Lucy was able to read and write, and it is quite possible that she sent written menaces to her neighbour herself or helped her husband to do it.[7]

Sinister messages, and anonymous written threats to those identified as enemies of the cause, had been part of the lexicon of rural revolt for decades. The 'Swing' riots of the 1830s had also seen cryptic slogans written on walls, and a blizzard of notes distributed to farmers and gentry, making demands and issuing warning. One of these, sent to a Norfolk parish officer in 1833, gives a flavour of their contents: '*You G.F. shall be a dade man, prepear yourself to die for a mess of lade is got fit for you... you shall be shot like a dorg before long.*' George Francis just happens to share the initials of the recipient; might something similar have been sent to him?[8]

John Nicholls Tom was at Hernhill and Fairbrook on that same Sunday, visiting Elizabeth Arnold and then William Wills at their cottages. The parish constable James Gorham saw him later in Boughton Street, leading his grey horse and accompanied by William Price and Thomas Tyler Mears. Gorham saw them again at seven o'clock, coming down the lane from Hernhill and crossing the highway towards Dunkirk Common. There had been one more message circulating that day too, though probably a verbal one: a summons to the faithful. Now, as the shadows lengthened towards evening, the faithful assembled.

Accounts of these events give the site for the meeting at various places around Boughton Hill. Gorham gives the correct location: Sir William Courtenay had gathered his followers outside the house of Thomas Kennett in Dunkirk, at the foot of the hill. This had been one of his earliest stopping places when he first visited the area, back in the winter of 1832–33, and clearly he had maintained his connection with Kennett ever since. At the nearby highway junction stood the Woodman's Hall, licensed by Charles Pay. The large brick-built pub that bore that name and stood on the corner plot until its recent demolition was a later construction, and Mr Pay probably ran his pub as a cottage beershop; the 1830 Beer Act allowed any ratepayer to open their premises as a public house for a small fee, and thousands of these ad-hoc beershops had sprung up almost immediately. It was also a convenient place of assembly: just on the Boughton parish boundary, close enough to Hernhill and the scattered hamlets beyond it, and within easy reach of the Blean woods and Bossenden. A place outside of the immediate regard of the authorities too. Constables like Gorham might have been loitering about, spying out what they could, but it would be several days before the likes of Charles Handley or Dr Poore found out about the meeting.[9]

There were between 100 and 200 people assembled in the broad lane outside Kennett's cottage and the Woodman's Hall. Some may have climbed onto carts or sat along the fences of Thomas Wraight's field opposite. Among them was a woman called Elizabeth Brunsdame, who lived a few cottages away in Boughton. She had heard that Sir William was going to make a speech outside Kennett's and was drawn by curiosity to attend. Many of those among the crowd perhaps felt the same. But at their core must have been the true believers. William Wills would have been there, with Price and Tyler. William Burford was probably there, too, as he likely lived very close by. Emily Burford may have been with him. Sarah Culver might have ventured down the hill from Bossenden to join the throng. The grieving, desperate George Branchett likely attended, and a man named Thomas Brown who lived nearby, and would later act as Courtenay's groom.[10]

Nicholas Mears, brother of the Boughton constable John Mears, owned a cottage only three plots to the rear of Kennett's and he too may have attended the gathering. According to later testimony from George Francis, Nicholas had visited Fairbrook earlier that day with six or seven other men and spent some time in the cottage of William Wills. John Nicholls Tom had been there, too, and had given the men three shillings and sixpence for bread, cheese and beer. Nicholas Mears had eaten and drunk, and according to Francis – although how he knew about it is a mystery – he had told John Tom that *he never would leave him*. Was this a pledge of allegiance or of loyalty? Or could Mears have been acting as a spy for his brother, and trying to discover Sir William's plans? Either way, if Francis was not mistaken, it places Nicholas Mears squarely in the impostor's retinue, only a few days before he became his first victim.[11]

Addressing the crowd of his supporters, John Nicholls Tom first proposed a toast – Mrs Brunsdame did not catch what it was, but 'Health to the Poor' was one of his favoured cries. We might assume that he had bought beer for the throng as well, so all could drink his toast with him. According to Constable Gorham, this was the only occasion that he saw Sir William bareheaded. He had removed his broad-brimmed hat because he was about to preach a sermon. This was Sunday, after all.

His text, so Charles Handley's informant later told him, was the first line of the fifth chapter of the General Epistle of St James, with additional quotes from the twentieth chapter of the Book of Job. Did John Tom read from the pocket Bible he always carried with him? That alone would have been impressive. Perhaps more impressively still, he might have recited the lines from memory, while holding up the holy book for all to see. Gorham, lingering on the margins of the crowd, heard Tom giving his address; the people, he reported, were 'very attentive.' Not surprisingly, this was nothing like the lengthy, uninspiring sermons they might have heard from the conservative Reverend Charles Handley at Hernhill, or the octogenarian Reverend Thomas Wright at Boughton. Nor was it the sort of performance that Sir William had once given from the balcony of the Rose Inn in Canterbury, full of radical bluster and evocations of the lost world of roast beef and nut-brown ale. This was less a sermon than a call to arms.

'*Go to now, ye rich men,*' the Epistle of St James reads, '*weep and howl for your miseries that shall come upon you.*' The twentieth chapter of Job is filled with violence, and the vengeance of God against the wealthy and wicked man: '*Because he hath oppressed and hath forsaken the poor; because he hath violently taken away an house which he builded not... God shall cast the fury of his wrath upon him... The heavens shall reveal his iniquity; and the earth shall rise up against him.*'

And the hundred or more gathered in the early summer dusk to hear those words, all of them poor, all of them people of *the earth*, must have recognised why Sir William had selected those passages, and the powerful threat they contained to those who stood above them. Did they also recognise the irony of a man who claimed to be Viscount Courtenay, Earl of Devon and one of the wealthiest landowners in the land, declaiming such words? The irony too, perhaps, that the lines from Job 20 are spoken by Zophar the Naamthamite, one of Job's unwanted comforters, trying to counsel him in his distress but only adding to his misery?

Elizabeth Brunsdame left the gathering after only quarter of an hour, perhaps sensing trouble ahead. James Gorham stayed until the end. He heard John Tom telling the crowd that they could go about their usual labours on the following day, but that on Tuesday they should join him once more and prepare themselves for what lay ahead. Gorham went on up Boughton Hill to the Red Lion pub and was still there a short while later when Tom and his retinue passed by in the gathering twilight, heading for the track that would return them to Bossenden.

Monday was quiet indeed, but that night a great storm swept across eastern Kent, buffeting the woodlands of the Blean. The next day, 29 May, was Oak Apple Day, the traditional celebration of the restoration of King Charles II. As Barry Reay points out, protests often began on holidays, when a spirit of festivity could easily tip over into riot. As a staunch patriot and monarchist, John Nicholls Tom might have considered the day appropriate for what he had in mind.[12]

He was up early that morning, passing through the wind-blown woodlands from Bossenden. Days later, the *Times* correspondent noticed a direct path into the wood marked by hatchet cuts in the bark of the trees – a secret route, known only to those who could pick out the signs, leading towards Dunkirk Common. By eight, Tom was making his way along Boughton Street, a small band of men accompanying him, all of them from Dunkirk. William Burford was with him, and the ex-militiaman George Branchett, and Thomas Dalton, and Thomas Brown leading his horse. But they were gathering supporters as they went. William Blanchard, standing at the door of his cottage, saw Tom and his men passing. 'Do you want bread?' the impostor called to him. Blanchard did, and followed them. At Mrs Palmer's grocery Tom paused to buy four half-gallon loaves and a big wheel of cheese, and to exchange money for smaller coins, then used it to buy two more loaves at Mr Smith's bakery along the street.

Alfred Payne, a harness-maker from near Canterbury who was working that morning in the yard of Colonel Groves's house, overheard two women saying that Sir William Courtenay was giving away free bread. He later claimed that he had been ordered by John Mears, the parish constable, to observe Courtenay and his followers and discover his plans. He left off his work and joined them. By the time John Nicholls Tom passed the White Horse pub and turned up Bull Lane towards Fairbrook, his retinue had grown to a dozen or so. The day was bright after the night's storms, the wind still gusting. Crossing the ridge beneath the turning sails of Richardson's Mill, they descended into the next valley and climbed again to join the lane from Staple Street towards Faversham. Thomas Tyler and around ten others fell in with them along the way.[13]

Up at Fairbrook, farmer George Francis must have viewed the approach of Sir William Courtenay and his followers with trepidation, especially if the mysterious 'papers' he had received had contained threats against him. Wisely, he kept himself out of sight until he was sure that the approaching band were heading for the neighbouring house of William Wills, and not his own. By then, Tom's support had grown greater still; Alfred Payne counted thirty people in all, between twelve and fourteen of them women. About half remained outside, in Wills's small garden, while the rest entered the house. Sir William called Payne in and ordered him to sit.

'This is the twenty-ninth of May,' the impostor told his followers, 'and a glorious twenty-ninth of May it shall be for the poor who stick by me.' They had been long enough imposed upon, he told them, for truth and liberty, but he would 'head them through it.' He ordered Thomas Tyler to bring beer, and others to fetch the bread and some cheese, so all could 'fill their bellies.'

Also inside the cottage, Payne reported, was a 'respectable looking female' wearing glasses, who appeared to be deaf. This was Miss Mary Horne, Mr Francis's sister-in-law, who must have come across from Fairbrook to join the gathering. She told Sir William to take off his hat and give it to her, then she kissed him in front of the assembled people. Shortly afterwards Tyler returned with the beer, three or four gallons of it, and the disciples ate and drank. Sir William ate a crust himself and then called a toast: 'Health to the poor, and may they gain independence!' He gave somebody a couple of shillings to go and buy tobacco to share among his followers.

'I am not an earthly man,' Tom told the people in the cottage, and once more returned to his claim that he had 'fallen from the clouds.' He would leave them again at some point without any knowing when – we might imagine this last claim caused some consternation. But his powers were unabated: he could slay ten thousand of his foes, he explained, merely by striking his right hand against his left bicep. He could then vanish completely, without his enemies being able to find him.[14]

In the midst of this bizarre scene of indulgence and violent fantasy, some of the women present sang a song. 'It seemed as if they had composed it themselves,' Payne suggested, 'against some person that had injured them.' William Blanchard, who had followed the party from Boughton, claimed that the women sang a hymn – he had heard it sung at the Wesleyan Chapel, he said, and the chorus went *'The shepherd guards his sheep by night and day.'* They were to sing that same hymn three times over the course of the day, but it is hard to identify; one possibility might be an American Methodist anthem from the early 1800s, later popular with the Mormons, which features the lines *'Day and night, the lambs are crying / Come, good Shepherd, feed thy sheep …'* If so, it is strange that John Nicholls Tom should have chosen it, or that a group of Kent labourers' wives would have been familiar with it.

After about ten minutes of hymn-singing, Lucy Wills pointed out a figure crossing a field of ripening wheat in the middle distance. This was Mr George Francis, who had finally made his escape from Fairbrook and was off to find a magistrate and report what was happening. 'There goes Francis,' Lucy called.

'There goes the first that wants to be topped!' He was afraid to approach, she said, as he did not know who had 'written some papers,' but would soon find out.[15]

It was around eleven in the morning when John Nicholls Tom emerged from the cottage and mustered his supporters. He had changed his dress and now wore a smock and overalls of brown Holland, like a labouring man. In his leather belt he carried a brace of pistols, and his sword hung at his side in a steel scabbard. By a cord around his neck, he carried a bugle, and in his hands he carried a loaf of bread stuck on top of a pole, a traditional symbol of popular unrest in rural England. 'Here is bread before us,' William Wills declared. 'We only have to follow it, and we shall have more.'

Wills himself was carrying a flag, white silk bordered in blue. On one side was painted the figure of a rampart lion in red and gold, surrounded by a wreath of green laurel. The flag had most likely been painted back in Canterbury during Sir William Courtenay's election campaigning – one very similar appeared during his triumphal return to the city in April 1833. It still survives to this day, much restored, kept with a collection of other artefacts by the Dawes family at Mount Ephraim. The rear of the flag is blank, and it was perhaps intended originally to hang from a window or on the side of a cart rather than being carried on a pole.

'I am going for a jubilee,' the impostor told his men, and assured them that if they followed him, he would 'fill their bellies with victuals,' and nothing bad would happen to them. Ordering his men to fall in by threes, like soldiers in line of march, he pointed at the flag and told them to have hearts as fierce as the lion, and to be as hard as heart-of-oak. He appointed Edward Newman, who lived in Wills's cottage, as the 'general' of his army. Then he blew on his bugle and told them the sound had been heard at Jerusalem, where ten thousand awaited his command.

And so the army set off on its march, Wills at the head with the flag and Tyler leading the horse, while a man named William Price carried the bread on its pole. Alfred Payne, lingering near the back of the column, noticed that the man ahead of him was carrying a blue bag that he believed contained pistol bullets. Passing Fairbrook House, they rejoined the road and turned right towards Faversham. After a few hundred yards Tom led them off down another lane, running north through the hamlet of Goodnestone and towards Graveney on the edge of the Seasalter levels. He called to two men he saw working in a hop garden. 'The loaf, the loaf, my boys!' he cried, pointing to the pole that Price was carrying. 'Come on, or you'll be sorry for it!'

But the two men were unimpressed, and the column marched on.[16]

A little beyond the Three Horseshoes pub, Tom sent Tyler on up the road to Graveney church with the horse, while he led the rest of the band over a stile and across a field of oats. With a smaller group he approached a bean stack in the adjoining meadow – these stacks could be as large as hayricks, and some had thatched covers to protect them from the elements. It appeared to those watching from the oat field as if he might be trying to set fire to it. They would have remembered the severe penalties for incendiarism, and the Packman brothers hanged on Penenden Heath back in 1830.

But there was no smoke, and no flame. Somebody – probably Tom himself – had apparently put a match into the beanstack, but it had not ignited. Undeterred, Tom returned and addressed them all. The time had come for him to strike the bloody blow, he said. Streets that had lately run with water would soon run with blood, for the rights of the poor. One witness claimed that he fired off his pistol and then reloaded it. At this point the harness-maker Alfred Payne decided to melt away between the hedgerows, no doubt deciding he had seen enough.

Tom and his band moved off again, up the lane to the little twelfth-century church at Graveney, then swung eastwards along the edge of the marshlands, heading for Waterham. His route might appear bafflingly random to us now, but he was making a circuit of the margins of Hernhill parish, passing through as many hamlets and isolated farms as possible. This was a recruitment march, but his numbers had grown only slightly by the time he reached Lavender Farm, past Waterham. Several men, like Alfred Payne, had dropped away along the route, put off by Sir William's antics with pistols and matches. The farm was owned by Julius Shepherd, but his bailiff John Hadlow ran the place, and he was married to Lydia, William Wills's sister. In the yard of the farm Tom and his weary followers could break their march and refresh themselves with yet more bread and beer.

What did those followers think they were doing? Very likely some of them had just tagged along for the free food and drink and tobacco. Others could have been curious to see what would happen, and what this man, who talked up so bold a storm, was going to do next. But at the core of that throng of marching men in smocks and fustian jackets, swinging along empty-handed behind the lion flag and the loaf, were Courtenay's true believers. Wills and Price, Tyler and Newman. Perhaps Burford, too, the elder Wraight, and Alexander Foad. For them this was not a mere ramble around the parish boundaries, but a holy expedition. They would have heard the stories in the New Testament and known them well. Did Jesus not lead his disciples on lengthy journeys, for mysterious reasons? Did he not often say and do cryptic things, which baffled many at the time? With faith would come understanding, and the miraculous light; some were already explaining that it was a miracle that the bean-stack was *not* set ablaze. Sir William had commanded it not to burn![17]

This sort of thinking was, of course, what the clergy and the gentry and the journalists would later call *delusion* – that term so firmly denied by Sarah Culver in her poem. But those men striding along the lanes after Sir William had lived their whole lives in a society permeated at every point by religion. Many of them kept religious books in their homes and hung cheap prints of Biblical scenes on the walls of their cottages. Their understanding of the world was sustained by the vital importance of faith, and belief in the literal truth of Christian miracles. For these men truly to believe in Courtenay's message, they had to imagine that a better world was possible, and imagine that they themselves could live in it, and play a part in its creation. If they were as dim-witted and gullible as some would have them – if they were no more than 'simple Kentish yokels', as P. G. Rogers described them in 1962 – they could not have stretched their minds to encompass so radical an idea.[18]

In part, theirs was a faith born of limited possibilities: in the harsh confines of a rural existence growing ever less tenable, even the impossible seemed preferable to their current reality. Who among them would not take solace and inspiration from those passages of Revelations 21 – '*I saw a new heaven and a new earth ... the holy city, new Jerusalem, coming down from God out of heaven, prepared as a bride adorned for her husband*' – passages that Sir William Courtenay knew so well and could recite with such eloquence and conviction? '*And God shall wipe away all tears from their eyes; and there shall be no more death, neither sorrow, nor crying, neither shall there be any more pain: for the former things are passed away.*' How could the likes of George Branchett, who had known such terrible loss, or Emily Burford, whose whole life had been marked by suffering, not be moved by these words?

And if anyone had the power to reshape their world and *make all things new*, it was surely Sir William Courtenay. As a religious leader, a Messiah, he was not the gentle cheek-turning Christ beloved of the gentry, but a muscular six-foot man of the people, who spoke with confident command, feared nothing, and seemed capable of anything. He came not to bring peace, but fire and the sword – and a brace of loaded pistols too.

'If anyone comes to take me now,' he told his followers as they rested at Lavender Farm, 'I am at leisure. But if they should, I shall try my arm. I have done nothing wrong. I only come for a day's pleasure, to give these men that have no employ, food, and drink ... If they come,' he said, drawing one of his pistols, 'I shall cut them down like grass.'[19]

Alarming tidings swirled in the wake of John Nicholls Tom's progress around the boundaries of Hernhill that day. The Reverend Charles Handley had first heard between nine and ten that morning that 'Thom' was 'going about the country exciting the people.' He went at once to find his 'worthy neighbour and friend' Colonel Percy Groves, whose messenger had probably brought him the news. Groves, an elderly gentleman, had commanded the 3rd Foot (the Buffs) early in the French Revolutionary War, but for several decades had been living in genteel retirement with his unmarried daughters in a large walled house in Boughton Street. Alfred Payne had been working in the colonel's stableyard when Tom and his band had passed along the street earlier that morning, and the colonel had doubtless heard about it soon enough.

Conferring, Handley and Groves agreed that there was peril in this popular 'excitement', and that Groves should seek out a magistrate to report what was happening. Mounting his horse, Groves set off west along the London road. He went first to find Norton Knatchbull, son of Sir Edward Knatchbull MP, who lived at an old house called Provender, up a lane a few miles past Faversham. Knatchbull was not at home, so Groves rode west once more, along the straight highway to Murston Rectory on the outskirts of Sittingbourne. Here, he found that the other magistrate, Dr John Poore, was also out. Already it was mid-afternoon on a warm day, but Groves — no doubt perspiring heavily and feeling all of his sixty-five years — was undeterred. He soon located Dr Poore, halting him in the street of Sittingbourne and telling him of his news: Courtenay was gathering a mob, inflaming them with language 'of a most exciting description,' and promising that if they followed him, he would deliver them from oppression. In particular, Groves told the magistrate, he was claiming that he would 'rescue' them from the hardships of the New Poor Law.[20]

Dr John Poore was also an elderly man, sixty years old. He was neat and rather precise, and not inclined to take fright or act with undue haste. Had he not faced down the rioters in his district in 1835, even when they had imprisoned him in his own justice chamber? He knew the law and was determined to follow correct procedure. In order to issue an arrest warrant, he explained, he must first have a sworn affidavit by an eyewitness, testifying that Sir William Courtenay had broken the law or disturbed the peace. Without that, he could not legally

'The Earth Shall Rise Up'

act. Groves declined to swear: all he knew was hearsay, and he had seen nothing of the man himself. Dr Poore instructed him to return home, find witnesses to attest to what he had claimed, and then to meet him at ten the following morning, at the Faversham office of Julius Shepherd – who alongside being a landowner and the proprietor of a brewery was also clerk to the magistrates. There, Poore said, he would hear the evidence and take steps accordingly.

But Groves was not the only concerned member of the gentry flitting about the countryside. George Francis of Fairbrook, after beating a swift retreat from the assembled followers of Sir William Courtenay, had crossed the fields to Boughton Street and called upon the Reverend George Pierce Marsh, another local clergyman, for advice. Mr Marsh was also away from home, so Francis went next to Brenley House, the home of Mr Jarman, 'one of our respectable gentlemen of the parish,' to consult on the best course of action. Like Handley, Jarman advised notifying the magistrates, and sent Francis hurrying off in the same direction that Groves had taken hours earlier.

It was six in the evening by the time Francis arrived at Murston, and this time he caught the magistrate at home. He was able to tell Poore everything he had picked up: the previous Sunday at the foot of Boughton Hill, he explained, Sir William had mustered two hundred followers and 'excited' them by 'stating the hardship the poor were labouring under from the New Poor Bill.' That very morning, he went on, Courtenay had been in the field outside his house with twenty followers; he believed they might be heading for Ospringe Fair. Presumably he did not tell Poore about the mysterious 'papers' he had received, which would surely have provided more concrete evidence of threat. Maybe he believed they reflected poorly upon him. Or maybe, even at this stage, he was trying to keep his former friend Sir William out of too much trouble?[21]

Once again Poore had to explain that he could do nothing without a sworn witness statement. Patiently he instructed Mr Francis to return to Boughton, collaborate with Colonel Groves in finding witnesses, and return with them to the Faversham office the next morning. Once Francis had departed, however, Dr Poore sent an express message to George Poynder at the Kent Country Lunatic Asylum, to discover what authority had granted the madman's release the previous autumn. Even at that stage, it seems, he was beginning to consider what the consequences of all this might be.

After covering over nine miles, with frequent pauses, John Nicholls Tom and his band had reached Dargate, a settlement at the far edge of Hernhill on the fringes of the Blean woodlands. Here they paused again to rest and hear the master's words. He took off his shoes, according to one witness, and in his bare feet he proclaimed 'now I stand upon my own bottom!' Nobody was sure what he meant, but like so many of Sir William's statements nobody was sure that it was not in some way profoundly important.[22]

Dargate was the home to a large number of those who would follow Tom to his final confrontation. James Goodwin, publican of the Dove beershop on the common, would be one of them. Edward Wraight the Elder lived next door, and owned chunks of the surrounding arable land. Alexander Foad's smallholding was just along the lane, and Phineas Harvey, a literate and hardworking young labourer, lived across the common. Five of the workers on Osborn Snoulton's farm would desert their posts and follow Sir William when he left Dargate.

But first there was singing – the hymn about the shepherd and his sheep once more – and then a session of mass prayer with all kneeling upon the grass of the common together. Then, as the light began to fade, the cavalcade swept on up the hill and into the woods, towards Bossenden.

They all slept at the farm that night, most of Tom's new followers on the straw of the old barn. Ten miles they had covered that day – no exceptional distance for labouring men accustomed to working on distant farms. But the festive mood of the day endured: there was more beer, and more bread and cheese for all, women as well as men joining the assembly. Some may have come along just for the free food, the company, and the novelty of it. The impostor 'used to treat his followers and have parties,' explained William Packman years later. He had gone up to Bossenden himself that evening and met John Nicholls Tom at the forge near the Gate public house on the main road. Packman mentioned talking with him at the forge, but tactfully did not say whether he had accompanied him back to the farm. He would have been wise to keep clear. 'Once they went with him,' he told the interviewer, 'they would have to continue to do so, or he would threaten to shoot them.'[23]

There were others loitering around Bossenden that night who were not attending Sir William's 'party'. James Gorham, the Boughton constable, went up to the farm at eleven and remained on watch through the midnight hours, concealed in the fringe of the woods. At one in the morning, he saw John Nicholls Tom emerge from the house and walk up and down in the open. The night was warm and close, and he looked like he was taking the air, but he carried a sword in his hand. Little more than an hour later Tom emerged once more, this time dressed in a shepherd's gabardine smock. As

Gorham watched, thirty or forty men assembled in the yard of the farm, coming from the barns and outbuildings where they had slept for only a few hours. In the darkness they formed up in a column and moved off along the farm track, towards the highway that would take them past the Red Lion and down the hill into Dunkirk.

Gorham followed them as far as Boughton Street, where he saw one of them rap at the shutters of William Blanchard's house. Blanchard had gone with them the day before, but somewhere along the way had dropped out and returned home. Gorham heard their mocking cry, 'Blanchard, did you see it smoke?' Perhaps they guessed that somebody had been investigating the bean stack the day before. It was too mysterious for Gorham, who followed them no further. They were close to his own house by that point, and he would surely have needed to get some sleep.[24]

John Tom and his men moved onward, flowing along Boughton Street and westward across the dark countryside, following the straight ribbon of the London road towards Sittingbourne. Alfred Payne the harness maker later claimed that he had encountered them at Boughton Chalk Pits that morning. An 1801 map of the district shows these pits on either side of the road. It was shortly after three in the morning by then, and still a pitch-black night. If Payne met them here it must have been a strange and eerie sight indeed, and a terrifying one; he was probably on his way to Faversham at the time, under cover of darkness, to give evidence against them to the magistrates. They now numbered forty-one men, so he said – he would have counted them off as they passed him, streaming out of the night – most of them with flayed sticks or bludgeons in their hands. Thomas Tyler was leading Sir William's horse. They were carrying Courtenay's lion banner too, and the loaf on its stick, though Payne would not have been able to distinguish them in the blackness.[25]

By the time the first daylight appeared in the sky the marchers had left the turning to Faversham behind them; they would have been trooping past the house of General Gosselin JP just as the first cocks began to crow. As the light rose, they pressed on through Ospringe and Teynham, then through Bapchild with a fine morning sun at their backs. By six in the morning they had covered over eleven miles, all the way to Sittingbourne.

The Reverend Dr Poore was alerted at that hour and told that Sir William Courtenay had arrived in town with his followers – the number given now as thirty – who were having breakfast at the nearby Wheatsheaf, which Poore calls 'a public-house of the lowest class.' Sir William was armed with a sabre and pistols, and his followers carried clubs, and a flag with a lion on it; another witness later reported that he was wearing a military-style cloak. We might imagine that Dr Poore was both surprised and rather alarmed to discover that the former lunatic he had only yesterday heard was inciting rebellion was now only a few hundred yards from his own home with a large band of armed men. His account of proceedings, however, remains brisk and unflustered. He went to the Wheatsheaf himself shortly afterwards, having sent men on ahead to observe the activities of Sir William and company. Presumably he then stationed himself at some convenient vantage to keep watch on them. But the impostor and his gang were, he discovered, 'conducting themselves peaceably and quietly.'[26]

The Wheatsheaf was a small brick pub, standing to the left of the road as it entered the old town of Sittingbourne. Asked why he was there, John Nicholls Tom replied insouciantly that he and his friends had got up, gone for a walk, and decided to visit the Wheatsheaf of Sittingbourne, of which they had 'heard much talk.' His followers drank beer and ate bread and cheese, but Tom himself took only a glass of sherry. He was scrupulous about paying for it all, too – the bill came to 25 shillings.

It was nine in the morning by the time the disciples roused themselves and set out once more, and by then Dr Poore had already departed for his meeting with Colonel Groves and Mr Francis. At the Faversham office the magistrate found Groves and his fellow clergyman George Marsh waiting for him. Edward Curling, the Hernhill farmer and poor law guardian, had accompanied them as well, to get a warrant for the return of four of his men 'enticed away' by Tom. There was no sign of George Francis, but as it happened his input was not required. The visitors had brought a pair of witnesses with them: one was Alfred Payne, the harness maker who had followed Tom and his men the previous day, and the other a labourer named Dunkin.

Both Dunkin and Payne made sworn statements of what they had seen. Dunkin had been carrying dung from his mistress's yard, he said, when he observed Sir William Courtenay and several others in a neighbouring field, apparently trying to set a bean stack on fire. After the party had departed, he went to the stack and retrieved a spent match, which he exhibited to Poore and the other gentlemen. Payne was able to testify that Sir William had made several bloody boasts and threats, had carried loaded pistols, had drilled his men to march like soldiers, and had called one of them the 'general'.

This was evidence enough even for the scrupulous Dr Poore that the madman Sir William Courtenay had been 'tampering with and exciting the people.' He issued warrants for the arrest of Courtenay himself, together with William Wills and his housemate Edward 'General' Newman. His visitors departed

'The Earth Shall Rise Up'

with the warrants, intending to pass them to the Boughton parish constables to serve the following morning. Dr Poore, meanwhile, made his way back to Sittingbourne, only to discover that Tom and his men were already gone.[27]

Rather than retracing their route back along the main road towards Faversham, Tom had led his followers off to the right somewhere east of Murston and began a lengthy march through the villages of the hinterland: Linstead and Doddington, Eastling and Throwley, Sheldwich Lees and Selling. These had been among the districts most affected by the anti-Poor Law rioting back in 1835, and he perhaps hoped that he might find recruits there. On the outskirts of Sittingbourne, he passed a gravel pit where thirty men were at work, likely on parish relief and labouring for their dole. He told the labourers that they were oppressed by the laws, and by the New Poor Law in particular. Was it ever ordained by God, he asked rhetorically, that the Union workhouses should separate married couples? But the workers in the pit were not interested; they would need sufficient cause, one said, to put their own necks in the noose and throw the country into chaos. Tom dismissed them as a 'set of Methodists,' and led his band onwards, deeper into the countryside.[28]

They would cover nearly thirty miles that day, a punishing hike in the warmth of early summer. Even with frequent stops at public houses, and at one point in a chalk pit, Tom's ragged little army must have been close to exhaustion by the time they stamped back across the parish boundary into Dunkirk and followed the road up to the Common. Their numbers had not grown by much since their departure and may even have decreased. Even the fervent enthusiasm of men like William Wills, the dogged tenacity of William Burford and George Branchett, must have been depleted by that point. Was John Nicholls Tom himself beginning to doubt his mission?

Around this point, probably as they passed back through Dunkirk Ville, the band were joined by a number of women and children. These would have been the wives and families of the marchers, come to greet them on their triumphant return. Together they swelled the number to fifty or sixty, as Tom led them up between the scattered cottages and past the tile works to the edge of the woodland. They followed him up the trail, tracing the route by the barked trees, towards Bossenden. At some point along the way, Tom halted. He lay down across the path and seemed almost to be sleeping. His followers halted, too. Silently, wondering, they formed a circle around him. Amid the woodland bracken, on the soft matting of dead leaves, men, women and children sat or squatted in small groups, and they waited.

It was now between seven and eight in the evening. The sun would not set until nearly nine, but already the light beneath the coppice oaks and hornbeams would have been growing dim. A woodcutter, returning along the path with his son and his dog, chanced upon the scene and was later able to describe it. One of the earliest reports confused the time of this encounter and placed it at seven the following morning. A later report corrected the date, although several subsequent accounts and histories have repeated the error and even embellished it. There would not have been sufficient time on the following morning for what followed to have taken place. But it fits perfectly on the Wednesday evening: after the long, dispiriting day of marching, John Nicholls Tom needed to rouse the fire and fervour of his disciples once more, and truly become the divine leader they wanted to follow. At such moment, perhaps, perceptions fogged by long toil or exertion become softer and more malleable.[29]

The woodcutter joked that they resembled a regiment of soldiers, waiting concealed in the bushes around the path. But he soon fell silent. Sir William Courtenay was muttering as he lay flat on his back, his lips moving as he formed the words. Abruptly he awoke from his trance and got to his feet. In some versions of the woodcutter's story, he simply greeted the man, with a slightly manic look in his eye, then gathered his followers and moved off. But it seems likely that the interloper witnessed most of what followed. If he did not, there were others present who certainly would have done. The impostor began one of his speeches, addressing all of those gathered in the glades around him, new followers as well as old disciples, women and children besides men. He spoke of great oppression and coming glory. He promised he would seize the lands and property of the gentry and the elites and partition them among the poor: each of his followers would have a farm of forty or fifty acres. He repeated the claim that he had come to earth on a cloud, and that one day he would ascend once more into the sky. He said that he was immune from earthly weapons, the bullets of his enemies could not harm him, and if ten thousand enemies came against them, he could slay them all with a word of command.

He had said as much before, but this time he would give his supporters something new. If they had faith in him, he could grant them the same magical protection that he enjoyed. And there was more: a 'sacrament' in bread and water, shared by all. Liardet later heard the scene described by a charcoal burner, who he reckoned may have witnessed it himself:

'... and then he giv'em all the sacrament, and after that he anoints himself and all of 'em with oil, and tells 'em that then no bullet nor nothing could harm 'em – and

> Sir William, he sat upon the ground with his back against a tree like, and there was all the women a crying and praying to him, and they says to him, "Now do tell us if you be our blessed Saviour, the Lord Jesus Christ!" and says he, "I am he ..." and then he shows 'em the mark of the nails in his hands which was made when he was put on the cross ...'[30]

Now Sir William Courtenay was not just a celestial being, a messiah with a divine commission: he was the literal reincarnation of Jesus Christ himself, the blessed redeemer in the flesh. He even had the marks to prove it, the nail-scars on his hands that several people later claimed to have witnessed. 'He showed us his wounds,' one old man said, 'and how could we dare to disobey him?' There in the dimming woods they must have clustered around him, creeping forward on their knees perhaps. Sarah Wraight was among them, and later described Sir William taking up the children and blessing them, and the women weeping over him, and kissing him, and worshipping him as the Christ.[31]

Alexander Foad, the sober and parsimonious small farmer from Dargate, also knelt at the messiah's feet and worshipped him. George Branchett, the Dunkirk ex-militiaman who had lost most of his family in the workhouse, was gripped with 'enthusiastic fervour,' and did the same.

Despite his enthusiasm, Foad seemed a little conflicted as to the role he might play in the forthcoming Apocalypse. Should he follow Sir William in the body, he asked, or might he be permitted to go home and merely follow him in spirit? But none could leave: any who departed, Sir William told them, would be consumed by fire and brimstone raining down from heaven. They must follow him in the body, and none could be excused.

'Oh be joyful!' Foad exclaimed, springing to his feet. 'Oh be joyful! The Saviour has accepted me. Go on, go on: till I drop I'll follow thee.'[32]

There were a few, nevertheless, who slunk away between the bushes. Edward and Sarah Wraight seem to have departed at this point, taking their children with them. Quite a few other witnesses chose this moment to vanish into the twilit woodland. But John Nicholls Tom gathered the rest of them and set off once more, following the pale hatchet-scars on the trees, towards Bossenden.

Some of them, together with their leader, would never see another sunset.

7. 'TO THE WORLD'S END'

Edward Curling of Hernhill was either a very brave man or a very foolhardy one. He had gone to the magistrates on Wednesday morning to get a warrant for the return of four of his regular labourers; he had sent them to work in his fields, but instead they had laid down their tools and gone off to join Courtenay. The warrant that Dr Poore had issued for Sir William's arrest did not immediately aid Curling in getting his men to come back and resume their work. So, that evening he decided to ride on up to Bossenden and set about retrieving them himself.

Born a labouring man, Curling owned little land in his own name. But he was the principal tenant and farm manager, and therefore the leading employer, in Hernhill. He was also the churchwarden, the poor law guardian and the roads surveyor. While the Reverend Charles Handley might have been, as Liardet put it, the only gentleman residing in Hernhill, the fifty-nine-year-old Curling occupied a more central role in the life of the parish. In Barry Reay's telling phrase, he was 'the cock of the village.' The very model, perhaps, of the old-fashioned English yeoman: tough but fair, earthily unpretentious, Tory-voting and tautly pious. And he was not accustomed to being crossed in his desires.[1]

By the time Curling rode up Boughton Hill, the impostor and his ragged army had returned from their lengthy march around the countryside. Past the Red Lion, Curling turned onto the track that led to the farm. He intended a ruse, claiming that he had come to collect a poor rate payment from old William Culver, supposedly the man of the house. But when he arrived in the yard he was met at the back door by the real master of Bossenden, the impostor John Nicholls Tom himself. It must have been getting dark by then, as Tom did not recognise the visitor as his 'determined opponent' Edward Curling. But he would have guessed that a man on horseback was unlikely to be a friend and demanded to know his business. Curling began asking for his workers by name, perhaps hoping that they were within earshot – was George Griggs there? William Knight? George Hawkins, or Charles Hadlow? With gathering annoyance, the impostor replied that they were not. 'They are my men,' Curling explained, 'and they have left their work improperly. I am anxious to get them back, as their wives are uneasy about them.'

The impostor wanted to know why he asked for these men.

'Because I provide for them,' Curling told him.

'I don't know that you do provide for them,' John Nicholls Tom replied. He went back into the house, only to be told that he had just been speaking to Edward Curling, one of his most vigorous adversaries; at once he seized a brace of pistols, loaded them and ran into the yard again. Curling, however, had turned his horse and ridden for safety, and by the time the impostor emerged from the house he was out of range.[2]

At some point that evening or the following morning, John Nicholls Tom demonstrated to his followers his miraculous ability to withstand gunfire. He had claimed as much during the sacramental ceremony in the woods, but clearly some of his disciples needed further persuasion. He first had one of them – perhaps William Wills – fire a pistol at him, and then fired one back at a gathering of the more faithful. In both cases, the lead pistol balls seemed to vanish into thin air. Truly, Sir William was *bullet proof* – and now those that believed in him were too: 'neither wounds nor death could be inflicted upon them, while they possessed the power of destroying all others.' Presumably there was some sleight of hand involved, and the pistols were subtly loaded with blank charges. But many of those present accepted what they saw.[3]

It was also around this time, too, that Sir William started exhibiting the marks of the crucifixion upon his body, in particular the scars on the palms of his hands, supposedly left by the nails of the cross. Scattered mentions of these wounds or puncture marks imply that a number of people witnessed them, but by no means all or most of the impostor's followers. It may only have been over this last night, following the strange assembly in the wood, that the mysterious wounds first became visible. There was apparently a scar in Tom's side as well, supposedly the spear wound dealt to Christ as he hung on the cross; the impostor 'was accustomed to show [this] to his disciples when he represented himself to them as the Messiah,' saying that it was the wound into which the doubting apostle Thomas had 'thrust his hand.'

Nowhere in the scant descriptions of these wounds does anyone claim that they were fresh or bleeding, or that they only appeared occasionally. Strictly speaking, therefore, they were not *stigmata*; Tom was not miraculously emulating the wounds of Christ, he *was* Christ, and still bore the old scars upon his body. But what did his followers, and others who witnessed it, make of this? All of them, like John Nicholls Tom himself, inhabited an entirely Protestant, and largely Anglican, religious environment. Reverence for the wounds of Christ, like the miraculous *stigmata*, has largely been confined to Catholic spirituality. None of the English prophets and messiah-figures of the eighteenth and early nineteenth centuries – neither Wroe nor Ward, Brothers nor Southcott, nor even the 'Quaker Messiah' James Naylor back in the seventeenth century – had exhibited Christ's wounds upon their flesh. The appearance of these scars seems to have been an innovation, intended further to convince the doubtful among Tom's retinue of his true identity.[4]

Accordingly, it was over this final night and the following morning that he issued his most grandiose statements and made his most bloodcurdling threats. 'I am the resurrected body of Gideon,' Tom told his disciples at Bossenden. 'This is the day of judgement, the first day of the Millennium, and this day I will put the crown upon my head. Behold, one greater than Sampson is with you!' Perhaps by this point he was aware that the moment of crisis was approaching, and he needed fully to secure the allegiance of his followers. If any of them wished to leave him now, he said, they could go. 'But, if you desert me, I will follow you to the furthermost pits of hell and invoke fire and brimstone from heaven upon you!'[5]

Between five and half past five, soon after sunrise, the clergyman Mr Marsh's servant, Isaac Philpotts, together with another man came to the farm, probably sent up to spy on what was happening. They were later able to name several of the impostor's supporters, seen walking in the garden with their master. Thomas Tyler Mears was there, with Thomas and Peter Adams. Peter had no shoes on, Phillpotts recalled. He and his colleague were not the only spies lingering around the margins of Bossenden in the early hours; Stephen Gorham had taken up the observation post

'To the World's End'

of his brother, Constable James Gorham, on the edge of the woodland.[6]

The statements of these witnesses suggest that Tom and some of his followers had slept little, if at all, over the preceding night. *The Saviour never slept*, the impostor had told the asylum superintendent, *as the Holy Ghost would not let him sleep* ... But the reference to the men 'walking in the garden', one barefoot, summons a deeper echo. Bossenden was Sir William's Gethsemane. His disciples had been keeping the night vigil. And soon enough, Judas would appear.

Nicholas Mears awoke early that morning. He put on his best coat, blue with gilt buttons and a swallow tail, and knotted a yellow and blue checked handkerchief around his neck. The day was already warm and close, the air sultry, and a light mist hung over the woodlands of the Blean. According to 'Canterburiensis', Nicholas and his wife parted with great affection – which might seem strange if, as John Nicholls Tom later suggested, he had 'used her like a dog.' He did not like this business, he told her. He knew, as his brother John Mears the parish constable perhaps did not, that he had pledged only four days ago that he *never would leave* Sir William. Now he had to accompany his brother to arrest him.

The day before, Nicholas and another man, a labourer named Daniel Edwards who lived up at Fairbrook, had been sworn in as petty constables to aid in executing the warrants of arrest on Sir William Courtenay, William Wills and Edward Newman. None of them were armed. In fact, John Mears later claimed, they had no intention of trying to arrest the named men if there was any sign of resistance. They would simply make an effort at doing their duty and then retreat. Even so, Nicholas seems to have had a premonition of the violence ahead. If one of them should die, he told his brother, it had best be him; unlike John, he had no children, and there would be none left fatherless.[7]

It was around six in the morning when they reached Bossenden, and full daylight. The lane from the highway took them up to the central yard of the farm, which lay at the rear of the main house. As they approached, the Mears brothers could see figures in the yard, and among the outbuildings to either side. These would have been the men and women who had slept the night in the barn. A later source claimed they were sharing 'a basin of milk.' Emily Burford was probably among them; the reports on her actions later that day suggest that she entered the wood *from* Bossenden, and she had likely spent the night there.

Deciding to circle around the farm buildings and present themselves at the front door instead, the constable and his assistants crossed a stile from the lane and made their way along a path to the left of the house. Accounts vary as to where they were intercepted; some suggest that the fatal clash happened as they crossed the stile. But drawings and plans of the scene of the murder, and the statements of eyewitnesses, make for a clearer reconstruction.[8]

A second fence divided the northerly field at the front of the house from the one to the west. This fence ran up to the northwest corner of the building, with either a gate or a gap – depictions vary, and one eyewitness mentions a *wicket* – to allow access from the garden plot at the side of the house to the front. It was at this second fence that Nicholas Mears met his end.

Several of the impostor's disciples – William Burford, William Price and Thomas Tyler Mears among them – were waiting on the path as the constable and his men circled the house. They carried oak cudgels in their hands. Tyler, the Mears brothers' cousin, went ahead of them to the house corner and called a warning through an open window. Shortly afterwards, John Nicholls Tom emerged from the front door. He was dressed in a shepherd's gabardine smock and carried a knife or a short sword in one hand and a loaded pistol in the other. His readiness suggests that he had been anticipating this encounter.

He met the Mears brothers as they came through the gap in the fence at the corner of the house. Nicholas was in the lead, with the third man, Daniel Edwards, hanging back at the rear. 'Are you the constable?' Tom demanded. He must have recognised him; this man had accepted food from his hands and pledged never to leave him. Now he was leading other men to arrest him.

'Yes,' Nicholas Mears replied, or 'I be.'

Without another word John Nicholls Tom raised the pistol in his right hand and fired it at close range. The lead slug punched into Nicholas Mears's chest just above his jacket lapel, passing between two of his ribs. Mears staggered backwards, falling against the railings of the fence. Already Tom had thrown down the spent pistol and lunged at John Mears with his blade. 'And you are the other!' he cried.

The constable turned to run, heading obliquely across the field behind him towards the nearest fringe of the woods. Tom came after him, still trying to strike him with his sword. Stephen Gorham, concealed at the edge of the trees, saw the impostor stumble as his foot caught on brambles. John Mears bolted clear, crashing through the undergrowth and into the woods close to where Gorham was watching. Daniel Edwards, the other assistant constable, was still lingering at the side of the house; he saw Thomas Tyler gesturing to him and took the opportunity to flee. After regaining his footing, John Nicholls Tom walked back up the field to where his victim lay sprawled against the fence. He went back into the house, and emerged moments later carrying his second pistol.

'What am I to do?' the wounded Nicholas Mears cried. Daniel Edwards also heard him ask, 'am I to lie here in this *dishabille*?' – a curious statement, but Edwards was probably running for his life by this point and may not have heard clearly what followed.[9]

'You must do what you can,' John Nicholls Tom told Mears. Then he raised his sword and stabbed him three times in the shoulder, the blade slicing through his neckerchief. He was still striking wildly at the fallen man as Edwards snatched a glance behind him. Mears rolled over on his side, and Tom shot him a second time in the back, his pistol so close to the victim's body that the muzzle-flash singed the wool of his coat.[10]

By now a crowd had gathered around the door of the farmhouse and the gate from the yard. John Field, the Culvers' servant, reckoned that fifteen to twenty men had witnessed the killing, but none tried to prevent it. George Hawkins, who had slept in the straw of the barn overnight, claimed to have witnessed the scene from a distance. Alexander Foad and George Branchett, the men who had worshipped Tom as Christ the evening before, had also joined the crowd of spectators. Perhaps some of the women had come from the barn too, Emily Burford among them, and Sarah Culver from inside the house.

John Nicholls Tom stood before them all now. He appeared 'frantic', according to Field, like a 'crazy madman.' Brandishing his bloodied sword over his head, he cried 'I am the only saviour of the world! I am your shepherd, and you are my true lambs, every one of you!'

On his orders, four of his disciples – Burford and Tyler, with William Price and another man – took the body of the murdered Mears by each limb and lugged him, hanging face down between them, back along the path at the side of the house to the garden plots. Here they slung the corpse into a dry ditch. 'Though I have killed his body,' Tom told them when they returned, 'I have saved his soul.'

Then he invited them all to join him at breakfast.[11]

Courtenay has shot Mears. Sir William has killed the constable. Along the woodland tracks and the highways the news spread, over fields and hop gardens, from cottage to cottage. John Mears and Daniel Edwards carried it westwards as they fled the scene, through Boughton towards Faversham. Edward Curling, mounted and dressed in his rudimentary camouflage of a labourer's smock, carried it east towards Canterbury. The sound of those two pistol shots, and those savagely hacking blows, would echo over greater distances still. An hour after the murder of Nicholas Mears, young Henry Hadlow unhitched his ploughhorse, swung up onto the animal's back and rode it over the hill through Hernhill towards his home at Waterham, yelling his threatening taunt: '... and he'll shoot a hundred more of you buggers before night!'[12]

It was nearly ten in the morning by the time the news reached Provender, the magistrate Norton Knatchbull's house a few miles beyond Faversham. Knatchbull would later claim to have known nothing of the activities of John Nicholls Tom until the evening of 30 May. But he had been aware for many years of the impostor Sir William, who had appropriated two of his assumed names – Honeywood and Courtenay – from Knatchbull's mother's family.

Back in 1832 Norton had accompanied his father, Sir Edward Knatchbull, to the hustings on Barham Down, and would have witnessed the impostor's bizarre pitch for the East Kent parliamentary elections. Five years later he read in the *Kentish Chronicle* of the release of Sir William from the asylum and had asked George Francis in vain for news of his whereabouts. But in May 1838 he would be unaware of Tom's 'tampering with the people' until after his death. Apparently, his mind was on other things.

Aged twenty-nine, Norton was a very different sort of character to his blunt, brusque, traditionalist father Sir Edward. Ten years before, Norton had gone off to Italy to complete his education in the accepted manner. In Rome during a rainy *Carnevale* season he had become acquainted with a wealthy Staffordshire family, the Watts Russells, and travelled with them down to Naples and Sorrento in the spring. Somewhere between touring the ruins of Pompeii and Paestum and climbing Vesuvius by night as lava streamed and fiery projectiles arced overhead, Norton fell helplessly in love with seventeen-year-old Mary Watts Russell. She was gorgeous and vivacious, wealthy and cultured, fluent in Italian and German, and shared his passion for the poetry of Schiller and Southey. By the time they returned to Naples, the couple were engaged.[13]

None of this pleased Sir Edward Knatchbull, who initially refused his consent for the marriage. The Watts Russells might be rich, and politically conservative, but Mary's grandfather had been an East End soap boiler, and her father had made his fortune in industry. Sir Edward found his new teenage daughter-in-law deplorably thoughtless and impudent, and careless with money, and decreed that his eldest son would not inherit the baronetcy, or the Palladian family mansion of Mersham Hatch. Instead, they would go to his second wife's children.

The newlywed Norton and Mary Knatchbull had to make do with Provender, a smaller and more rustic country house near Faversham which dated in parts to the fourteenth century.[14]

In the years that followed, while Mary dutifully produced a succession of children and sank into moods of gloomy religiosity that read in her diary very much like episodes of depression, Norton attempted to live up to his father's expectations of him. He became a captain in the Ashford troop of the East Kent Yeomanry. He also became a magistrate and a Justice of the Peace, but left most of the duties to the older local gentlemen, Dr Poore in Sittingbourne and General Gosselin in Faversham. Norton was perhaps not too suited to the active life anyway. He was a slender young man of refined constitution, much given to fits of weeping – or so he portrayed himself in early letters to Mary, perhaps accentuating his romantic pallor and delicacy. Even playing cricket was beyond him: 'I find the ball hurts horribly,' he told her, 'what a coward I am, am I not? My hands are black and blue – you know it does not take much to bruise them.' He seems to have preferred less strenuous pursuits: botany, for example, and gardening. He was also partially deaf, and made use of an India-rubber ear trumpet.[15]

It was with considerable dismay, therefore, that Norton learned on the Wednesday evening that the maniac Sir William Courtenay was 'parading the country at the head of 60 or 70 persons.' How could he not have noticed this beforehand? The impostor and his band had passed twice within a mile or two of Provender earlier that same day, and Colonel Groves had come from Boughton the afternoon before to inform Knatchbull of Sir William's antics. By the time news reached him the following morning of the murder of Nicholas Mears, Norton Knatchbull was prepared at last to take action. No doubt he was spurred by the thought that he had failed in his duties by remaining unaware of the disturbances for so long. But perhaps he was driven, too, by the realisation that, in demonstrating prompt and manly courage in confronting the threat, he might have finally found the opportunity to impress his father, and to mend relations between them.[16]

An eyewitness account reports Knatchbull travelling in a 'carriage' as he set off to apprehend John Nicholls Tom. This was perhaps a curricle, a light two-wheeled vehicle of the sort favoured by wealthy young men. Alert to the possibility of violence, Knatchbull was careful to arm himself before leaving Provender with more than one firearm, including a double-barrelled pocket pistol. He reached Faversham to find constable John Mears and Daniel Edwards already waiting at the clerk's office, ready to give their sworn statements on the killing at Bossenden. Knatchbull issued further warrants for the arrest of Sir William Courtenay – this time for murder – along with William Burford, William Price and Thomas Tyler Mears, whose culpability the witnesses attested.

Knatchbull next assembled the local officers of the law, led by Bartlett Chambers, high constable of Faversham. Together they enrolled a number of others as special constables, including George Catt of the Good Intent beershop, who was enthused by the rumour of a reward for taking Sir William Courtenay dead or alive. By the time Knatchbull set off in his carriage once more, along the highway towards Boughton, a band of mounted men were riding in his wake.[17]

Despite John Nicholls Tom's warnings of hellfire and brimstone, several of his supporters had returned to their homes rather than accompanying him back to Bossenden the evening before. Among them was Edward Wraight the younger, the handsome, mild-looking smallholder from the hamlet of

'To the World's End'

Bessborough. Wraight and his wife had witnessed the sacramental ceremony in the woods, but had chosen to go back to their cottage, rather than continuing to follow Tom and his close disciples. It might be tempting to imagine that Edward Wraight was the man who lay sleepless and trembling in his bed that night, terrified that fire would come from heaven to destroy his family.

Wraight knew nothing of the murder of Mears when he left his cottage on Thursday morning. In the lane outside he met Edward Rigden Curling, a distant and much poorer relative of the Hernhill farmer Curling, who lived up at Waterham and worked as a shepherd, or 'sheep looker', out on the marshes. Wraight suggested, so Curling later claimed, that they 'go and see what Courtenay and his men were up to.' Rather a casual notion, it might seem, and doubtless they had a stronger motivation than mere curiosity. Both would be in shackles by the end of the day, accused of riot and murder.[18]

By the time Wraight and the shepherd Curling fell in with John Nicholls Tom, he was on the march once more. An illustration in the *Weekly Chronicle* of 10 June, perhaps based on eyewitness testimony and later sketches from the scene, shows 'Courtenay with his Troops leaving Bosenden Farm, Culver's residence', either on the Thursday morning or the day before. Tom is marching in the lead, his sword in his hand as he points the way ahead. He is shown wearing a large hat, and a jacket with thickly braided lapels which also features in several other illustrations; this may have been the black velvet garment he appears to have worn underneath his shepherd's gabardine.

Behind him comes a man in a smock carrying a stick and leading Tom's saddled horse. The illustration identifies him as Thomas Tyler Mears. There is no mention of the horse during this day's events, and Tom may in fact have left it stabled at

Bossenden or taken it to Fairbrook and left it there. In the illustration, the column of men following the horse curls out from the yard of the farm, forty or so men marching in single or double file, cudgels on their shoulders like soldiers' muskets. A man in the lead carries the lion banner; another report names this standard-bearer as William Rye, an 'industrious labourer' from Hernhill. The picture shows the house very clearly. The window shutters and perhaps the door stand open, but nobody else is in sight. The women – Emily Burford, Sarah Culver and her mother among them – must have been watching from within as their menfolk marched off that morning. What did they think was going to happen? How many truly believed that this was, as Sir William had promised, 'the day of judgement', and the 'first day of the Millennium'?[19]

Leaving Bossenden by the woodland paths, an hour or so after the killing of Nicholas Mears, Tom and his band descended to Dargate Common, where constable James Gorham spied them from a distance around ten in the morning. From Dargate they paraded westward along the lanes, once more gathering strength. James Goodwin, publican of the Dove beerhouse on Dargate Common, had joined them by this time, leaving his pregnant wife Mary Anne – the daughter of Edward Wraight the Elder – and their five children behind him. Noah Miles, the small farmer who ran the Noah's Ark beershop at Bessborough, also fell in with the march. Miles, aged fifty-six, had been setting out for a morning's work with his hoe when he met John Nicholls Tom and his followers parading along the lane. One of his daughters – all 'exceedingly pretty, and having an air of extraordinary gentility' – persuaded Miles and his son to accompany Tom and discover what he had to say.

Another new recruit was an elderly man named Thomas Ovenden. A lifelong inmate of Whitstable poorhouse, Ovenden was later described as 'wretched-looking,', an 'imbecile', and 'little better than an idiot'. He had been wandering the lanes from Whitstable towards Boughton that morning when he met Tom and his band, who persuaded him to join them. He probably needed little inducement.[20]

At Lavender farm near Waterham, west of Dargate, Tom rested his men once more. Elizabeth Arnold, the waggoner's wife who had been so terrified of Sir William when he took tea at their cottage, went up to the farm with a message for the bailiff John Hadlow, and found them all there. In old age, she remembered what she saw that morning:

> '... the men were seated beside the granary eating bread and cheese and drinking beer. They were bringing the beer out of the cellar in pailfuls. I went to the door to deliver my message and Courtenay came to the door and he said, "Good morning, Mrs Arnold," and I said, "Good morning, Sir William," and he said, "I have done one deed and had a hearty breakfast and I will do another and eat a hearty dinner. He (meaning Mears) used his wife like a dog, and like a dog he dies." These were the very words he used, sir.'[21]

As they marched on through the hamlet of Bessborough, Tom and his men passed the cottage of the younger Edward Wraight. Wraight himself had joined the band by that point, but as his wife Sarah watched them streaming along the lane she noticed Alexander Foad at the rear of the column and went out to speak to him. She knew Foad to be a sober and respectable man, if a parsimonious one, but the evening before she had seen him kneel before Tom and acclaim him as the Messiah.

'Do you, Muster Foad,' she asked, 'believe he is our blessed Saviour?'

'Oh, yes,' Foad replied. 'Mrs Wraight, for certain sure he is, and I'll follow him to the world's end!'[22]

The second 'deed' that John Nicholls Tom intended was perhaps to take place at Fairbrook. Rumours of Tom's intentions passed between his followers during the march: he would lead them to Canterbury and burn the city, he had boasted, or to the Milton Union workhouse and tear it down. Or he would lead them to Fairbrook, and put to death Farmer George Francis *and his whole family* for having declined any further acquaintance with Sir William Courtenay.[23]

Eliza Jane Francis and her aunt, Mary Horne, had no foreknowledge of these threats as they saw Tom and his dusty little army straggling up the lane towards Fairbrook. The morning mist had burned off and the day was growing hot, though the sky was still overcast. John Tom must have been sweating in his black braided jacket and gabardine, and burdened with his heavy pistols and sword. His men, too, having walked off the pailfuls of beer they had drunk at the farm, would be in need of further refreshment. Some of them were still carrying the leafy green boughs they had brought from Dargate Common, apparently waving them before their master 'as the Jews preceded Christ into Jerusalem, bearing branches of palm in their hands … lauding him as their God and Saviour.' Eliza and Mary came out of the house and waited at the garden fence as the men approached.[24]

Sir William called for gin and water, and drink for his troops, and the women brought out two big brown jugs of beer and six half-pint mugs. Mary Horne fetched a bottle of gin as well and passed it across the fence. Around this time

Mr George Francis joined them, having lingered for some time indoors, probably debating with himself how he should respond to this unwelcome intrusion. He later told the Select Committee that he had been concerned for the ladies, thinking they would be frightened, but confessed that he was frightened himself. When he finally emerged, it was to forbid the men outside from drinking his beer – too late, as it happened.

John Nicholls Tom greeted him with rather condescending goodwill. 'Francis, I am come here to make my peace with you,' he said. 'We have not been upon terms for some time. I forget and forgive you all that has passed, and I hope you will do the same and shake hands.'

Francis responded guardedly. 'Sir William,' he said, 'I regret seeing you in this situation; you are not only getting into trouble yourself, but by coming to my house you are getting me into trouble also. I must request that you will immediately take your party off my premises.' He assured his former friend that he felt no animosity towards him. However, he said, 'if you are not the man you have pretended to be ... there is no punishment too bad for you.'[25]

Nevertheless, Mr Francis shook hands with him, as did his daughter Eliza. Mary Horne instead flung her arms around Tom, hugging him and kissing him, according to an onlooker, 'as if she would bite a piece out of his cheek.'[26]

Tom's men, meanwhile, were gathered along the fence drinking beer from the jugs. Abruptly one of them raised the alarm: soldiers were advancing upon them on horseback. John Nicholls Tom at once ordered his men to cross a stile into the field and follow him obliquely down the slope to an osier bed, or plantation of coppiced willows, in the vale below. There, he said, they would have open ground in which to fight, and the protection of the osiers should they require it. As Tom and his men crossed the stile and made their way down the slope, George Francis waited for the riders who were coming up the lane towards Fairbrook. Rather than a troop of dragoons, he saw Norton Knatchbull in his carriage, followed by a dozen or so constables, local gentlemen and yeoman farmers. John Tom had forty-two men with him at this point, and while the newcomers now commanded the higher ground at the top of the slope, they lacked the strength to flush him out of his position among the osiers.

Knatchbull had arrived in Boughton only shortly beforehand, riding in from Faversham with his mounted escort, and Dr Poore had joined him at the house of the clergyman Mr Marsh. Marsh and Colonel Groves had been alerted earlier to the murder at Bossenden, initially by Marsh's servant and then by Mears and his assistant Edwards, who confirmed the facts. The clergyman had already sent his son William off to Canterbury to summon help from the magistrates and the military garrison there. Edward Curling had also set off on the same mission, some time in advance, but neither had yet returned. Dr Poore should have been aware, of course, that neither Marsh nor Groves were magistrates, and so could not authorise a request for military assistance. Besides, with both the witnesses to the killing having travelled on to Faversham and then returned with Knatchbull, nobody in Canterbury could have sworn an affidavit that a crime had been committed.

As usual, the slow and deliberate working of local justice was counting against a swift resolution to the problem. Nevertheless, Dr Poore counselled waiting for the arrival of military support before attempting to move against Sir William Courtenay and his followers. By now, the scouts and observers posted across the surrounding countryside had reported that Courtenay and his band had moved towards Fairbrook.

It would be dangerous and foolhardy, Poore reasoned, for the civil power to attempt to execute the arrest warrants. Norton Knatchbull disagreed. He was determined to confront the madman and his deluded followers himself, with anyone who would volunteer to accompany him.[27]

This mood of resolute determination, even bloody-minded courage, seems oddly contrary to the view that Knatchbull had once presented of himself: the pale and fragile youth who had returned from Europe filled with romantic longings and German poetry. Norton had never, as far as we know, encountered physical peril or violence. In Rome he had seen a man knifed to death during a street brawl below his window, and the sight had horrified him. But he would have known, as he turned his curricle and whipped the horses up the lane towards Fairbrook, that all eyes were on him. He was performing a role, one that would be seen and appraised not only by his fellow magistrates but by his potential future constituents. His father would hear of it too, of course. It might be discussed in Parliament. It was vital that he make a bold show and demonstrate a courage and fortitude that did not come easily to him.

Charles Neame, a local yeoman farmer, went up to Fairbrook with Knatchbull, together with Mr Edward Jarman, of Brenley House, and the witnesses Daniel Edwards and John Mears. We can assume that George Catt, the special constable from Faversham with his eyes on the reward for Sir William's capture, was accompanying them. Knatchbull also had four policemen from Ospringe and two or three others with him, and one of these companions – called only 'a gentleman' – subsequently left one of the best accounts of what followed.[28]

As they approached Fairbrook house, they saw Tom and his band retreating down the field towards the osier beds. Knatchbull left his carriage in the lane and proceeded on foot past the house. From the front garden, George Francis 'endeavoured to enter into explanations,' but Knatchbull indignantly shouted him down; Francis had 'harboured the madman,' and upon his head rested much of the blame for what had happened since.

His mood of nervous bonhomie unabating, Francis next called out to some of the other gentlemen, in a 'manner more befitting a racecourse salutation' – would they care for some refreshment? Edward Jarman replied, with astonished disgust, 'refreshment, Mr. Francis! Will you lend me a brace of pistols?' Francis, determined not to take sides in the developing confrontation, still believed that Sir William Courtenay was 'a good man'. But the small band of gentlemen and constables were following Knatchbull's lead now. Ignoring Francis, they crossed the stile into the field.

The osier bed was a large and very dense plantation, roughly square with a stream on one side and ditches on the other three. Entering it from the field, Tom and his men could feel secure. By now, however, they had realised that rather than retreating from a company of soldiers, they had withdrawn in the face of a mere dozen or so civilians, most of them unarmed. Twice Tom recrossed the ditch and advanced a short way up the field towards the cordon formed by Knatchbull and his companions. They were cowards, he yelled, and would not dare approach him. He challenged any one of them to go 'foot to foot' with him, in single combat. Then he returned to his redoubt among the osiers, his men cheering and brandishing their clubs in defiance.

Wisely, Knatchbull was keeping his distance; seeing that Tom and his followers meant 'serious mischief', he had determined to await the support of the army. Back in Boughton, meanwhile, Edward Curling's son had found Dr Poore and told him that the authorities in Canterbury needed a signed letter from a magistrate on the scene before they could sanction military deployment. Poore duly wrote the letter, and the young man swung back into the saddle and rode off towards Canterbury again. It would be at least another hour before any troops could come to their aid.[29]

In the field below Fairbrook, the stand-off continued. It was now approaching noon, and another couple of horsemen had appeared on the eastern slope of the vale, at the far side of the osier beds to Knatchbull and his posse. Reverend Charles Handley and his brother had learned of Nicholas Mears's murder some hours before, and the reports of the murderer's unchallenged tour around the surrounding countryside must have alarmed them considerably. At some point they decided to set out themselves and see if they could reason with Tom's supporters; we might assume that the impetuous Major Benjamin Handley was behind the scheme. Riding westwards from Hernhill, they came down towards Fairbrook through the woods where Kemsdale House would later stand. From the slope here they could look out across the valley towards the farm, and see Knatchbull's party gathered on the far side, and Tom and his men in the osier bed below them.[30]

Charles and his brother were not the only Handleys at Fairbrook. The Dawes archive at Mount Ephraim holds the typed transcript of notes attributed to 'Lt J Handley Jr', who was also observing the events in the osier beds. The transcriber is slightly mistaken in his identity: John Handley Jr, nephew of Charles and Benjamin, was not a military man but a barrister and a partner in the family bank. He, too, must have been visiting Hernhill at the time, although there is no mention of his presence in any other accounts. The notes states that he 'made use of the glass', or telescope, so he must have been observing from a distance. One of the early *Times* reports mentions 'an individual ... reconnoitring the party from the top of a mill at some distance with a glass' – the vantage point was perhaps Richardson's windmill, above the western end of Boughton Street and the tallest in the area. From up there, sixty feet above the ridge, an observer could have scanned the countryside for several miles in any direction, and tracked the progress of John Nicholls Tom and his band. The man on the mill cap would also have been ideally placed to pass signals between Knatchbull's party at Fairbrook, three quarters of a mile away, and Dr Poore and his men waiting for the soldiers down in Boughton Street.[31]

Handley Jr claims to have changed his position more than once. There were other observers in the vicinity, too – a band of men had climbed to the top of Hernhill church tower and were keeping watch from there. Edward Curling had reappeared on the scene, still dressed in his smock, with a fresh horse beneath him and a pistol in his hand. He was not about to risk any more unarmed encounters with Tom or his disciples.

Charles and Major Handley chose their moment well, waiting for the impostor to make one of his sallies from the osier beds to taunt and challenge the constables. Only then did they ride closer from the opposite side, calling out to the men sheltering amid the willow coppices. Their leader Sir William Courtenay had criminally murdered one of their neighbours, Charles declared to them; they must desert him, or share in his guilt.

It seems that this short speech, or the stress of the overall situation, was telling on some of Tom's supporters. James Goodwin, the publican of the Dove who had joined the march at Dargate, was already talking about quitting and going home. John Nicholls Tom returned to the osiers filled with wrath, and confronted Goodwin and any others who shared his faintness of heart. One greater than Samson was with them, he reminded them – if they deserted him now, he would chase them down to hell and shower fire and brimstone upon them. Then he drew his pistol and pointed it at Goodwin, demanding to know whose side he was on. If he belonged to the other party, he would not live.

'If anyone tries to leave me,' he told them, 'I will blow his bloody brains out!'[32]

One witness expected to see 'Goodwin's brains blown into air' at that very moment. Instead, John Tom stalked across to the opposite side of the osier beds and confronted the Handley brothers, who were still on horseback on the far bank of the stream. Major Benjamin Handley called that they wanted to come to a parlay with Tom and his men. But the impostor was not backing down now; drawing his sword he began to flourish it in the air above his head with a 'demoniacal look.'

This display was too much for Major Handley. 'My men,' he called to Tom's supporters, 'your infatuated leader knows not how to use his sword! What are you afraid of?'

Tom sheathed his sword and raised his pistol instead, pointing it at the major. 'I will plant a ball in your heart, sir!' he shouted.

'You are a madman!' the major called back.

Tom fired – the constables on the far side of the valley and the observer with the telescope heard the shot. But his aim was poor, and the bullet missed. Unconcerned, he turned 'in an insulting manner' and strode back into the osier bed to rejoin his cowed troops.[33]

That shot at least had required no additional witnesses: dozens had seen the maniac Courtenay attempt to murder Major Handley. Overcoming their shock, the brothers continued to attempt reason for a few minutes more, the major informing Tom's men that they were guilty of high treason, but soon afterwards they gave up. Keeping clear of the osiers, they crossed the stream and rode up the far slope to join Norton Knatchbull and his constables.

From his point of observation, the Handleys' nephew saw something which everyone else appears to have missed: a woman came down to the osier bed to speak with Tom. Handley Jr identified her as Sarah Culver, and claimed later to have seen her after the encounter in Bossenden Wood. It is possible that the woman he saw was Mary Horne, from Fairbrook – both were around the same age, and John Handley knew neither of them well and was watching from a distance. But quite possibly Sarah had followed the march, and joined John Tom now. Was she – or Mary – trying to persuade him to end the confrontation?

A short while later, the impostor decided to emerge from cover. He sounded his bugle, and his men marched out from the osier bed and advanced in file up the field towards Knatchbull and the constables. Various estimates put their number between thirty-five and forty at this point. Those who had carried leafy branches had thrown them aside and armed themselves with cudgels made from osier roots. Knatchbull considered making a stand but was aware that the rest of his posse had already retreated up the field behind him towards Fairbrook Lane. They were greatly outnumbered, and few of them were armed. Steadily they fell back, opening a path for Tom and his men to move through their cordon and recross the stile into the lane. Charles Handley called out to them again as they filed past him, addressing his parishioners by name – Edward Wraight the Elder and his son, Noah Miles, Thomas Tyler Mears, Alexander Foad, William Knight and the

Hadlows – and begging them to desert their leader. Had they no regard, he asked them, for their families? Noah Miles called back that he certainly did. It was, as he later claimed, his family that had got him into this situation.[34]

According to one of the gentry volunteers, as Tom and his men crossed the stile and passed a cottage just beyond it, 'certain incidents occurred, which it is expedient to pass over without further allusion.' This mysterious comment receives little support from other accounts – quite possibly nobody else was close enough to see what took place, but the hint of impropriety or disgrace might suggest that the women of Fairbrook were involved once more. Did Eliza Francis and her aunt Mary Horne bestow further congratulation on their hero, for evading his foes? The *Times* correspondent later wrote that many local people 'blame Miss Horne and Miss Francis, aunt and niece, for the encouragement they gave to this vagabond. It is said ... that these ladies waved their handkerchiefs to Thoms [sic] as he left them after murdering the constable.'[35]

Forming his men into a column four abreast outside Fairbrook, Tom led them down to the junction and turned left along the road, heading back towards Hernhill, Dunkirk and Bossenden. Knatchbull mustered his own party and set off in steady pursuit, the magistrate's carriage taking the lead. Daniel Edwards, the petty constable who had fled Bossenden that morning after the killing of Nicholas Mears, had gone to his cottage at Fairbrook and fetched his gun. He offered to run on ahead, conceal himself in the hedge, and shoot Courtenay as he crossed the bridge over the stream. His companions talked him out of it.[36]

By this point Tom's hold over his men was slackening, and their morale was fraying badly. Noah Miles and his son took the opportunity to slip away from the rear of the column, surrendering to the yeoman farmer Charles Neame. They were tired, they told him – they were probably terrified as well. Eager to prevent further desertions, Tom dropped back from the front of the column to the rear, taking the role of a 'whipper in' during a hunt. A witness saw one man, John Fuller, driven along by repeated prods from the muzzle of Tom's pistol.[37]

Along Staple Street they marched, past the Three Horseshoes pub, the Hernhill turning and the gates of Mount Ephraim. Norton Knatchbull was 'hanging on their skirts' all the way, holding his carriage horses to a slow steady walk. At one point during that strange pursuit, Tom halted and turned in the middle of the lane, raising his weapon to aim back at Knatchbull.

Norton had his own carriage pistols with him. He levelled one of them at John Nicholls Tom and fired. If he was aiming at him, he missed. Tom did not return the shot; he eased down the hammer of his pistol, lowered the weapon and then moved on after his retreating men.[38]

Down the slope, the column of men passed through the upper fringes of the settlement of Dunkirk Ville and past the tile kilns. From here the path led on through the woodlands towards Bossenden Farm; Knatchbull did not dare follow them in there. As he saw the lion banner vanishing into the gloom beneath the trees, constable James Gorham, who had tracked the band since Dargate, fired his brass blunderbuss at the rear of the column. The spray of shot only managed to clip a cudgel that one of Tom's men was carrying over his shoulder. Then the last of them hurried off into the protective cover of the trees.[39]

Norton Knatchbull ordered his scouts forward to follow the band, and report back to him if they came to a halt. Matters elsewhere were developing, he had learned. After all the confusion of that morning, Dr Poore had managed to convey his written authorisation to their fellow magistrates in Canterbury, who in turn had issued the order for military support to the civil power. Turning his carriage once more, Knatchbull ordered his men down towards the highway and up the long hill that led towards the Red Lion pub. Charles and Major Handley went with him, and their nephew John with his telescope. Charles Neame and Edward Jarman joined them, and the constable Edward Catt.[40]

Finally, after much delay, the troops were on the march and rapidly approaching, and the forces of law and order readied themselves for a confrontation.

8. 'I HAVE JESUS IN MY HEART'

Few in Canterbury had heard anything of Sir William Courtenay for the last five years. Even so, many remembered him fondly. Those who had supported him and voted for him in the elections of 1832, and cheered him through the streets after his release from jail the following year, still considered him a champion of the common people. When news spread through the city on that sultry Thursday morning that Sir William had killed a man in the Blean woods, and had started a riot, and that the magistrates were sending troops against him, many came out on his side. Some – perhaps those who had jeered and thrown stones at the Yeomanry after the riots of 1835 – declared that Sir William was surely raising a revolt against oppression, and the New Poor Law. He would 'break open the Whig bastilles' and restore justice to the land. Sir William was 'nothing but a good one,' they said. He was 'a trump to the backbone.'[1]

The first word of what was happening at Bossenden had arrived in the city shortly after seven in the morning, carried by Edward Curling. Shortly after him came Mr Marsh's son William, and later still Curling's son with the signed authorisation from Dr Poore in Boughton. By then it was approaching midday. The city magistrates, Mr Baldock and Mr Halford, sent the order on to the commander of the military detachment at Canterbury barracks, who gave the order to march. It was nearing one in the afternoon by the time the soldiers set off.

The 45th Foot (Nottinghamshire Regiment) had only returned to England that spring, after a long and exceptionally unhealthy nineteen-year posting to British India. Six of those years they had spent in Burma, in the aftermath of the British defeat of the Kingdom of Ava in 1825. Cholera and tropical fevers, and a series of minor anti-insurgency operations against what the regimental history calls 'marauders' in the jungles north of Moulmein, had thinned their ranks horribly. Only twenty-two of the original eight hundred enlisted men who left for India with the regiment had returned with it.[2]

Soldiering was unpopular in the 1830s. The troops of the young Queen Victoria sweltered and died in fever-ridden colonies overseas, fought in savagely inglorious brush wars around the margins of the Empire, and acted as riot police, strike breakers and convict guards at home. Many civilians of all classes would have agreed with John Nicholls Tom's comment in the *Lion* about the 'red coated puppy' as the enforcer of a 'despotic government.' Soldiers could also be punished with the lash even for relatively minor offences; Tom was not alone in decrying 'the infamous practice of flogging'. When the 45th Foot was inspected at Canterbury barracks in mid-May 1838, a local paper reported that the ranks were filled mainly by newly recruited young men. Many of them were Irish immigrants who had come to England for the harvest the previous summer and then joined the depot company at Chatham – in 1830, 42.4 per cent of the British Army was made up of Irishmen. Others had been enlisted more recently still, to bring the regiment back up to strength. Aside from the veteran corporals and sergeants, few had any experience of active service. Some would have received only a month or six weeks of training in basic drill before they marched out at the end of May to confront John Nicholls Tom and his men at Bossenden.[3]

British soldiers of the 1830s were armed, uniformed and equipped much as their forebears had been at Waterloo. They still wore the red short-tailed coatee, with the cuffs and the high collar in regimental facing colour: dark green for the 45th. Beneath the coatee collar, they wore a stiff leather stock that chafed at the throat but kept the soldier's head rigidly upright. The 'stovepipe' shako headgear of the Waterloo era had been changed to a 'bell topped' model, heavy and cumbersome but in keeping with the latest French military fashion. They still carried the familiar 'Brown Bess' flintlock musket, a muzzle-loading smoothbore of 0.76-inch calibre, weighing nearly 10lb. A trained soldier was expected to fire three shots a minute. Accuracy was poor at anything greater than fifty yards, but that mattered little: troops were drilled to load and fire in perfect unison, crashing out mass volleys that sprayed a hail of lead. After a few of these volleys the soldier's lips would be stained black with gunpowder from biting open the paper cartridges, his eyes stinging and his face smirched by the smoke. At close quarters there would often be no time to run through the loading procedure, and the bayonet – a sixteen-inch steel spike fixed to a socket beneath the muzzle – or even the brass-bound butt of the musket made a handier weapon.[4]

Elliot Armstrong, appointed to lead the detachment that day, was an unusual soldier. A major at only thirty, he had experienced in his youth a religious epiphany. Now he was a strict teetotaller and a member of the dissenting Plymouth Brethren. While stationed in India he had gained a reputation as a zealous Christian: 'fearless and ardent in the service of his earthly Sovereign, he was equally, if not more so, in the cause of his Heavenly Master.' His second in command, Captain James Reid, was over a decade older, and had served with the 45th since the Peninsular War, fighting at the battles of Nivelle, Nive and Orthez and taking a severe wound at Toulouse in 1814. Reid was accompanied by another captain, and the detachment also included at least three lieutenants, two of them Irish. Thomas Prendergast was a thirty-eight-year-old officer from Tipperary, who had fought with the 89th Foot in the Burma War, distinguishing himself in storming the enemy stockades at Prome and at the capture of Bagan, before transferring to the 45th. The second Irish lieutenant, Henry Boswell Bennett, was twenty-nine but appeared younger. He had joined the regiment while it was already in Burma and had little or no experience of combat. 'Small, handsome featured, dark-haired,' he was a sociable man, popular in Canterbury's more refined company, and had been on furlough and visiting friends in the city when the order came to deploy in support of the civil power. He volunteered to join the detachment as a supernumerary officer but requested special permission to return to Canterbury before six o'clock, as he had a dinner engagement that evening. Presumably he did not anticipate anything too serious.[5]

Rather than marching his troops all the way to Boughton, or wherever they might be required, Armstrong commandeered a stagecoach and several carts or fish vans as transports. The detachment numbered a hundred men, plus officers and NCOs, and some must have been seated precariously on the roofs of the vehicles as they set off up Harbledown Hill and away from the city. The troops were accompanied by Mr Baldock and Mr Halford, the Canterbury magistrates. After them came a wave of civilians, both the curious and the eager, some riding in the wake of the troops while others made their way across the fields. The enterprising journalist Henry Ward was quick to follow them, with a number of other local newsmen. George Mount of Canterbury, aged twenty-five, walked and ran the distance in stages and arrived at the Gate public house on the highway into Dunkirk at the same time as the military detachment. He followed them on down the road to the Red Lion and estimated that between 100 and 150 other civilian onlookers were soon gathered there.[6]

It was now around two in the afternoon, and barely an hour had passed since the troops left barracks. Dr Poore had met the advancing convoy at the Gate and given Major Armstrong and his fellow magistrates his appraisal of the situation. Norton Knatchbull and his band of constables, mounted yeomen and gentry joined the soldiers at the Red Lion as they scrambled from their vans and vehicles. Under whose orders, Armstrong asked, were he and his men to act, and what nature of service were they required to perform?

'I suppose this man Courtenay is to be taken?' he asked.

'Oh yes, you must take him dead or alive, for he is a murderer,' Dr Poore replied. The troops should also capture as many of Sir William's followers as possible, he told the major, while 'emphatically cautioning him to avoid the effusion of blood.' This rather contradictory order was overheard by many of those present. At some point Dr Poore apparently read the Riot Act, although this was not mentioned in the earliest reports. Several commentators on subsequent events assumed that it had not been read at all, and that the magistrates had forgotten in the heat of the unfolding moment to perform the vital public ceremony which would legalise violence and indemnify the troops, their officers and themselves from any culpability in the bloodshed to follow.[7]

'*Our Sovereign Lady the Queen,*' the Act states, '*chargeth and commandeth all persons, being assembled, immediately to disperse themselves, and peaceably to depart to their habitations, or to their lawful business, upon the pains contained in the act made in the first year of King George the First, for preventing tumults and riotous assemblies. God Save the Queen.*'

To be truly effective, of course, the Riot Act should have been read in the hearing of the presumed rioters themselves – any group of twelve or more could be so designated – who would then be given an hour to disperse before force could be used against them. At the time of the reading, assuming Dr Poore remembered to do it, John Nicholls Tom and his followers were half a mile away in the depths of Bossenden Wood and could not possibly have heeded the warning, had they chosen to do so. But the crowd gathered in the road outside the Red Lion would have heard the fateful phrases, and presumably Dr Poore considered that sufficient legality to proceed.

By this time Knatchbull's scouts had returned and informed him that Tom and his followers, rather than continuing through the wood to Bossenden Farm, had halted in a clearing bordering a stream or drainage ditch. Sources at the time refer to the place as 'Mash Fall' – a 'fall' being perhaps the contemporary local term for an area of older fallen or windblown trees, a clearing, just as 'springs' seems to refer to new growth or shrubs. Major Armstrong swiftly consulted with the magistrates and his officers and decided to divide his force in two. One fifty-man section from his own company, under his command with Dr Poore and Mr Halford, would march up a lane into the woods to the west of Tom's reported position and swing around to intercept him. The second section, drawn from Captain Reid's Light Company with Norton Knatchbull and Mr Baldock, would move up the track to Bossenden Farm and then advance through the woods to come at Tom's party from the other direction. With luck, Armstrong must have assumed, the murderer and his followers, on finding themselves surrounded, would surrender or flee.

This was a type of operation that Major Armstrong and at least some of his officers and NCOs would have found very familiar. They had engaged in much the same in Burma, against the 'marauders' north of Moulmein. It was, in effect, a colonial-style anti-insurgency action. In his trial statement Armstrong describes Bossenden as 'a thick wood or *jungle*' – using the British form of an Indian word for scrub forest or wasteland that he would have known from his days in Burma and the Madras Presidency.[8]

As the soldiers divided, the major addressed the great crowd of civilian onlookers who had gathered around the Red Lion to watch the proceedings. 'My good people,' he told them, 'I advise you all to keep well back. Do not attempt to follow the soldiers into the wood, because if you do I shall charge you to assist them. From the character I have heard of this man, I am afraid there will be something serious.' Even so, a number of local farmers rode forward with the troops as they set off along the lane into the trees. Armstrong called back to them once more. 'No, gentlemen,' he told them, 'you may not come in here. We will likely have some hot work, and I advise you to get off your horses.'[9]

The day by now had grown heavy, the afternoon sky weighted with cloud and the air humid and close. The troops assembled in their sections and moved off, each soldier burdened with musket, bayonet and marching kit, and those of Armstrong's company carrying in addition a heavy black knapsack with 45 painted on it in white. This section turned off the road at a saw mill, following a lane that led deeper into the woods. The Reverend Charles Handley was accompanying them by this point, with Major Handley and their nephew John. The constables John Mears and Daniel Edwards, James Gorham and George Catt also joined the party. As the woods closed in around them, Armstrong and Poore sent scouts on ahead, coursing through the undergrowth and the coppice thickets to seek out their enemy.[10]

They were only a short way into Bossenden Wood when the skies suddenly darkened. Thunder rolled. Back on the highway the crowd of spectators ran for shelter in the Red Lion. Then the rain came down in a torrent, hissing through the trees.

At Bossenden Farm, Emily Jane Burford would have seen the fifty soldiers of Captain Reid's section coming up the track from the highway and known for the first time that Sir William Courtenay was now facing serious opposition. She and the others remaining at the farm would have witnessed the murder that morning – and those who had not would have seen the corpse of the murdered man, Nicholas Mears, still lying in the dry ditch where he had been thrown. They must have known that the deed would summon a response. But even so, it must have been a shock to many of them as the fifty redcoats came stamping through the yard outside, with Edward Curling's son and the yeoman Charles Neame following on horseback.

They would have watched the troops moving on across the meadow to the north to a cornfield at the edge of the wood, where they divided again. Those with sharp eyes may have picked out the thin young magistrate who accompanied them, perhaps still wearing his long carriage coat. He and a smaller band of soldiers went on into the woods, while the rest remained in the cornfield.[11]

Emily, at least, had seen enough. We don't know what she thought or felt, then or at any time, about Sir William Courtenay,

'I Have Jesus in my Heart'

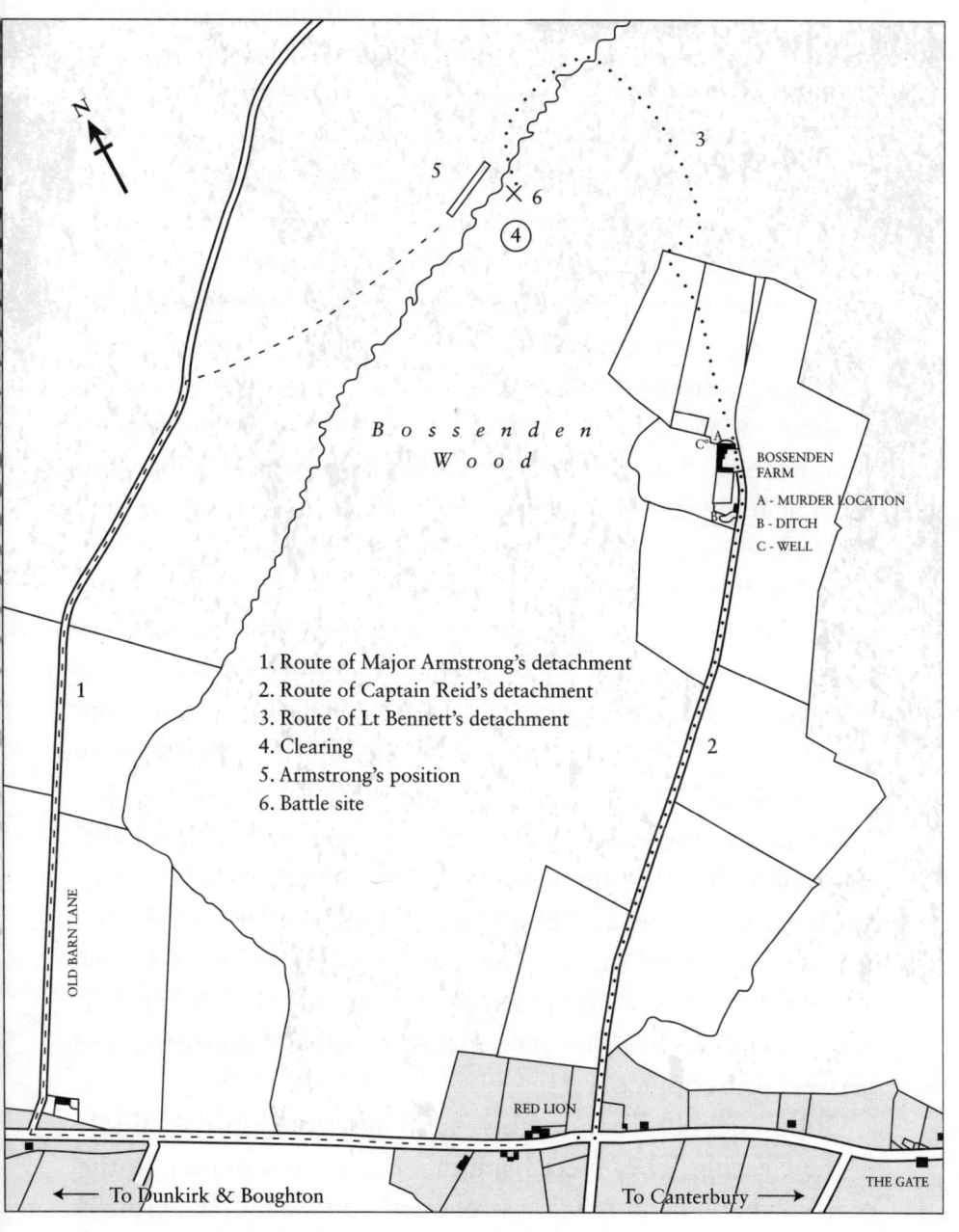

his divine claims and his crusade to bring the Millennium. Nor do we know how she felt now about William Burford, the abusive husband who had become one of Sir William's closest disciples. It's not impossible that she was driven by love or marital devotion, even for a man who had tormented and humiliated her. Not impossible that, having risked so much – both her reputation and her safety – in bringing him to justice for his crimes against her, she was unwilling now to let him throw himself away for a lost cause. More compellingly, she must surely have guessed her own fate and that of her child if William were to die or be imprisoned. Under the harsh rule of the New Poor Law, she and her son would be unlikely to escape the workhouse. And she would have been all too aware of what happened to people in that place. Preserving her husband's life could have been a simple matter of survival.

If Emily had brought her five-year-old son Edward to the farm with her, she would have had to leave him there. They would not be reunited for some time. Entering the woods, she followed the straight track marked with bark-cut trees, the route that John Tom's followers knew well but the soldiers and those guiding them did not. It was about quarter of a mile through the woods to the clearing known as Mash Falls. At some point the thunderstorm would have struck, if it had not done so before, and Emily would have had to take shelter. A little further on she may have passed Sarah Culver, hurrying through the wood in the opposite direction. Further still, and she would have become aware of other figures moving between the coppice trees.

John Nicholls Tom and his men had paused in the middle of the clearing. They were lying in a circle, Tom himself at the centre, where the lion flag was planted on its pole. The ground around them was covered with scrub bushes and surrounded by low hornbeams and a few taller oaks and whitethorn trees. Less than fifty yards beyond the clearing was a stream with deep earthen banks; the 1827 map calls it Denstrode Bourne, but later plans refer to it as a land drain, or ditch. The stream still flows today, although now at the edge of the wood rather than through its heart. Quite possibly, as she entered the clearing, Emily Burford would already have been able to see the red coatees and white crossbelts of the soldiers approaching through the thin woodland on the far side of the stream. She would have heard the scouts, too, hallooing through the bushes as they sighted their quarry.[12]

Emily ran to her husband William, lying in the circle with the other disciples. What she said to him we do not know, only that she tried to persuade him to leave with her. Edmund Foreman, the son of the undertaker, had been tracking Tom's men since they entered the wood. He saw Emily in the clearing talking to her husband. But her attempt at making William see reason was quickly interrupted: John Nicholls Tom told Emily that he would shoot her if she did not leave them, and he would shoot her husband if he tried to go with her.

By now the first scouts had appeared at the edge of the clearing. Tom recognised one of them as Thomas Millgate, a coach porter from Canterbury. Perhaps he had known him in his electioneering days? Swinging the pistol, he pointed it at the man, calling out 'Millgate, move no closer.' Millgate retreated smartly into the bushes, but other men were all around the clearing now, and the soldiers were closing in.[13]

'Up, men,' John Nicholls Tom commanded his followers, and as one they rose, with cudgels in their hands.

Norton Knatchbull had accompanied Captain Reid's section through Bossenden Farm to the cornfield at the edge of the trees. Here Reid had split his force, remaining behind with the bulk of his men while Lieutenant Henry Boswell Bennett and Sergeant Langley took ten soldiers on a circling manoeuvre through the woods that would bring them around the far side of John Nicholls Tom's supposed position. Presumably Reid was hoping that Bennett and Armstrong's sections between them would herd the rioters back through the trees, and that his own men would then trap them at the edge of the woodland. Knatchbull, with young Curling and the yeoman Neame, joined Lieutenant Bennett's party.

They moved on, passing through some taller older growth to an area of four-year-old 'springs', where Bennett dispersed his men in a skirmishing line to move up on the enemy position. Crossing the stream and wheeling to the left, they could now see the red coats of Major Armstrong's section through the trees on their flank. Almost at the same time they caught sight of John Nicholls Tom and his band of followers, rising from the concealment of the low bushes in the clearing. None of Bennett's section had yet loaded their muskets, but Bennett at once ordered them forward. Sergeant Langley came close at his heels, with bayonet fixed. Knatchbull went after them. They had to recross the stream, leaping over the earth banks, and as they reached the far side, Tom and his men charged at them. The impostor had a sword in his left hand, a pistol in his right. One of the yeomen in the wood heard his cry, 'Come on my men, don't prove yourselves cowards!'[14]

In the dripping *jungle* on the far side of the stream, Major Armstrong had moved his section up in a disciplined march, deploying them directly into a firing line as they sighted the clearing. Careful to cede authority to the civil power, he asked Dr Poore if his men should load their muskets with ball cartridge; 'Certainly,' Poore replied. The cartridges had been tied in bundles, and it took a few minutes to free them and for the soldiers to go through their loading drill. By the time they had done so, John Nicholls Tom was on his feet and his men already in motion. The stream lay between them, and Armstrong could see Lieutenant Bennett, distinctive in his blue uniform coat and peaked cap, crossing it to his far left with his small party.[15]

Tom's men were carrying the lion flag before them. But as the rampant lion was painted only on one side of the silk, from the other side the flag appeared to be plain white. Both Armstrong and Major Handley believed they were carrying a flag of truce and spurred their horses forward. 'You misguided and deluded men!' Handley called to them, 'are you coming to reason, or to speak with us?'

Snatching off his hat, the impostor waved his men forward, directly at Bennett's advancing soldiers. 'Fall back, Bennett, fall back!' Armstrong shouted. At any moment the lieutenant's party would be directly in his own field of fire. But Bennett did not slow, and neither did the impostor. 'Good men, he is deceiving and deluding you!' Benjamin Handley cried desperately. 'He is leading you to destruction!'

A couple of witnesses claim that Bennett called out a demand to surrender. Then, with only a stride or two between them, John Nicholls Tom leaped a fallen log and levelled his pistol. The lieutenant swung up his sword to strike, but before he could do so, Tom fired, shooting Bennett in the chest below his raised arm. A jolt ran through the lieutenant's body, his sword sliced down and missed his killer, and then he fell on his back.

At once a 'scream of horror' went up from Armstrong's men. They saw Sergeant Langley lunge at John Tom with his bayonet, across the fallen body of his lieutenant, only to be bludgeoned to the ground by William Wills. The coach porter Thomas Millgate had dashed in and managed to strike Tom over the head with a truncheon, almost knocking him down. Then Millgate himself was felled, John Tom standing over him and battling furiously against the constables as they tried to seize him.

'Dr Poore, where are you?' Major Armstrong shouted. 'Dr Poore, am I to fire?'

But the magistrate had no time to respond. The recruits of the 45th heard only one word – *fire* – from their commanding officer. As one, they slammed their muskets to their shoulder and discharged a single crashing volley. Fifty lead bullets shredded the trees and the bushes of the clearing, and then a choking cloud of dirty grey gunsmoke concealed everything.

John Nicholls Tom was one of the first to die. A bullet struck him just below his collarbone, piercing straight through his body and out behind his shoulder. He staggered a few steps and then fell at the base of a whitethorn tree. His last words, heard by those around him, were 'I have Jesus in my heart.'

Several of his closest disciples probably fell alongside him. George Branchett, the ex-militiaman who had lost his wife and children in the workhouse the previous winter, was shot through the breast and his fallen body stabbed with a sword or bayonet. Another bullet struck Phineas Harvey of Dargate, a 'sober industrious labourer' of twenty-nine and a regular churchgoer, passing through his torso and fracturing the top of his spine, killing him instantly. William Rye had carried Tom's lion flag earlier that day, and perhaps into the final battle, too. He was killed with one bullet through his hip and lower abdomen.[16]

Norton Knatchbull had followed close behind Lieutenant Bennett and had seen him cut down. He claimed to have fired one barrel of his pistol at John Tom, moments before the first blast of musketry crashed through the trees. Three men armed with clubs then charged at him; Knatchbull had time to fire his second barrel before turning to flee with the rest of Bennett's soldiers, back across the stream. 'How I escaped I know not,' he wrote to his father; 'men were dropping before & behind me & I heard the balls whistle by my head.' He hoped he had not hit anyone with either of his shots, he wrote, though 'it would not lay very heavily upon my conscience had I done so.'[17]

While some of Tom's men went after Knatchbull and Bennett's remaining soldiers as they retreated in confusion, the main force turned to attack Armstrong's section. Charging out of the fog of gunsmoke, they rushed the banks of the stream to assault the soldiers before they could fire a second volley. Seeing the horde of screaming men coming at them with cudgels raised, some of the 45th fixed bayonets, while others fell back as they tried to reload. For several minutes a ferocious struggle surged along the line of the stream, steel bayonets and musket butts against oak clubs, hobnailed boots and gnarled fists. William Burford, Emily's husband, had joined the charge against Armstrong's section. As he reached the stream a musket ball struck him behind his left ear and then blasted out through the back of his skull. A soldier stabbed him in the left eye with a bayonet, but he was already dead.

Witnesses later estimated they had heard at least sixty shots fired; John Handley Jr reckoned more than a hundred. Knatchbull had noticed some of Bennett's section frantically loading their weapons after they crossed back over the stream, and some of Armstrong's steadier men, with amazing discipline, must have managed to run through the musket drill a second time as the frenzied melee erupted right in front of them. Then they fired, blazing away into the smoky chaos between the trees, and the mad whirl of bodies locked in combat.[18]

Young George Griggs had been one of the regular farm workers who left Edward Curling's fields. He had long been a student at Cassandra Handley's Sunday School at Mount Ephraim, where he had made 'great progress in religious knowledge'. He was shot through the liver and spleen as he pursued the retreating men of Bennett's section. Falling at the side of the stream, he managed to crawl a short distance and rolled over onto his back, bleeding heavily and clasping his wounded belly. On a mound of dirt he lay in agony, 'holding in his intestines with his hand.'[19]

With the fighting boiling ferociously along the banks of the stream, Armstrong gave the order for the men of his section to charge with fixed bayonets and push the 'rioters' back into the clearing. Many of the injured and slain bore bayonet wounds, although none were mortal, which suggests that the 45th had not yet been trained to use the weapon effectively. Instead, they used the steel points to drive their opponents before them, until one of their number could fire the killing shot from a loaded musket.

Knatchbull later wrote to his father that the troops 'behaved steadily & well without showing any passion or excitement whatsoever.' Scraps of other evidence, however, hint that the soldiers were rather less restrained and disciplined than their officers, and magistrates like Knatchbull, would claim. One of Catt's fellow constables was almost shot in the chaos: 'Several muskets were presented at him by the soldiers ... when he, in an agony of fear, threw himself on his knees and implored them not to kill him, declaring he was not a rioter.' Bartlett

Chambers, chief constable of Faversham, was shot in the lower lip, although he could not tell by whom. To the men of the 45th, in the frenzy of hand to hand fighting and the fog of hanging gunpowder smoke there may have been little to distinguish Tom's followers from those on their own side.[20]

Special Constable George Catt of Faversham had run forward from Armstrong's line the moment he spotted John Nicholls Tom, still determined to claim the reward for his capture. A bullet struck him in the face, passing through his cheek and mouth to pierce his brain. The place of his death remains mysterious: one report says he was killed as he crossed the stream to the right, near where William Burford fell. Another witness, William Champ, claimed that Catt was already close to Lieutenant Bennett when Tom shot him, and that he saw him die there. The surgeons were convinced that Catt had been slain by a musket ball, as the wound did not resemble those dealt to Bennett or Nicholas Mears by Tom's pistol. Major Armstrong subsequently denied that Catt was within the field of his soldiers' fire when he died and believed that another rioter had shot him with a pistol. William Wills had been briefly spotted carrying such a weapon before the fighting started but does not seem to have had it with him later. Still, the possibility remains that Catt was killed by someone other than the soldiers, and the position of his wound suggests that the shooter was ahead of him, rather than at his back. Might one of Norton Knatchbull's errant bullets have struck him instead? If anyone suspected it, they obviously chose to say nothing.

Lieutenant Thomas Prendergast of the 45th had also charged into the fray just before the initial volley, believing that Bennett was only wounded and determined to protect his brother officer with his sword. He fell under a rain of cudgel blows, struck on the head and the arm, and in the side, and then clubbed as he lay on the ground. Major Armstrong too was beaten, after riding forward into the melee in support of his men. He managed to bend the blade of his sword while trying to cut a path through the tangled scrub and was then struck on the legs with a bludgeon by William Wills. 'I never saw men more furious or mad-like in their attack upon us in my life,' he said.[21]

Despite having been at the heart of the combat, Tom's principal evangelist was taken alive. William Wills had followed Tom in his charge against Bennett's detachment, fought furiously against the constables, and then attacked Armstrong, who had managed only to wound him slightly. Thomas Tyler Mears was captured too, despite 'acting with great violence during the affray,' and bludgeoning several of the constables who tried to seize him.

Edward Wraight the Elder, the surly old farmer who refused to attend church, was shot once through the ribs, again in the shoulder blade, and was then bayoneted in the right armpit. Any of his wounds could have been the one that killed him. His son, Edward Wraight the Younger, was fighting furiously at his father's side when he was wounded in the hand, probably by a bayonet. He was taken prisoner moments later.

Others, too, were captured after being wounded. Alexander Foad, the small farmer who had worshipped John Nicholls Tom as the Saviour, had fled the clearing when the firing commenced and tried to hide. Moments later, perhaps remembering his promise to follow Tom 'to the world's end', he had emerged from cover, only to be instantly shot in the face. The bullet smashed away part of his lower jaw, and he was taken soon afterwards, bleeding 'like a bullock', his face a mess of gore.[22]

Several of Tom's other supporters had scattered even before Lieutenant Bennett was shot down. William Couchworth, 'the stoutest and most healthy man in the group,' was running from the clearing when a spent musket ball pierced his neck and caught in his mouth. Miraculously, Couchworth survived otherwise unscathed, but was captured soon afterwards. Thomas Ovenden, the elderly poorhouse inmate from Whitstable, was still clutching the bludgeon that Tom's men had given him as he fled. Alfred Payne the harness maker levelled a pistol at him and ordered him to halt, but Ovenden kept running. Constable James Gorham truncheoned the old man to the ground before he could get much further.[23]

Edward Rigden Curling, the Hernhill 'sheep looker' who had met Edward Wraight that morning, also tried to flee the combat at first. Like Foad, he turned and came back, only to be seized and taken prisoner by the soldiers, who handcuffed him to Emily Jane Burford. Emily, too, had been captured as she tried to leave the clearing after her desperate attempt to rescue her husband from Tom's control. Many witnesses subsequently misidentified her as Sarah Culver; both women were wearing dark bonnets, it seems. It was Edmund Foreman who attested that Emily had been captured at the scene, and that he had seen her moments before the violence began, trying to reason with the impostor.[24]

Some time earlier that day, or the night before, John Nicholls Tom had told Sarah Culver that, if he was shot down and appeared to be dead, she was to moisten his lips with water. Either this would revive him, or he would rise again from death after three days. The exact instruction may have been left deliberately vague; however, shortly before the troops had closed in Sarah had realised that she had no water for this vital operation. The stream was apparently dry, or too muddy, and she set off at once for the nearest source she knew. Back through Bossenden Wood, along the path traced by the hatchet marks in the trees, she reached her family's farm. There was a spring close to the place where Nicholas Mears had been slain, where water flowed into a sunken wooden basin. Sarah filled a pail from the spring, then set off back though the wood again towards the clearing where she had left Sir William and his men. She would have heard the first volley of gunfire as she drew closer. By the time she arrived, her saviour had already been slain. Running between the soldiers, unnoticed at first in her black bonnet and long skirts, she crouched beside the fallen man and washed his face and mouth with water from the bucket. She was seized there, dragged aside and handcuffed.[25]

And John Nicholls Tom stayed dead.

The Battle of Bossenden Wood, as it was later called, began at 3pm on Thursday 31 May. After barely more than three minutes, Major Armstrong ordered his bugler to sound *cease fire*. That brief space of time had seen the fiercest and most savage violence that anyone present – even those who had seen action in Burma or Spain – had ever experienced. Nine men were dead, and another two subsequently died of their wounds. Over twenty were taken captive, many of them also wounded. A mere handful of John Tom's followers escaped, slipping through the cordon of soldiers and constables and concealing themselves in the depths of the woodland.

Even as the acrid wash of gunsmoke faded between the trees the soldiers moved into the clearing, securing their prisoners and gathering the corpses of the slain. They dragged the grievously wounded George Griggs from his mound of blood-soaked dirt to lie with his head against an oak tree, while the bodies were placed in a row beside him. He died there shortly afterwards. Attentive to his duties as a magistrate, Dr Poore went along the line of dead men, noting down their names – Charles Handley may have assisted him, as he knew many of them well. Alongside the corpse of Sir William Courtenay lay Edward Wraight the Elder, Phineas Harvey, William Foster and William Rye, all from Hernhill, George Branchett and William Burford from Dunkirk, and the now-dead George Griggs, formerly of Boughton.[26]

Many of the captives were wounded, some grievously. Griggs's brother Thomas had been captured after being shot through the lungs and was not expected to survive, having to suck his every breath through the bloody wound in his back. Stephen Baker, described as an 'inoffensive young man,' had been shot in the groin. He would die after two days of intense pain, as the wound mortified. Sixteen-year-old Henry Hadlow, the son of Lydia Hadlow, who had ridden through Hernhill earlier that same day on his plough horse, had his thigh smashed by a musket ball; he would spend many days 'lying in a dangerous state.' Alexander Foad was disfigured by his facial injury, his smock covered in blood, while Edward Wraight the Younger was weeping desperately as he nursed his wounded hand and gazed at his father's corpse. Of all the captives, only Sarah Culver remained apparently unmoved.[27]

The horde of spectators, local farmers and journalists who had accompanied the soldiers had hung back while the fighting was in progress, but as soon as the last shots had been fired several of them entered the wood and quickly located the clearing. The sight shocked them. In a radius of five hundred yards the undergrowth was trampled down and the earth churned by the stamping of boots. Blood pooled on the ground and spattered the surrounding trees and bushes. All around, the tree trunks had been shredded by musket balls, suggesting that many of the initial gunshots had been fired high, the barely trained recruits flinching as they discharged their weapons. John Tom himself was conspicuous among the slain, his corpse drawing immediate scrutiny and wonder. The correspondent of the *Morning Herald* later wrote of investigating Sir William's freshly bloodied body and finding the fingers still trembling and the muscles twitching.[28]

'The infatuation of the poor men was most surprising & dreadful,' wrote Norton Knatchbull. He spoke to one of the prisoners – it was possibly William Wills – who, with the body of John Nicholls Tom lying dead beside him, still maintained that he was 'the Christ'. But already the faith of some of the other disciples was fading. A gentleman arriving on the scene shortly after the battle asked another prisoner what had caused them to fight against the troops. 'Our belief that Sir William was Jesus Christ,' the prisoner replied. 'He told us that, if we went with him, we should share his glory, but if we ran away we would be damned everlastingly.'

And did he still believe this was true?

'No,' the prisoner replied. 'I see that he is only a poor worm like myself.'[29]

By evening, the settlements of Dunkirk and Boughton resembled a military encampment. Captain Reid's light company of the 45th Foot garrisoned the area around the Gate and Red Lion public houses, where the manacled prisoners had first been taken and where many of the bodies now lay. Captain George Minter's company had escorted the prisoners down the hill to Boughton Street, where they remained stationed on guard with muskets loaded and bayonets fixed. The captives had been locked in an upstairs room of the White Horse Inn, and there were rumours that the local people might try some desperate attempt at liberating them in the night.[30]

Despite the presence of the troops and the dangers of further insurrection, the crowds not only remained but grew greater as darkness fell. Still more spectators arrived before the day's end: both the curious and the morbid, the former supporters of Sir William Courtenay and his former adversaries too. The body of young Lieutenant Bennett was laid reverently on a bed in one of the upstairs rooms of the Red Lion. Bennett's injured colleague, Lieutenant Prendergast, had already been conveyed to Canterbury in a post-chaise by the magistrate Mr Baldock. But it was the mortal remains of the dead Sir William Courtenay and his fallen disciples that drew the greatest interest.

The bodies were laid out on the straw of the stable adjoining the main building. The impostor was in the middle, still dressed in his braided velvet jacket – his bloodied smock had been torn from his corpse and was subsequently ripped to pieces for souvenirs. Three dead disciples lay to either side of him: William Foster, George Branchett and Phineas Harvey (wrongly labelled 'Peter' by the sketch artist) to the left; Edward Wraight, William Rye and William Burford to the right. While many of the spectators were amazed at the stature of the fallen leader, his great breadth of chest and shoulder, his commanding visage even in death, the sight of his men was far less impressive. A witness to the scene was appalled at the state of two older men – probably Edward Wraight the Elder and forty-nine-year-old George Branchett – who had 'scarcely a tooth in their heads, and were shocking to behold.'[31]

While the Canterbury journalist Henry Ward had already clambered from his ditch and taken the first passing coach for London and the offices of the *Times*, the newsmen remaining on the scene harvested their quotes and anecdotes, trying to establish what had happened, and the chronology of events. Several of these initial accounts were to prove more confusing and contradictory than illuminating, but they provided plenty of colour. One correspondent claimed to have overheard the young Irish soldier who was amazed that the 'Englishers fought so cruel hard.' Another, indulging the contemporary relish for Irish mimicry, expanded the quote: 'Why, I never saw better men in Ireland! ... It goes to my heart to hurt the boys, they handle their shillelaghs so like the Mahonys.'[32]

But the supporters of the fallen messiah in the local area, and the wives and families of his followers, were receiving a very different sort of news. Many, even those who remained at home, had heard the sounds of the distant gunfire. Over the hours that followed they would hear the rumours, then the certain information of the disaster that had overtaken Sir William Courtenay and his band. At first many clung to their beliefs. 'We were told he would surely rise again,' Sarah Wraight told the interviewer Frederick Liardet. After hearing of the battle, and her husband's capture, 'me and a neighbour sat up the whole of that blessed night reading the Bible, and believing the world was to be destroyed on the morrow.'[33]

Lydia Hadlow, leading evangelist of the new messiah, was also unwilling to accept the truth, even when she was informed of the imprisonment of her husband and the critical wounding of her son. The disappointment, once she was induced to accept it, would prove hard to endure:

> When the soldiers were heard to fire upon the rioters, Mrs. Adlow, who was at the time in her garden at Herne Hill, fell upon her knees, and 'prayed to see fire and brimstone pour down from Heaven, and destroy the enemies of Sir William'; and in a frenzy of religious exultation she cried out, 'I'll die too; I'll die too.' She then looked up in the clouds to discover a lion (a rampant lion was John Tom's device), but perceiving no such figure, this wretched woman sat down and wept bitterly.[34]

9. 'MAD TOM OF CANTERBURY'

They cut up John Nicholls Tom the following day, in an upstairs room of the Red Lion, less than a mile from the spot where he was slain. His body was laid on a trestle table, stripped to the waist, and at least three surgeons from Canterbury and Boughton went to work on him with their scalpels and their saws, their bone-breaking chisels. First they razored off his hair and his famous beard, so a plaster cast could be taken of his face. Then the medical gentlemen opened his skull to examine his brain, finding it very much inflamed. They broke upon his chest and sliced open his abdomen, tracing the course of the killing bullet from his left shoulder through both lungs and out through the upper right of his back, then they hacked out his heart. The description of their operations, printed in unusual detail the next morning in the *Canterbury Chronicle*, reads in part like a dutiful post-mortem autopsy, and partly the fascinated examination of a rare scientific specimen.[1]

Tom's hands were still clenched tightly into fists, but the surgeons determined that the 'nail marks' in his palms were only skin deep. They observed with interest the cicatrice in his side but discovered when they briefly removed his stockings that he had no marks at all on his feet. A journalist permitted to view the mauled corpse some time later noted no fatal wounds upon it other than the killing gunshot; the clotted blood around the head was perhaps caused by the stamp of a soldier's boot or a musket butt, and the wound on the cheek may have been the work of a bayonet, or more likely the razor used to shave the dead man's face.

When they were done, they sewed the body up once more, wrapped it in linen and laid it in a coffin packed with sawdust, leaving the head and face exposed. One of the surgeons, Dr Chisholm of Canterbury, was permitted to take John Tom's heart home with him as a curiosity, carrying the wrapped morsel in his hat. After all, they might have reasoned, how could the local people continue to believe that their champion would rise from the grave if his heart was missing?[2]

Once the surgeons had finished their gory examination, the body in its coffin was returned to the stable and placed once more between the other corpses. In the damp warmth of early June, the process of decomposition would be quick, but the authorities believed the grisly display was necessary, nonetheless. Only by seeing their supposed messiah dead in his open coffin, flanked by the bodies of his disciples, could the local people be induced to accept his mortality, and his defeat. The public exhibition of the dead was a means of 'beating down their delusions by the evidence of their own senses.'[3]

But many continued to believe even so, and the vast public fascination held a strong element of reverence. The crowd around the Red Lion had not diminished, even twenty-four hours after the battle, and as news of the events spread so increasing numbers came to view the site and the bodies of the dead men. Mail coaches brought spectators from Canterbury and London and further afield. People came in steamers down the Thames to Herne Bay and Margate, just to visit the scene. The crush around the stable doors became intense. More than one young woman fainted and had to be carried from the press.

Not all the visitors to the stable were merely curious: some appeared with springs of green foliage they had cut from the battle site, speaking of the fallen men as martyrs and Sir William as a saint. A brisk trade in souvenirs sprang up – any old button could be 'Courtenay's button', any lead slug could be 'the bullet that killed Sir William.' Fragments of the dead man's blood-drenched smock were rare treasures. Locks of his hair and beard were prized. For some, these mementos had holy significance: 'Women,' one newspaper noted, 'seek these relics with great avidity, and are described as receiving them with enthusiastic devotion.'[4]

The site itself had already become a place of fervent pilgrimage, the clearing in Bossenden Wood trampled by hundreds of feet, the bark of the surrounding trees stripped off, every bullet gouged from the timber as a valuable keepsake. Patches of gore-soaked dirt were scraped up and preserved. Local people crafted their own cudgels and stained them with animal blood, to sell to morbid visitors. The gate that led to the lane that Armstrong and his men had taken into the wood was soon chalked with a sign: *This is the Way to Courtenay's Fall*. The whitethorn tree where Sir William had died was marked out with a board bearing the declaration: OUR REAL TRUE MESSIAH. KING OF THE JEWS.[5]

On Friday evening, after the initial inquests on the victims of the tragedy, the body of Lieutenant Bennett was removed from the upper room of the Red Lion and conveyed to Canterbury in a hearse. The sociable young officer would be buried the next day in the cathedral precinct, with six thousand people attending his funeral service. By special permission, the men of the 45th Foot fired volleys over his grave. You can still see the marble tablet dedicated to his memory, on the north wall of the cathedral nave close to the pulpit: Lieutenant Bennett, the inscription reads, '*fell in the strict and manly discharge of his duties, in Bossenden Wood, in the Ville of Dunkirk ...*'

That same evening, the remaining soldiers were withdrawn from Boughton and Dunkirk and sent back to Canterbury aboard their carts and coaches, each man firing off his musket as he passed the Red Lion to clear the charge from the barrel. By then it had begun to rain. The dampness, the crackle of musketry and the lingering stink of gunsmoke did nothing to deter the sightseers. The landlord of the pub later estimated that twenty thousand people had flocked to Dunkirk over those days, thirsting for a glimpse of the dead Sir William. By Sunday, the crowd had grown so boisterous, their weird intensity so overwhelming, that he feared a riot and had to close his premises, nailing the doors and windows shut against the ravening throng.[6]

For those captured in the immediate aftermath of the fighting, or in the dragnet that swept through the local communities in the hours that followed, justice was inexorable. The initial inquest on the murder of Nicholas Mears was conducted on Friday afternoon by the East Kent Coroner, Mr Thomas Delasaux. In the parlour of the White Horse Inn down in Boughton Street, the jury assembled, while the prisoners were locked in an upstairs room and an adjoining barn. It had been an uncomfortable night for them; many were wounded, and all doubtless dreaded what might follow. The yard at the back of the inn had been packed with the wives and families of the captives, weeping and distraught as they called up to the rear windows for news. Stephen Baker had died in the night, of the gunshot wound in his groin. His body was placed on the straw in the inn stable, beside the corpses of George Griggs and the constable George Catt. In a final indignity, Catt had already been pointed out to visitors as one of the slain rioters, and identified as the most notoriously ferocious of them all.[7]

The jury inspected Nicholas Mears's body and heard statements from several witnesses, including the dead man's brother John, constable Gorham, and Daniel Edwards. The coroner explained the legal principle under which the jury were to proceed; when 'divers persons' assemble together to 'raise tumults and frays,' and in the process an officer of the law is killed – here taken to include special constables and men aiding those officers – all of those present are considered guilty of murder.

So the accused men were to be treated as principals in the murder of Nicholas Mears, and not as mere accessories. The arbitrary nature of this concept is underlined by the identity of those indicted for the offence. Knatchbull's original arrest warrant had named Sir William Courtenay, William Burford, William Price and Thomas Tyler Mears. Courtenay and Burford were dead, but the coroner now widened that indictment to include the appallingly disfigured Alexander Foad and one William Nutting. Foad was well known in the area, and a committed and public disciple of the impostor Tom. But why had William Nutting, the twenty-one-year-old son of a Boughton shoemaker, been included? His name is only mentioned once in the recorded witness statements, as being present at Bossenden farm. And yet here he was, indicted for a capital crime, solely on the basis that somebody remembered seeing him at the scene. By the evening of that day the jury had returned a verdict of wilful murder against all four surviving men – Price, Mears, Foad and Nutting – and the coroner had despatched them to Maidstone Prison in a guarded carriage.[8]

It was late in the day, and the inquest on Lieutenant Bennett was adjourned until Saturday morning – the jury had only time for a visit to the Red Lion and an official viewing of his corpse before it was taken away to Canterbury for burial. The remaining prisoners were sent to Faversham, packed into omnibuses with soldiers riding on the roof with fixed bayonets, to be locked up securely for the night. The next morning, some at least were back at the White Horse. The second inquest proceeded much like the first, but with many more witnesses: Dr Poore and Norton Knatchbull, Major Armstrong and the Reverend Charles Handley, a phalanx of constables and others who had been in the clearing on Thursday afternoon and seen the lieutenant shot down and the chaotic frenzy that followed.

The jury, so the coroner explained, were to sit in judgement both on the living and the dead. By the time the witnesses had concluded their evidence, he was able to present twenty-two names for indictment. Among them was Sarah Culver. She was present in the inquest room and provided a focus of interest for the more prurient of the reporters, whose record of her features and clothing suggests a certain breathless relish at her predicament. Rumours of the strange sexual magnetism of the fallen messiah Courtenay had followed him from Canterbury. Here, perhaps, was one of his concubines. But the chance to see such a person indicted for murder was denied. Edmund Foreman, the son of the Hernhill coffin-maker, attested that Miss Culver had not been in the wood at the time of the killing. Instead, the woman in a dark bonnet seen with Tom and his gang immediately beforehand was Mrs Emily Burford. Sarah Culver was absent when the murder was committed, on her water-gathering mission. She was discharged, together with a couple of other random men. But she does not appear to have been particularly moved by her near escape from imprisonment.

The rest were not so lucky. All were loaded into vans and sent to Maidstone to stand trial for their lives.[9]

Emily Burford was brought before the magistrates' petty sessions at Faversham Town Hall the following Monday. By then she had been a prisoner for over three days and had spent the last forty-eight hours locked in a cell. Before that, she had seen her husband and many of her neighbours shot dead, and been taken captive herself, presumably none too gently. She had probably seen or heard nothing of her five-year-old son since her arrest. Even her own mother may not have known what had happened to her. As she was brought into the courtroom to be identified by witnesses, she saw arrayed on the bench before her several of the same men – Dr John Poore, Norton Knatchbull, Charles Handley – who had led the military forces against her husband and his friends, now assembled to pass judgement upon the survivors.

Before she could be brought to the bar, Emily fell into what the newspapers described as 'strong hysterics'. After everything she had endured, this was too much for her. The assembled witnesses and spectators found her 'sobs and groans ... most distressing.' In a rare display of compassion, Dr Poore ordered her to be removed from the chamber; hers was a most painful case, he explained, and the attendants were to tell Mrs Burford that 'she was no occasion to alarm herself about her fate.' That, he rather complacently suggested, would 'compose her mind.'

He went on to tell the court that Mrs Burford had only gone to the wood to 'exhort her husband to quit the rioters,' and he therefore took great pleasure in ordering her to be discharged. Quite why he could not have done this three days beforehand remains a mystery, as it doubtless was to Emily herself. But with her husband dead, and no means of support for herself or for her child, it is unlikely that her mind would have been much composed by her release, despite Poore's further order that 'in consideration of her melancholy lot' she would not have to find monetary surety for her future good behaviour.

Emily remained under custody, however, until the conclusion of the petty sessions, when one of the attorneys present had to remind the magistrates to release her. Having recovered from her hysterics, the attorney said, Mrs Burford now appeared 'as if her mind was gone, from the grief and terror she has recently undergone.'[10]

In the meantime, after going through the evidence, Dr Poore and his fellow magistrates had found it necessary to commit four of the accused to Maidstone. The remaining eight were discharged, on finding a £50 recognisance for their future good behaviour. Among them were Noah Miles, the publican of the Noah's Ark beershop, and his son, James; Noah had explained to the court that he had been happy to escape from Tom and his band and had only joined them on his daughter's persuasion. But Poore had cut him off.

'I don't want to hear you talk,' the magistrate told him curtly. 'Women,' he went on, 'have been the great cause of these melancholy disasters.'[11]

For five days, the corpse of John Nicholls Tom lay in its coffin in the stable of the Red Lion public house. The weather was warm, close and humid. Several times the thatch above it had been drenched by rain. On Tuesday morning, the coffin was reopened for the benefit of visiting reporters, and the body presented 'a loathsome picture of decay.' The correspondent of the *Times* described 'a livid greenness on the countenance, and a sinking in of some of the features, which had completely altered their expression, and though his eyes ... were now closed, his aspect was infinitely more horrible.' Nobody mentioned the other six corpses, lying in their own coffins to either side. Presumably they were considered unimportant.

The magistrate's clerk, Mr Shepherd, had just ordered the undertaker to seal the coffin lid when a lady burst into the stable in great agitation, demanding a last glimpse of the dead man. Mr Shepherd obliged her, but when two more arrived moments later he refused their request. By then the undertaker was driving in the screws. One of the journalists noticed that there was no name upon the coffin.

'What would you have me call him?' the undertaker replied.[12]

Hurried into a van outside, special constables on all sides and a posse of local gentlemen riding behind, the body of John Nicholls Tom was driven off at a brisk pace. Those few lingering souls who had remained at the Red Lion to see Sir William's coffin brought forth could only run along after it as the van rattled down Boughton Hill and then up the undulating lanes towards Hernhill church.

Despite the hurry, and the lack of public notice, a crowd of over a hundred had gathered around the churchyard gate. The Reverend Charles Handley, who was to conduct the funeral service, would not allow the dead man to be carried into the church but rather met the burial party and led them to the graveside. He went through the most perfunctory service, avoiding any display of emotion and omitting the passage about the resurrection of the body: nobody needed any reminder of that sort of thing. Sunday had come and gone – the third day, when many local people including Lydia Hadlow and Sarah Culver still maintained that the saviour would rise again. But few in the churchyard seemed to hold with such notions. 'Cover him up quickly,' somebody cried, once the coffin had been lowered into the shallow four-foot-deep pit. 'Let us have no more of him.'

The Home Secretary, Lord Russell, had suggested that John Tom might be buried in secret and at the dead of night, somewhere far away, lest his grave become a place of pilgrimage. But it was better by far, Mr Handley and the magistrates' clerk Mr Shepherd had decided, to have him interred in the full view of the local community, so none could doubt that he was truly dead and buried. The exact site of the grave was left unmarked, and no headstone commemorated his mortal remains. Even so, Edward Curling appointed a guard of his own labourers to stand over the plot by night for the following two weeks and ensure that none of the impostor's followers attempted to dig him up again.

That same afternoon, the other dead men were buried, too. This time the solemnities were observed in full, each coffin carried into the church to the tolling of the passing bell and taken to stand before the altar. The correspondent of the *Times* had delayed his departure from Hernhill especially to attend the burials, but found himself overwhelmed by the scenes of grief and anguish that had consumed the entire community. Thirty-one people in the parish were missing, either dead, wounded or in prison. Hernhill was a place of widows, orphans and the bereaved. 'I heard the voice of wailing in every house,' the correspondent wrote that evening on his return to Canterbury. 'Never was I more pained than I was by the spectacle of universal sorrow, amounting almost to despair, which it was then my misfortune to behold.'[13]

Prominent among the mourners was Emily Jane Burford, who alone accompanied the coffin of her dead husband William into the church. She had recovered only slightly after her mental collapse in the courtroom in Faversham. 'Her grief was not so boisterous as formerly,' the journalist noted, 'but still she appeared deeply affected.' The sorrow of the widows and orphaned children in particular struck the correspondent keenly. 'Deprived of their natural supporters and protectors,' he had written after his first visit to the district, 'starvation or the workhouse stares them in the face!'[14]

The Reverend Charles Handley, too, was overcome by emotion. His voice broke as he read the funeral service, and he had to pause for some time with his face pressed into the folds of his gown. In this, and in his performance of the burial rites that followed, none seemed to doubt the sincerity of his feelings. One by one, he accompanied the bodies of Stephen Baker, William Foster, William Rye, Edward Wraight the elder, Phineas Harvey and William Burford from the church to their individual graves outside.

Originally the authorities had decreed that all the men should be buried together, 'in the vicinity of Mad Tom', but all were allowed to be interred separately, close to their families. None appear to have been permitted a grave marker or tombstone even so; only in recent decades was a wooden plaque erected beside the path leading up the church porch, listing their names and ages. George Branchett is also listed among them and described as forty years old; both age and burial place are incorrect. Although the Dunkirk resident William Burford had been buried at Hernhill, the church authorities decided that the forty-nine-year-old Branchett, also from Dunkirk, should be sent elsewhere. A grave had already been prepared to receive him in the churchyard of St Michael's, but his funeral was delayed until the following day, when his coffin was taken on a cart to Boughton and buried there instead.[15]

The funerals at Hernhill might have seemed the emotional finale of the Courtenay debacle, but they would have an odd sequel the following Sunday. Once again, the local people assembled at the church of St Michael, most of them still clad in mourning clothes. Outside, the attending correspondent from the *Times* witnessed a group of men, many wearing black bands in their hats, standing directly on the muddy patch of ground where John Nicholls Tom was buried. As if, he thought, they were trampling his remains underfoot, 'exhibiting their abhorrence and detestation of the wretched maniac who ... had so cruelly misled so many of their friends,' and stamping the earth down over him.

Once again, Charles Handley addressed the congregation, in a long and heartfelt sermon that the journalists present did not see fit to record. When he reached the point in the order of service during which a hymn or psalm would normally be played, there was silence. The choir gallery high at the western end of the nave was empty. William Wills the flautist and all the rest of the men who formed the church choir were either dead or in prison. Instead of passing over their lack, Handley let the moment resonate. For two or three minutes, the duration of the psalmody – and by chance almost the duration of the fighting in Bossenden Wood – the packed church remained in total and profound silence. No sermon could so eloquently have conveyed the loss that the community had suffered, or the absence at its heart.[16]

Two months later, in the same sweltering Maidstone Assize Court that had seen Sir William Courtenay's trial for perjury in 1833, eighteen of his surviving supporters stood in the dock as the Grand Jury assembled to prove an indictment for wilful murder against them.[17]

Amazingly, the prosecutions of eight of the men were dropped on the first day. The randomly-accused William Nutting of Boughton, young Henry Hadlow, beershop owner James Goodwin, poorhouse inmate Thomas Ovenden and the bullet-catching William Couchworth, together with John Spratt and an itinerant labourer named John Silk, all found themselves unexpectedly free to go home. Two days later, however, the serious business commenced. William Price and Thomas Tyler Mears were up first, on the charge of murdering Nicholas Mears. Lord Chief Justice Denman, the former Attorney General, presided. The jury took only half an hour to agree their guilty verdict, with a recommendation to mercy. Denman placed the black cap upon his head and pronounced the sentence of death. Only once that terrible formality was concluded did he announce that the lives of the prisoners would be spared.

On the following day the performance was repeated. Eight men stood indicted for the murder of Lieutenant George Bennett. Thomas Tyler Mears was there again, this time his companions included William Wills, the disfigured Alexander Foad, Edward Wraight the younger, and Thomas Griggs, who had unexpectedly survived the bullet through his lungs even after being given the last rites. Edward Rigden Curling the 'sheep looker' joined them, with Charles Hills and Richard Foreman. This time, all of the men pleaded guilty, on the advice of their lawyers. Again, the sentence of death, and the granting of life. Three of the prisoners would be transported to Van Dieman's Land, now Tasmania: William Wills and Thomas Tyler Mears for life, and William Price for a term of ten years. The remaining six would serve a year in Maidstone prison, with hard labour and one month's solitary confinement.

Lord Chief Justice Denman then ordered Lydia Hadlow to the bar. She was not one of the prisoners, and had not been accused of any crime, but the judge took the opportunity to admonish her publicly for her encouraging so many to join the criminal activities of the madman John Tom, and in particular for having led her son Henry into 'this horrible and dangerous transaction.' Despite this thundering appraisal, Mrs Hadlow left the court 'without much apparent feeling of contrition.'[18]

Before the month was out, a petition was going around Canterbury and the neighbourhood requesting that the Home Secretary grant still greater leniency to the three men condemned to transportation:

> ... for we believe they were so infatuated by their leader, who had previously induced them to believe he was their Saviour come again on earth and it was impossible for them to do wrong provided they acted according to his guidance. In their behalf we therefore do now and most earnestly, imploringly and respectfully beg to intercede, and we humbly trust Your Majesty will not refuse our Prayer, that there may be a mitigation of their punishment as we trust they are already convinced of the enormity of their conduct, which we hope and believe will have a salutary and lasting effect on their future lives ...

The petition eventually gathered several hundred names, including the mayors of both Canterbury and Faversham, and the coroner Mr Delasaux. It was even signed by a 'Mr Collard', presumably the man who had once acted as Sir William's valet and had sore experience of being duped by the impostor. The Home Secretary, however, was unimpressed. He may have been swayed by a letter addressed to him by Julius Shepherd, clerk to the magistrates in Faversham, stressing that 'should a remission take place and the parties be again let loose upon Society in this neighbourhood, life would assuredly be at stake here.'

Wills, Tyler Mears and Price were despatched to the *Fortitude* hulk, to await the next transport to Australia.[19]

Dr Poore had claimed that women had been the cause of the 'melancholy disasters' that had beset Hernhill, Dunkirk and Boughton. Certainly, the likes of Lydia Hadlow, Sarah Culver, Eliza Francis and her aunt had added considerably to John Tom's messianic allure. But the question of who bore the greatest responsibility for what had happened soon came to obsess many others. *Blame*, like an indelible black cloud that besmirched all on which it settled, was drifting across the country. John Nicholls Tom and his closest disciples were dead, the rest had been brought to justice; their guilt was obvious, but the cloud of blame soon found new targets. Poore himself felt the brush of it: in his initial report to the government on what had happened in Dunkirk parish he was careful to stress that he lived fifteen miles away from the scene and had not been made aware of what had been going on there until Tuesday evening.[20]

Charles Handley felt it, too. He and Poore were directly named in a doggerel verse printed in the *Sunday Satirist* a fortnight after the events. Handley is depicted as a drunkard, 'mad with wine or porter,' and the two 'parsons' as urging on the slaughter of the 'peasants' by the military, 'with words of war instead of peace':

Forget, forgive, hope better deeds,
When poor men meet with nicer feeds
Than bullets hot from holy bores
Of muskets 'sauced' by Handley's roars.[21]

Charles Handley received much other criticism, both immediately following the events and in subsequent history. Many found his care for his parishioners negligent, his attitudes towards them condescending, his cursory and deliberately brusque treatment of John Tom's mortal remains disgraceful and his attitudes towards the likes of George Francis hypocritical. It would be easy to paint him as a pompous bigot, accusing others to hide his own failings. But this same Charles Handley had overseen the schooling of generations of local children, in his own house – as he was quick to remind the Archbishop of Canterbury, when the cloud of blame drifted closer.

Fifty years later, a chance remark revealed that Handley had aided in the escape of one of John Tom's wounded followers. The man – another of the Hadlow family – had fled the scene at Bossenden and concealed himself deeper in the wood, and later in Edward Curling's oast house. Curling himself had given food to the fugitive and then told his son to take him to Handley, who in turn conveyed him to Faversham and enabled his escape. Since Hadlow would surely have had to stand trial for his presence at Bossenden, and quite possibly would have faced a capital charge of murder, this act of aiding the escape of a fugitive was itself criminal. Both Curling and Handley must have recognised that the Hadlows had suffered enough, and that the imprisonment or transportation of another of their menfolk would leave them unable to support themselves. As an act of mercy, it stands in dramatic contrast to the more usual reputation of both men. Curling had already demonstrated the finer aspects of his nature, personally accompanying Edward Wraight's widow at the funeral service and then escorting her home after it. Both he and Handley had been the enemies of John Nicholls Tom, and of his supporters, but now that the community was united by a sincere common grief both stepped up quite adequately to the role of leaders.[22]

Some time later, Handley happened to meet his parishioner Alexander Foad, recently released after his spell in prison, and asked him why he had chosen to follow the impostor. Foad replied that he could not say how he had been so deluded. Handley was quick to stamp down such a notion. 'You must not talk of delusion to me, Foad,' he told the man, 'for I maintain ... that there was more wickedness than delusion in the matter.' But a decade and more later still, Handley was still feeling the prickling need to explain himself. In the blank pages of an old tithe book, a slim rectangular volume kept today in the archives of Canterbury Cathedral, he recorded his own account of the Courtenay Affair. 'Such an account may be useful to my successors,' he wrote, 'for there is no saying what follies & absurdities may even yet be imagined or what wickedness may even yet be added to that which has been caused by this individual.'[23]

Meanwhile, even Dr John Poore, that stickler for correct procedure, had petitioned the Home Secretary to grant an official pension to the widow of Nicholas Mears. The murdered man had not been an officer of the law or of the government, but in the circumstances, Lord Russell agreed that Mrs Mears should receive a stipend of £40 a year for life. A considerable sum, and some recompense for all she had endured. The officers of the Faversham Poor Law Union were also moved to charity: they paid for the coffins of the dead men buried at Hernhill and Boughton, and later agreed to extend 'outdoor relief' to the families of the victims – as they were now increasingly seen – for several months. None, just yet, would be consigned to the workhouse. But a petition for the widow of George Catt, the special constable shot during the battle, merely gained her a single payment of £10 compensation for her loss.[24]

Norton Knatchbull received little of the contemporary blame directed at the two clergymen, although subsequent history has been less understanding. He had first written to his father on the Thursday evening, as soon as he arrived home after the fighting at Bossenden. He was called away before he could finish writing, and the letter was completed by his wife Mary. 'What a dreadful dreadful day this has been,' she told Sir Edward, 'but I thank God who has preserved my dear husband; he tells me that under Providence he owes his life to Mr Marsh & others at Boughton whose advice he took in not approaching too near …' In reality, of course, Knatchbull had ignored the elderly clergyman's advice, at first anyway. Perhaps this was the story he had told Mary afterwards?

Sir Edward must already have been informed otherwise. In her diary that evening, Lady Knatchbull recorded the 'sad riot at Boughton in trying to take Sir W.C…' – and noted that 'Norton had a narrow escape, being close by the affray at the time.' The following day, Norton wrote a much fuller account for his father, including many details not recorded in the witness testimonies. Already he was aware that these details might prove crucial in any legal proceedings, and in repelling what were certain to be spirited accusations against him and the other magistrates present.[25]

He was adamant that he and Poore had gone about tackling Tom and his uprising in the only way possible. If they had not called for military assistance in confronting the madman directly, he wrote, 'he would in a few hours time have [had] at least a thousand followers behind him, & hundreds might have fallen before the disturbance could have been quelled.' This suggestion that large numbers of men were about to join Tom's flag, triggering a mass uprising across Kent, appears in the accounts of other witnesses as well. Little evidence supports it, but it shows that the fear of popular insurrection still echoed from the great riots of 1830.[26]

'You may perhaps hear,' Norton went on, 'that I exposed myself more than was necessary; I do not believe upon reflection that I did more than you yourself would have done, if similarly situated.' Of course, we might consider it unlikely that the ageing and rather hypochondriacal Sir Edward Knatchbull would have done anything similar at all. Norton here is making a deliberate bid for parental approval. No longer, he was saying, was he the trembling romantic youth who had returned from his Italian tour to his father's frank displeasure. He was a firm and manly fellow now, decisive and commanding, heedless of danger. A true son of the Tory gentry, fit to succeed one day to the Knatchbull baronetcy. And Mary, as the addition to his first letter implied, was now a proper wife to such a man: pious and protective of her husband.

By that evening, Sir Edward himself was at Provender, 'in consequence of the riot,' and he stayed the night there. What passed between father and son is sadly unknown. Did the strain between them endure, even in such trying circumstances? By the following month, Sir Edward's attitude towards his son appeared as lukewarm as ever. 'Norton's birthday, 30,' Lacy Knatchbull wrote on 10 July. 'Sir E very indifferent from exhaustion & nervous affection.'[27]

But the baronet's visit to Kent had not been mere paternal duty. He was also gathering political ammunition. Lord John Russell, the Whig Home Secretary, had signed the order discharging Tom from Barming, despite the assessment of the asylum superintendent, Mr Poynder, that the patient was still insane. Was it not true, Knatchbull demanded soon afterwards in Parliament, that Russell had pushed through the release as a favour to his fellow Whig, Sir Hussey Vivian? Was it not also true that Vivian had been petitioned by the madman's father, who had agreed to vote for the Whigs in the forthcoming general election? Was not the father a constituent of the Whig member for Truro, Edward Turner, who had once employed the madman John Nicholls Tom as an articled clerk in his business? Was this not, in fact, all an inside job of the Cornish Whig faction, intended to destabilise the Tory stronghold of East Kent?

The Whigs returned the attack. Sir Hussey Vivian found it appalling to be so accused – 'a calumny more foul, a charge more false,' he claimed, 'was never yet made against any man on the face of the earth!' The whole affair had been the result of Tory misgovernment and the deep state of ignorance among the common people in Kent. But what, both Tories and Radicals asked, about the Whig imposition of the New Poor Law? And was not the church also to blame, the Radicals added, and the local gentry? Sir Edward's own son, also a Tory, had been among those magistrates on the scene, who had ordered the military to take John Tom 'dead or alive' …[28]

And so it went on, the accusations reverberating through the opinion columns of newspapers and journals of all shades. The *Weekly Despatch* wrote of 'the late horrible butchery near Canterbury,' describing the actions of the magistrates and military as 'cowardly' and attributing them (in a neat reversal of the usual evocations of lower-class ignorance) to the 'superstitions of clergy and aristocracy.' Even the correspondent of the *Times*, after speaking to some of the people living around Dunkirk and Boughton, compared the acts of Sir William Courtenay to those of Robin Hood, which 'could not be very culpable in these later days, when *grinding the face of the poor* was become a little more the practice.'[29]

Some of the most spirited commentary came from the radical reforming activist James Bronterre O'Brien, who in a letter to Feargus O'Connor, published in the *Northern Star*, wrote that 'our countrymen have been assassinated, basely and cruelly assassinated ... It is the murderers who have taken recognizance of the crime, and the murdered men are at this moment *branded as murderers*.' Rather than being a madman, O'Brian believed, Sir William Courtenay was a respectable figure whose political writings demonstrated a refined sensibility. Stories of his supposed claims to divinity, his miracles and the worship of his disciples were mere fabrications, cooked up to discredit him. He was shot while trying to defend himself against an unwarranted attack; not only that, the magistrates – those 'magisterial and military monsters' – had neglected to read the Riot Act, and 'therefore had no authority, and they are consequently the illegal and guilty parties.'[30]

By the end of June, however, neither Tories nor Radicals had succeeded in using the events in Bossenden Wood to seriously embarrass or destabilise the Whig government, still less to bring down Lord Russell or any of his fellow ministers. Sir Edward Knatchbull had managed only the appointment of a Select Committee to enquire into the circumstances of John Nicholls Tom's release from Barming. He must have known that the bout was lost; such a committee had limited powers, and by then everyone was far more excited about the imminent coronation of Queen Victoria. The Courtenay scandal was rapidly becoming old news.

The findings of the committee would prove invaluable to subsequent historians, however. Among those called to give evidence was George Francis of Fairbrook, whose halting and rather baffled testimony includes many dramatic details that might otherwise have been lost to obscurity. Francis himself, by then, had also felt the black cloud of blame settling around him. 'There is a strong feeling among the poor people,' Norton

Knatchbull had written to his father, 'that George Francis ought to be punished as well as their Husbands and Brothers and I wish something could be *done to him*.' The *Times* mentioned a rumour that Francis had actually been arrested and sent to Maidstone Prison; false, as it happened, but many welcomed it.[31]

A few days later the same correspondent passed Fairbrook and was outraged to see George Francis and a party of friends, presumably in the front garden, 'laughing and joking, as if Thom had been no friend of theirs, and as if they had not been mainly instrumental in spreading his delusions throughout the country.' Mr Francis was subject to no punishment or official censure for what had happened, except for having all the possessions that John Tom had left at his house – including his famous horse – removed as evidence and later sold. The strongest criticism levelled against him came from Susan Tom, the dead impostor's stepmother, who wrote to him at Fairbrook only a few days after the events. Why, she asked, had Francis persisted in humouring her stepson's delusion that he was Sir William Courtenay, when he must surely have known the truth? Why had he allowed him out of his care, and without informing his family of what had happened to him? 'I cannot avoid, sir,' she wrote, 'reflecting on you for aiding him in his delusions; but for going to your house, I am certain he would have returned to his friends, and, like the prodigal son, been received joyfully.'[32]

Tom's wife Catherine had apparently been informed of his death by a curt and anonymous note, saying only 'Your husband is dead. Come and bury him.' The handwriting suggested that it had come from Commander James Gordon, the impostor's former supporter in Boughton, whom Mrs Tom seems to have encountered at Barming asylum years before. If Gordon wrote anything more to her, or if George Francis ever replied to the letter above, no record of their correspondence has survived.

John Tom was dead and buried, but the ghost of Sir William Courtenay still walked the earth. Having 'voluntarily relinquished his connexion with the flesh,' his surviving disciples claimed, he was compelled to take spectral form for a certain period, before he could rise from his grave and become once more 'a sojourner upon the earth.' Others suggested that the rising had already occurred; Sir William had been seen in the flesh, in Canterbury, where his resurrected corpse had entered the chambers of the surgeon Dr Chisholm to demand the return of his heart.[33]

The impostor's reputation also lingered, for a time. For the next few years, journalists and social commentators would refer to 'Mad Tom of Canterbury' and his disciples as examples of the ignorance, political credulity, and religious superstition abiding even in the heartland of Victorian England (the name was perhaps a play on the traditional ballad *Mad Tom o'Bedlam*). But it was Chartism – the mass movement for radical democratic reform which first took official shape the same year – that at first made the best use of the Courtenay Affair. Briefly at least, some early Chartists adopted John Nicholls Tom as a champion of the people, and those who died beside him as revolutionary martyrs. One radical orator bade his crowd to 'remember Peterloo and Canterbury!'[34]

Soon, however, the new movement had martyrs of its own. While Bossenden was subsequently called the last battle fought in England, it would not be the last on *British* soil: that dubious honour perhaps goes to the armed uprising in the Welsh town of Newport in November 1839, when several thousand

Chartist supporters were fired upon by troops, and more than ten of them killed. The soldiers involved in the violence were from the Light Company of the 45th Foot, the same unit that had fought in Bossenden Wood the year before.

The national Chartist cause, and the violence at Newport, rapidly eclipsed the lingering phantoms of Sir William Courtenay and his luckless disciples. History was pointing clearly in a different direction, and the Kentish impostor's mystical Millenarianism and biblical prophecies now belonged to a fading and irrelevant age. Besides, much of the perceived darkness and ignorance in the districts from which his support had been drawn was soon dispelled: the barrister Frederick Liardet, having spent the summer of 1838 probing the lives of the people of Hernhill, Boughton and Dunkirk, presented his report to the Central Society for Education, and the following year Parliament passed a bill to increase the educational grant to the county of Kent by £10,000. With the support of an endowment fund set up by Lord Sondes and Charles Handley, the Ecclesiastical Commissioners reorganised Dunkirk as a parish, with a new church at the top of Boughton Hill. Christ Church was consecrated in 1841, and the resident vicar set about the work of 'reclaiming the neighbourhood from ignorance and immorality.'[35]

Many of the inhabitants of the new parish, we might imagine, were only too happy to be so reclaimed. Dunkirk, like neighbouring Hernhill and Boughton, had gained a grim and unwanted celebrity, and become the subject of an uncomfortable scrutiny. These were communities split down the middle, with relatives and neighbours who had fought and fallen on both sides of that strange conflict. Now they had once more to live together. Best put the past behind them, perhaps, and refer to what had happened only as *the fray*. Better to forget, or pretend to forget.[36]

While some of those affected by the strange career of John Nicholls Tom managed to regain possession of their lives over the years that followed, others could not. William Wills and his two fellow transportees had departed for Van Diemen's Land in November 1838 aboard the convict ship *Pyramus*. They would never return to England. William Price served his time and then settled down in the colony. Thomas Tyler Mears was granted remission of his sentence and later made a small fortune in the Australian gold rush of the 1850s. Wills, too, had his sentence remitted, after an exemplary servitude and showing an 'irreproachable character'. In 1852, he had a friend write on his behalf to Charles Handley, enquiring if he might be allowed to return home, 'to promote the moral and religious condition of his family.' Handley counselled against it: Wills had been granted no official leave to return. Besides, he told the correspondent in confidence, his wife Lucy Wills was now living with another man and had young children by him. The daughter he had named Helen Courtenay Wills had long ago died in infancy.[37]

Emily Burford evaded the workhouse, for a time at least. She and her son survived on the relief granted by the Poor Law Union, and the charity of their neighbours. Three years after her first husband's death she married a Faversham fishmonger and oyster dredger named Joseph Henry Clark. The marriage register lists her as 'Emma Jane Borfot', but the census of that year gives her new name as Emily Jane Clark, and her residence as Brent's Town, Preston, Faversham. Clark was a widower with two young sons, and Emily's boy Edward may have grown up with them. We can only hope that he was a better man, and a better husband, than William Burford had been. In 1851, the couple were still living in Faversham, but they do not feature on the census a decade later. By 1868,

Joseph Clark the oysterman was back, declaring bankruptcy, and is described as a 'widower'. The following year he was sentenced to twelve months' hard labour for taking a Guernsey sweater from a pub. By 1881, he was an inmate of Faversham Union Workhouse, and he died there four years later. We do not know where or when, in the interval between 1851 and 1868, Emily died. She slipped from life without leaving a trace. Her son worked for a while as a farm servant at Great Chart, before he too faded into the surrounding landscape of history.[38]

Up at Fairbrook, the much-maligned George Francis lived on into his seventies, although he was not permitted to rejoin the Faversham Farmers' Club. His daughter Eliza Jane never married. She died in the first days of 1844, at the age of twenty-eight, and was buried at the churchyard of Boughton under Blean in the shade of a sycamore tree. Mary Horne, the aunt who had shared Eliza's adoration of Sir William Courtenay, lived into her eighties but was buried alongside her.[39]

Courtenay's other great admirer, Sarah Culver, left Bossenden Farm shortly after her brother took it over. She moved to Kennington in Ashford parish and died there in 1875, but made no statements, left no record, and composed no more fervent poetry. None, at least, that has survived. Whatever she believed in her heart, whatever moved in her soul, remained unspoken.

Historians studying the nineteenth century have usually regarded the events of 1838 in Kent, if they regard them at all, as a minor aberration. Just as the main road from Canterbury towards Faversham now bypasses the villages of Dunkirk and Boughton altogether, so the highway of historical progress sweeps on past the Courtenay Rising, bearing its freight of great events: the Swing riots of 1830, the Reform Bill and the New Poor Law, then Chartism, industrialisation and the relentless rise of Empire. Marxist historian George Rudé, writing in 1964, described the Kent insurrection as 'only a localized movement, confined to a handful of villages in a single county,' and moved on.[40]

John Nicholls Tom has little to say to the scholars of labour struggle and proletarian advancement; similarly, he resists any easy incorporation into more sanitised evocations of history as a proud celebration of our national heritage and culture. But this neglect by generations of historians has in effect liberated him from the constraints of history itself. Larger than life, larger even than death, in his guise as Sir William Courtenay he seems a protean, timeless figure. No longer rooted in the Victorian past, he rather inhabits the dream state beyond history, the zone of myths, bizarre stories and unlikely legends; that rich seedbed that feeds so many of our ideas of landscape, belonging and possibility. Mad Tom's unquiet ghost disrupts the certainties that underpin our history, just as he once – so the local people believed – heaved at the foundations of the new church on Boughton Hill.

In Dunkirk itself, meanwhile, Sir William lives on. The sign outside the village hall proclaims that this is 'Courtenay Country'. Since my last visit, the three men I met years ago in Bossenden Wood have succeeded in having the battle site marked on the Ordnance Survey maps. A neat little crossed-swords icon now identifies the location of the clearing once known as 'Mash Fall', where John Nicholls Tom and his followers met the soldiers of the 45th Foot. There is a more solid marker at the site today as well: a stone slab, inscribed with the crossed swords and the words *The Battle of Bossenden Wood took place here on 31st May 1838*. When I last visited, however, the stone had been removed for repair. It had been broken in two, supposedly by a falling branch.

Over in Hernhill, the little wooden placard outside St Michael's church listing the names of Tom and his dead followers is cracked and peeling now. But a laminated notice pinned to the church door gives notice of an application to the Commissary Court of the Diocese of Canterbury to install a permanent memorial 'to commemorate the men who were killed at the Battle of Bossenden Wood in 1838 and are buried in the churchyard':

> The battle was the last one on English soil, and marked the end of a series of nationwide protest by impoverished farm workers. Most of the farm workers from Hernhill and the surrounding countryside were illiterate and easily deluded by the leader of the protest, John Tom. The proposal is to provide a stone memorial in the church to give a more sympathetic view of why the men lost their lives; this will be installed above two existing military memorials.

A note at the end states that if 'you wish to object to any of the works or proposals you should send a letter stating the grounds of your objection to the Diocesan Registrar.' I wonder whether the Reverend Charles Handley would have registered such an objection, had he known that one day the impostor's slain followers would be so commemorated. I like to believe that he would not.

Just as John Tom himself no longer appears as the quaint and rather ridiculous figure he might once have seemed to the historians of the later nineteenth and twentieth centuries – an embarrassing reminder of England's forsaken delusions and cranky religious fantasies – so his followers can no longer be dismissed as credulous 'yokels', or as a throng of identical 'peasants'.

Instead, they come to represent a rather contemporary-seeming public, dazed by contradictory messages, energised and terrorised by political threats, fake news and conspiracy, clashing versions of truth, and the possibility – and the plummeting fear – of change. In finding the implausible promises of a charlatan more enticing than the stark choices forced on them by their contemporary society, they provide a potent link between the early nineteenth century and today.

The rebellion that coursed through the Kent countryside, that strange fever that seemed to ignite from emptiness and burst forth into blood and fury, was just as much a part of England's history as the statesmen and clergymen who decried it, the magistrates who opposed it and the soldiers – veterans of empire's wars – who crushed it. Rather than inhabiting some murky back lane of history, John Nicholls Tom and those who followed him, fought for him and died in his name summon a different vision of England's past, part Millenarian dream, part bloodstained nightmare. A place where the irrational is seldom buried deep, and we too must wake in a sweat of dread, fearing the fires of morning. Where we too yearn for the new heaven and the new earth, and despair at the old earth we inherit instead.

The demons of our history stalk our present, and the events of May 1838, in a neglected corner of a Kent wood, seem not so very distant now.

Mad Tom's ghost is rising again.

NOTES AND REFERENCES

Abbreviations
CCA   Canterbury Cathedral Archives
KA   Kent Archives (Kent History and Library Centre, Maidstone)
NA   National Archives (London)
PP   Parliamentary Papers

Introduction
1. Charles Handley's account, CCA U3-235/3/E/3. Handley refers to the respondent only as 'Edward B'; an alternative might be local farmer Edward Browning, but since the 1841 census places Butcher's house 'near the church', and he was publican of the Red Lion opposite, he seems the more likely of the two men.
2. Norton Knatchbull to his father, KA U951/C37/5.
3. Dr Poore's account, PP Vol XLII, 1838; Norton Knatchbull, to his father, KA U951/C37/2.
4. Dr Poore to Sir Edward Knatchbull, KA U951/C37/3 / PP Vol XLII, 1838.
5. *Morning Herald*, June 2 1838.
6. *Times*, June 6 1838 / Anon. *A Canterbury Tale of Fifty Years Ago* (1888), p.58.
7. *Times*, June 2 1838.
8. Diary of Fanny C. Knatchbull (1838), KA U951/F24/35.
9. *Times* June 4, 6 1838.
10. *Times*, June 9 1838.
11. *Times*, June 4 1838.
12. *A Canterbury Tale* (1888), p.52; *Champion and Weekly Herald*, June 4 1838.

13. Victoria's journals are available online at: www.queenvictoriasjournals.org.
14. *Times,* June 1 1838; *Champion and Weekly Herald,* June 4 1838.
15. Dr Poore's account, PP Vol XLII, 1838.
16. *News and Sunday Globe,* June 10 1838.
17. *Times,* June 6 1838.
18. Boyd Hilton, *A Mad, Bad and Dangerous People?* (2006), pp.401–404.
19. *Times,* Oct 28 1831.
20. *Times,* June 2, 4 1838; on the public taste for physiognomy in criminal cases, see Sharrona Pearl, *About Faces: Physiognomy in Nineteenth-Century Britain* (2010), p.38. The plaster cast of John Tom's face has since been lost.
21. Frederick Liardet, *Riot in Kent: Report made to the Central Society of Education on the State of the Peasantry (in the County of Kent),* Publications of the Central Society of Education (1839).
22. 'Canterburiensis', *The life and extraordinary adventures of Sir William Courtenay: knight of Malta, alias John Nichols Tom... concluding with an accurate account of the trial of the rioters at the Maidstone assizes* (1838). Barry Reay (below, p.205) calls the book 'a turgid, convoluted work, a mixture of fact and fantasy.'
23. 'Minutes of Evidence taken before the Select Committee on the Discharge of John Nicholl Thom...' PP Vol XXIII, 1838; *Globe,* June 5 1838.
24. Philip George Rogers, *Battle in Bossenden Wood* (1962).
25. *Times,* June 4, 6 1838.
26. Barry Reay, *The Last Rising of the Agricultural Labourers: The Battle in Bossenden Wood, 1838* (1990).

Chapter 1
1. Tom's first appearance in Canterbury follows his own account in *The Lion,* Issue 4, April 6 1833, see also Anon. *Eccentric and Singular Productions of Courtenay* (1833). Varying sources give dates between late August and late September for his arrival. On beards: Anon, *The Toilette of Health, Beauty and Fashion* (1833), p.160.
2. Charles Dickens, *David Copperfield* (1850), 1881 edition p.208; Henry Ward, *The Canterbury Guide* (1833), p.13; Charles Wordworth, *The Law and Practice of Elections* (1832), p.230.
3. 'Canterburiensis' (1838), pp.215–217; Anon, *Essay on the Character of Courtenay* (1833).

Notes and References

4. *The Globe and Traveller*, June 4 1838.
5. *Essay on the Character of Courtenay* (1833).
6. ibid.
7. Charles Handley, CCA U3-235/3/E/3; 'Canterburiensis'(1838), pp.252–254.
8. *Globe and Traveller*, June 4 1838.
9. Tobias Hug, *Impostures in Early Modern England* (2010), p.111; Rohan McWilliam, 'Unauthorised Identities: the impostor, the fake and secret histories in nineteenth-century Britain', in Finn, Lobban, Bourne Taylor (eds), *Legitimacy and Illegitimacy in Nineteenth-Century Law, Literature and History* (2010), pp.76–77.
10. *Kent Herald*, Oct 25 1832.
11. John Philips, *The Great Reform Bill in the Boroughs* (1992), p.11; Creevey Papers, quoted in J.R.M. Butler, *The Passing of the Great Reform Bill* (1914), 1964 edition p.379.
12. Frederick Lansberry (ed), *Government and Politics in Kent, 1640-1914* (2001), p.139.
13. Frank O'Gorman, *Voters, Patrons and Parties* (1989), p.181; Antonia Fraser, *The Perilous Question* (2013), p.269.
14. Lansberry (2001), p.143, 164; Wordworth (1832), p.230.
15. *Times*, Sept 20 1832; Lansberry (2001), p.139.
16. *Kent Herald*, Sept 6 1832; 'Canterburiensis' (1838), p.218.
17. *Essay on the Character of Courtenay* (1833).
18. Lansberry (2001), p.143; *Kentish Gazette*, May 3 1831.
19. de Tocqueville quoted in Clive Emsley, *Hard Men: the English and Violence since 1750* (2005), p.118; Lansberry (2001), p.59; Robert Cowtan, *Passages from the Autobiography of a 'Man of Kent'*, 1866, p.66; Philips (1992), p.58.
20. Lansberry (2001), p.162; Philips (1992), p.126; on party colours, see James Vernon, *Politics and the People* (1993), pp. 164–67.
21. *Times*, Dec 11 1832; election address reprinted in 'Canterburiensis' (1838), p.219.
22. 'Canterburiensis' (1838), p.220.
23. *Times*, Dec 11 1832; *A Canterbury Tale* (1888), p.45.
24. John Belchem, *Popular Radicalism in Nineteenth-Century Britain* (1995), p.40; see also Hilton, (2006), p.627; *Eccentric and Singular Productions of Courtenay* (1833).
25. Charles Handley, CCA U3-235/3/E/3; *A Canterbury Tale* (1888), p.57, 64; *Times* June 6 1838.
26. *Kentish Observer*, Dec 13 1832.

27. Lansberry (2001), p.143; 'Canterburiensis' (1838), p.225; *Essay on the Character of Courtenay* (1833).
28. Reprinted in 'Canterburiensis' (1838), pp.225–26.
29. 'Canterburiensis' (1838), pp.228–29.
30. ibid, p.229.
31. *Kentish Observer*, Dec 13 1832; *Globe and Traveller*, June 4 1838.
32. *Globe and Traveller*, June 4 1838.
33. *Eccentric and Singular Productions of Courtenay* (1833); *A Canterbury Tale of Fifty Years Ago* (1888), p.61.
34. Canterbury poll book 1832, CCA-CC/R/P/7; *A Canterbury Tale* (1888), p.50.
35. *Essay on the Character of Courtenay* (1833); Charles Handley (CCA U3-235/3/E/3) writes that 'truth be told a clergymen of the established church voted for him,' and calls the electors of Canterbury 'the weak dupes of this impostor.'
36. Rogers (1962), p.26; *Globe and Traveller*, June 4 1838.

Chapter 2
1. Cowtan (1866), p.67; *Times*, Dec 19 1833; *South Eastern Gazette* Dec 25 1832; Lansberry (2001), p.139; Margaret Wilson, *Almost Another Sister* (1990), pp.78–79.
2. Knatchbull papers, KA U951/C43/1-7 / U951/C25; Journal of Mary Knatchbull, KA U3723/F3.
3. Lansberry (2001), p.164.
4. *Kent Herald*, Nov 22 1832; *Globe and Traveller*, June 4 1838.
5. Lansberry (2001), p.160.
6. Cowtan (1866), pp.66–67.
7. *Essay on the Character of Courtenay* (1833); *Times*, Dec 19 1832.
8. Handbill reprinted in 'Canterburiensis' (1838), pp.233–34; *Kentish Observer*, Dec 20 1832.
9. Charles Handley, CCA U3-235/3/E/3; *Kent Herald*, Dec 20 1832.
10. *A Canterbury Tale* (1888), pp.37–38.
11. The poll book for the East Kent election of 1832 is included in the copy of *Eccentric and Singular Productions of Courtenay* (1833) in the British Library bearing the shelfmark 809.f.32. (2.)
12. *Essay on the Character of Courtenay* (1833).
13. Charles Handley, CCA U3-235/3/E/3.
14. 'Select Committee on the Discharge of John Nicholl Thom...' *Reports from Committees*, Volume 17, PP Vol XXIII, 1838.
15. *Times*, June 8 1838.

16. Charles Handley, CCA U3-235/3/E/3.
17. Alexander Somerville, *The Whistler at the Plough* (1852), Vol I, p.42.
18. *A Canterbury Tale* (1888), p.43.
19. *Penny Satirist*, Jun 9 1838.
20. Canterbury Parish Registers, Kent History and Library Centre; Faversham Farmers' Club, KA U229/Z6.
21. John Marshall, *Royal Navy Biography* (1833), Vol. IV, 1, p.375; *Maidstone Journal and Kentish Advertiser*, Jul 30 1833.
22. *Kentish Gazette*, Feb 5 1833 / March 12 1833.
23. *Maidstone Journal*, March 5 1833; *Canterbury Journal*, March 5 1833; *South Eastern Gazette* March 12 1833.
24. *The Lion*, reprinted in *Eccentric and Singular Productions of Courtenay* (1833).
25. Ian Dyke, *William Cobbett and Rural Popular Culture* (1992), pp.169-70.
26. Joss Marsh, *Word Crimes* (1998), p.80; Frederick Liardet, *Riot in Kent* (1839), p.30.
27. Grande, Stevenson, (eds) *The Opinions of William Cobbett* (2013), p.78; *The Lion*, Issue 6, April 20 1833, all issues reprinted in *Eccentric and Singular Productions of Courtenay* (1833).
28. *A Canterbury Tale* (1888), p.51; *Kentish Gazette*, March 19 and 22 1833; *Canterbury Journal*, March 19 1833.
29. *Canterbury Journal*, April 2 1833; Quarter Sessions papers, CCA CC/J/Q/Box94.
30. *The Lion*, Issue 4, April 6 1833.
31. *Kent Herald*, April 4 1833; *A Canterbury Tale* (1888), p.48.
32. 'Select Committee,' PP Vol XXIII, 1838, p.14.
33. *Kentish Gazette*, April 16 1833; *A Canterbury Tale* (1888), p.62; Discharge papers from Canterbury City Gaol, CCA CC/JQ/257.
34. 'Select Committee,' PP Vol XXIII, 1838, pp.12-13.
35. *South Eastern Gazette* April 23 1833; *The Lion*, Issue 7, April 27 1833.
36. Faversham Farmers' Club, notes on members, KA U229/Z6.
37. *Canterbury Journal*, Jun 25 1833; Successive issues of *The Lion* are reprinted in *Eccentric and Singular Productions of Courtenay* (1833), as above.
38. *Times*, July 5 1833. Rogers (1962) provides a detailed narrative of the trial, pp.51-54.
39. Canterbury Quarter Sessions Order Book, CCA CC/J/Q/O/22; *Canterbury Journal*, July 2 1833; *Kent Herald*, July 4 1838.
40. *Times*, July 5 1833.

Chapter 3

1. Anon, *Essay on the Character of Courtenay* (1833), pp.9-20 contains a full description of the trial at Maidstone; several local newspapers sent reporters, and my account draws also on the *Maidstone Journal, Maidstone Gazette, South Eastern Gazette, Canterbury Journal* and *Kentish Gazette*, all of July 30 1833, together with *Kent Herald* Aug 1 1833. See also Rogers (1962), pp.57-68.
2. *Maidstone Journal*, July 30 1833.
3. *Essay on the Character of Courtenay* (1833), p.17.
4. 'Canterburiensis' (1838), p.371.
5. *Essay on the Character of Courtenay* (1833), p.20.
6. Now kept in the Dawes collection, Mount Ephraim, Hernhill.
7. *Maidstone Gazette*, Aug 14 1833; *Kent Herald* Aug 15 1833.
8. Reay (1990), pp.110-111; Rogers (1962), pp.1-3.
9. *London Despatch*, June 24 1838; *Maidstone Gazette*, Aug 14 1833. Kent County Asylum Admissions register No.107, KA MH/Md2/Ap1/1.
10. Reay (1990), p,111; see also Sarah Wise, *Inconvenient People* (2012), p.117.
11. 'Select Committee,' PP Vol XXIII, 1838, p.15; Len Oakes, *Prophetic Charisma: the Psychology of Revolutionary Religious Personalities* (1997), p.168. ibid pp.27-28.
12. 'Canterburiensis' (1838), pp.163-205; *Maidstone Gazette*, Aug 14 1833.
13. 'Canterburiensis' (1838), pp.206-214; *Morning Herald*, June 2 1838.
14. 'Canterburiensis' (1838), pp.62-70; Belchem (1995), p.22; *Penny Satirist*, June 9 1938; plaque text from Beverley Robinson, *The Red Lion* (1980), p.10.
15. Malcolm Chase, *The People's Farm* (1988), p.88.
16. 'Canterburiensis' (1838), p.215; *Morning Herald*, June 2 1838; *The Lion*, Issue 4, April 6 1833. George Francis's evidence to the Select Committee includes a confused reference to Tom's 'rescue' of 'a Jewess by the name of Solomons,' which might be connected to another of his scams.
17. 'Select Committee,' PP Vol XXIII, 1838, pp.8-9.
18. 'Papers Relative to John Nicholl Thom,' PP Vol XLII. 1838; Petition, NA HO 17/41/129.

19. Leonard Smith, *Cure, Comfort and Safe Custody* (1999), pp.20-22.
20. J.E. Huxley 'History and Description of the Kent Asylum.' in *The Asylum Journal of Mental Science* (1855), pp 39-45.
21. Smith (1999), p.165.
22. KA U1515/OQ/L1; Smith (1999), p.202-5.
23. KA MH/Md2/Ap1/1.
24. Rogers (1962) pp.71-72; *Times*, June 11 1838.
25. Smith (1999), p.199; 'Select Committee,' PP Vol XXIII, 1838, p.9.
26. 'Statement of Courtenay's Aberrations', KA U951/C37/47.
27. Smith (1999), p.100.
28. Reay (1990), p.123.
29. Ronald Matthews, *English Messiahs* (1936), 1971 edition p.213.
30. For example, 'The Man of Mystery' (1833, see Robinson (1980), p.xii), or 'The Knight of Malta; a Canterbury Tale of 1833', *Kent Herald* April 25 1833, or the publications *Eccentric and Singular Productions of Courtenay* and *Essay on the Character of Courtenay* (1833); petition: 'Canterburiensis' (1838), pp.273-75; *Weekly Chronicle*, June 17 1838.
31. William Harrison Ainsworth, *Rookwood* (1834), 1836 edition pp.274-277; Hilton (2006), p.626.

Chapter 4

1. Faversham Borough Register of Depositions, Upper Division of the Lathe of Scray, 1832-39, KA Fa/JP7/1. The script is difficult to read in places; words in square brackets are my own interpretation, with help from the staff at the Kent Archives in Maidstone.
2. Daybook of Constable John Mears, in Wendy Safe, *The Courtenay Affair, 1838* (1987), p.23.
3. Liardet (1839), p.18.
4. Edward Hasted, *The History and Topographical Survey of the County of Kent* (1798), Vol VII, p.3; Liardet (1839), p.11; For the weather, see *Times* July 2 / 4 1836; Princess Victoria's journal of July 3 1836 (www.queenvictoriasjournals.org) mentions that 'the heat since last Sunday has been intense.'
5. Reay (1990), p.8; Hasted (1798), Vol IX, p.3; *Times* June 11 1838.
6. Hasted, (1798), IX, pp.3-4.
7. *Times*, June 2 1838; Handley CCA U3-235/3/E/3.
8. Canterbury Parish Registers, Kent History and Library Centre; Hasted, (1798), Vol VII, p.19; Reay (1990), p.50.

9. NA MR 1/890, 'Map of Dunkirkville', 1828 / NA MPZ 1/26, 'Reference Book or Terrier to the Plan of the Ville of Dunkirk', 1827-28.
10. Indictment Roll, East Kent, Jan 1830, KA Q/SI/E/624 / East Kent Sessions Papers, Jan 1830, KA Q/SBe/117 / Quarter Sessions papers, 1826-1830, CCA CC/J/Q/Box93 / Pardon, July 13 1830, NA HO 17/113/94.
11. 'List of persons engaged in the Courtenay riot', CCA U3-235/28/1/1; 'Schedule of Persons involved in the Courtenay Riot', KA U951/C37/40; Liardet (1839), p.18; Reay (1990), pp.61-64.
12. Minghay, *The Victorian Countryside* (1981), Vol II, p.514; Reay (1990), pp.46-47; Reay, *Rural Englands* (2004), p.60.
13. *A Canterbury Tale* (1888), p.40; *Times* June 9 1838; Reay (1990), p.49, 54;
14. Edwin Hodder, *The Life and Work of the Seventh Earl of Shaftesbury, K.G*, 1887, p.368, quoted in K.D.M. Snell, *Annals of the Labouring Poor* (1987), p.380; NA MPZ 1/26, 'Reference Book or Terrier to the Plan of the Ville of Dunkirk', 1827-28.
15. George M Young, *Early Victorian England* (1934), Vol I, pp.137-38; Alan Major, *Kentish As She Wus Spoke* (2001), p.110-11.
16. Somerville, (1852), Vol I, p.120.
17. W.D. Parish, W.F. Shaw, *A Dictionary of Kentish Dialect and Provincialisms* (1888), p.52; Major (2001), p.72 / 75 / 76 / 117.
18. *Weekly Chronicle*, June 10 1838.
19. *Globe*, June 2 1838.
20. Carl Griffin, *The Rural War* (2012), pp.1-2; Eric Hobsbawm, George Rudé, *Captain Swing* (1969), pp.97-98; Reay (1990), pp.73-75; Cowtan (1866), p.53.
21. Robert Poole, *Peterloo* (2019), pp.16-19. Griffin (2012), p.139; Lansberry (2001), p.123.
22. Carl Griffin, 'Affecting Violence' (2008), p.153.
23. Griffin (2012), p.193; *Kent Herald* Oct 21 1830; See also John Stevenson, *Popular Disturbances in England* (1979), p.240, on the organisation of the 'rioters'.
24. Carl Griffin, 'Policy on the Hoof', *Rural History* (2004), pp.127-148.
25. *Times*, Oct 30 1830; Reay (1990), pp.75-77.
26. Hilton (2006), p.590. Lansberry (2001), p.106.

Notes and References

27. Nicholas Edsall, *The Anti-Poor Law Movement* (1971), p.5.
28. Hilton (2006), pp.593-94; Robert Lee, *Unquiet Country* (2005), pp.49-50.
29. *Morning Herald*, June 2 1838; Edsall (1971), p.14.
30. Hilton (2006), p.598; Assistant Commissioner Gilbert, quoted in Edsall (1971), p.38.
31. Hilton (2006), p.596; *Northern Star*, June 30 1838; Edsall (1971), p.32.
32. Edsall (1971), p.28.
33. 'Canterbury Convictions.' Accounts and Papers, Volume 11, PP Vol XLVII (1835); *Kent Herald,* July 2 1835; East Kent Special Session, June 1835, KA Q/SI/E/647.
34. Reay (1990), p.78; 'Canterbury Convictions' (1835); Safe (1987), pp.23-24.
35. *Times,* 14 May 1835; Reay (1990), p.77; Edsall (1971), pp.30-31;
36. *Kent Herald,* May 7 1835.
37. *Kent Herald,* May 7 1835; *Kentish Gazette,* May 12 1835.
38. NA MPZ 1/26; Reay (1990), p.70; *Kentish Express and Ashford News* Feb 12 1910 (clipping in Dawes collection, Mount Ephraim).
39. Safe (1987), pp.23-24; Liardet (1839), p.18.
40. East Kent Sessions, Michaelmas 1836, KA Q/SBe/146.

Chapter 5

1. John Barrow (ed), *The Mirror of Parliament* (1838), p.5122.
2. 'Papers Relative to John Nicholl Thom' PP Vol XLII (1838).
3. ibid.
4. 'Select Committee,' PP Vol XXIII (1838), pp.7-9.
5. ibid, p.10.
6. 'List of persons engaged in the Courtenay riot', CCA U3-235/28/1/1; 'Canterburiensis' (1838), p.475.
7. *Times*, June 9 1838.
8. Knatchbull letters, KA U951/C37/5; 'Select Committee,' PP Vol XXIII (1838), pp.9-10.
9. 'Canterburiensis' (1838), p.398; Charles Handley to Sir Edward Knatchbull, U951/C37/37. One of these pistols was supposedly recovered after the fight at Bossenden – it had a brass barrel, according to a newspaper report, and a bore nearly as large as a musket.
10. *Kentish Observer,* Jan 15 1838; *Times,* Jan 18 1838; *Canterbury Journal,* Feb 24 1838; Reay (1990), pp.81-82.

11. Canterbury Parish Registers, Kent History and Library Centre; Reay (1990), pp.140-1; *Times*, June 9 1838.
12. 'Canterburiensis' (1838), p.398.
13. Liardet (1839), p.18.
14. Liardet (1839), p.22.
15. Robert Clive Handley, *The Handley Family* (1992), p.51; Liardet (1839), p.21.
16. Charles Handley to Archbishop of Canterbury, KA U951/C37/34; Liardet (1839), p.35.
17. Liardet (1839), p.17; 'List of persons engaged in the Courtenay riot', CCA U3-235/28/1/1; Reay (1990), p.132.
18. Charles Handley, CCA U3-235/3/E/3.
19. Hilton (2006), p.401; *Revelation*, 20, 6-7.
20. Chase, (1988), p.50; Reay (1990), p.105-6.
21. Margaret Oliphant, *The Life of Edward Irving* (1862), p.397, in Hilton (2006), p.403. Kenelm Burridge, *New Heaven, New Earth* (1969), p.126.
22. Hilton (2006), p.401; J.F.C. Harrison, *The Second Coming* (1979), p.57.
23. Helen-Francis Dessain, 'Resisting mechanisation? Reading Shortshanks,' *Romance, Revolution and Reform* (2020), pp.41-42; Christopher Rowland, *Blake and the Bible*, pp.122-27; Harrison (1979), p.141, 147; Matthews (1936), p.82.
24. Ken Levi, *Violence and Religious Commitment* (1982), p.25; Liardet (1839), p.14; *Times*, June 9 1838.
25. *Kentish Express and Ashford News* Feb 12 1910 (Dawes collection, Mount Ephraim).
26. *Times*, June 9 1838; *Kentish Gazette*, Aug 14 1838; Liardet (1839), p.13; *Revelation*, 6, 2.
27. *Times*, June 6 / 9 1838; *Revelation*, 6, 13.
28. Liardet (1839), p.13.
29. *Times*, June 9 1838.
30. Anon. *Account of the Desperate Affray which Took Place in Blean Wood...* (1838), p.30.
31. Rogers (1962), p.91.
32. *Times*, June 4 1838; 'Canterburiensis' (1838), p.436.
33. *Desperate Affray...* (1838), p.30.
34. Rogers (1962), p.91; *A Canterbury Tale* (1888), p.38; *Times*, June 4 1838; Reay (1990), p.107.

35. Burridge (1969), p.161.
36. *Times*, June 1 1838.
37. *Weekly Chronicle*, June 10 1838.

Chapter 6
1. *Times*, June 6 1838.
2. *Times*, June 12 1838; *A Canterbury Tale* (1888), p.45.
3. Barry Turner, *The Victorian Parson* (2016), p.76, 84, 157.
4. Handley (1992), pp.48-49.
5. *The Examiner*, May 27 1838, p.330.
6. *Times*, Dec 15 1832; T.L. Richardson, 'The Labourers' Standard of Living in Lincolnshire, 1790-1840,' *The Agricultural History Review* (1993), p.16. Handley's combative attitude can be seen in his own *Facts Illustrative of the Mode by which the Law is Administered by County Magistrates...* (1839), detailing his dispute with a fellow magistrate in Lincolnshire.
7. *Times*, June 4 1838. *Globe*, August 10 1838, evidence of Alfred Payne.
8. John Archer, *By a Flash and a Scare* (1990), p.99; Lee (2005), p.16.
9. Hilton (2008), p.577; Tithe Map NA IR 30/17/41; *Globe*, August 10 1838. I am grateful to Melanie Backe-Hansen for her helpful suggestions on the probable construction date of the Woodman's Hall pub.
10. 'Select Committee,' PP Vol XXIII (1838), p.11.
11. *Globe*, August 10 1838.
12. Reay (1990), pp.102-3.
13. *Globe*, August 10 1838, evidence of Blanchard and Payne.
14. ibid, Payne.
15. ibid, Payne; *South Eastern Gazette* Aug 14 1838. Some later versions of this testimony change the word to 'stopped', but in context 'topped' – killed or murdered – seems to make more sense.
16. *Maidstone Journal*, June 26 1838.
17. *Times*, June 6 1838.
18. Liardet (1839), p.31, 40, 44; Rogers (1962), p.97.
19. *Globe*, August 10 1838, evidence of William Blanchard.
20. Charles Handley, CCA U3-235/3/E/3; John Poore to Sir Edward Knatchbull, KA U951/C37/3; 'Papers Relative to John Nicholl Thom' PP Vol XLII (1838).
21. 'Select Committee,' PP Vol XXIII (1838), p.10.

22. *Times*, June 1 1838.
23. *A Canterbury Tale* (1888), p.43.
24. *Globe*, August 10 1838.
25. 'Canterburiensis' (1838), p.407.
26. 'Papers Relative to John Nicholl Thom' PP Vol XLII (1838).
27. ibid, pp.9-10; *Maidstone Journal*, June 5 1838.
28. *Times*, June 7 1838.
29. *Times*, June 4, 9, 1838.
30. Liardet (1839), pp.11-12.
31. *Times*, June 4 1838; Liardet (1839), p.13.
32. *Times*, June 4 1838.

Chapter 7
1. Reay (1990), p.39; Liardet (1839), p.21: the 'meritorious individual' is Edward Curling.
2. *Times*, June 6; *A Canterbury Tale* (1888), p.54.
3. 'Canterburiensis' (1838), p.421.
4. *Times*, June 4 1838. Kristof Smeyers (in 'When Immortals Die' (2017), p.17) has so far been one of the only historians to discuss John Tom's miraculous wounds, which he refers to as *stigmata*; his forthcoming monograph on the subject should provide still greater illumination.
5. *Desperate Affray...* (1838), p.29-30.
6. *Globe*, June 5 1838.
7. *A Canterbury Tale* (1888), p.38, 40; 'Canterburiensis' (1838), p.410; *South Eastern Gazette* June 12 1838.
8. Most of the witness statements on the killing of Mears are collected in the *Globe*, June 1 / Aug 10 1838, and reprinted in 'Canterburiensis' (1838), pp.421-24 and p.468; additional reports in the *Times*, June 2, 9 1838. Contemporary drawings and plans in the Dawes collection, Mount Ephraim, show the murder site in detail, and the 1828 map of Dunkirk (NA MR 1/890) includes a measured survey of the farm layout.
9. *Globe*, June 1 1838: The French word *déshabillé*, meaning undressed or disarrayed, may have had a particular contemporary usage lost to us now; it appears in the poetry of John Clare, for example.
10. *A Canterbury Tale* (1888), p.38.
11. *Globe*, Aug 10 1838; *South Eastern Gazette* Aug 14 1838.

12. *A Canterbury Tale* (1888), p.54; Charles Handley, CCA U3-235/3/E/3.
13. Letters of Norton Knatchbull to his father and stepmother, KA U951/C54/8-11; Letters to Mary KA U951/C25.
14. Knatchbull letters, KA U951/C43/1-7 / KA U951/C9.
15. Mary Knatchbull journal, KA U3723/F3; Knatchbull letters, KA U951/C25/1-21.
16. Norton Knatchbull to his father, KA U951/C37/5.
17. *Desperate Affray...* (1838), p.4; *Morning Herald*, June 2 1838; *A Canterbury Tale* (1888), p.44.
18. *Canterbury Tale* (1888), p.60.
19. *Desperate Affray...* (1838), pp.29-30.
20. *Times*, June 7 1838.
21. *Kentish Express and Ashford News* Feb 12 1910 (Dawes collection, Mount Ephraim).
22. Liardet (1839), p.13.
23. *Times*, June 4 1838; *Examiner*, June 10 1838.
24. *Times*, June 4 1838.
25. *Globe*, June 4 1838, evidence of Edmund Foreman; 'Select Committee,' PP Vol XXIII (1838), p.11.
26. *Times*, June 7 1838.
27. Norton Knatchbull to his father, KA U951/C37/2.
28. *Desperate Affray...* (1838), pp.3-6.
29. Norton Knatchbull to his father, KA U951/C37/2; *A Canterbury Tale* (1888), p.55.
30. *Desperate Affray...* (1838), p.9; *Times*, June 4 1838.
31. Handley (1992), pp.48-49, 53; Dawes collection, Mount Ephraim; *Times*, June 4 1838.
32. *Times*, June 7, 9 1838.
33. *Globe*, June 1 1838.
34. Norton Knatchbull to his father, KA U951/C37/2; *Desperate Affray...* (1838), p.10.
35. *Desperate Affray...* (1838), p.5; *Times*, June 6 1838.
36. *A Canterbury Tale* (1888), p.56.
37. *Globe*, June 5 1838; *Times*, June 7 1838; Stevenson (1979), p.240.
38. Norton Knatchbull to his father, KA U951/C37/2.
39. *A Canterbury Tale* (1888), p.56.
40. Handley (1992), p.49; Dawes collection, Mount Ephraim; Norton Knatchbull to his father, KA U951/C37/2.

Chapter 8
1. *Morning Herald,* June 2 1838.
2. Philip Dalbiac, *History of the 45th, 1st Nottinghamshire Regiment* (1902), p.136, 140.
3. *The Lion,* Issue 5, April 13 1833; Kevin Linch, Matthew Lord, *Redcoats to Tommies* (2021), p.207; *Kentish Gazette,* May 22 1838; *Times,* June 6 1838.
4. Richard Holmes, *Redcoat* (2001), pp.194-95; Rory Muir, *Tactics and the Experience of Battle in the Age of Napoleon* (2008), p.85.
5. *Kentish Gazette,* June 16 1840; Henry George Hart (ed). *The New Annual Army List* (1840), p.196; Norton Knatchbull's letter to his father detailing the 'force used against Courtenay' (U951/C37/8) mentions one captain and three lieutenants. As he does not include Reid, an additional captain and one additional lieutenant must have accompanied Armstrong's detachment. The captain was probably George Minter (see below, note 30); *Globe,* Jan 1 1838; *Times,* June 4 1838.
6. *A Canterbury Tale* (1888), p.62.
7. *Kentish Gazette,* June 5 1838; *Desperate Affray...* (1838), p.6; *Times,* June 1; Two of the witnesses interviewed in 1888 remember the reading of the Act, while James Bronterre O'Brien in *Northern Star,* June 6 1838, disputes it.
8. Evidence of Major Armstrong, *Desperate Affray...* (1838), p.12.
9. *A Canterbury Tale* (1888), evidence of George Mount, p.62, and Mr Pidduck, p.65.
10. Handley (1992), p.49; Dawes collection, Mount Ephraim; *Times,* June 4 1838.
11. Norton Knatchbull to his father, KA U951/C37/2.
12. *Times,* June 4 1838; *Desperate Affray...* (1838), p.15.
13. ibid, evidence of Edmund Foreman, pp.16-17, evidence of Thomas Millgate p.15.
14. *Weekly Chronicle,* June 10 1838; *Kentish Gazette,* June 5 1838.
15. *Desperate Affray...* (1838), p.14. The description of the battle that follows is compiled from multiple witness statements given at the trials and inquests, together with contemporary newspaper reports.
16. *Times,* June 9 1838; *Globe,* June 2, 5 1838.
17. Norton Knatchbull to his father, KA U951/C37/2.
18. *Desperate Affray...* (1838), p.20; *Kentish Gazette,* June 5 1838, claims that ten rounds of cartridge were issued to each soldier before the firing commenced; Handley (1992), p.49; Dawes collection, Mount Ephraim.

Notes and References

19. Liardet (1839), p.18; *Times*, June 9 1838.
20. Norton Knatchbull to his father, KA U951/C37/2; *Maidstone Journal*, June 5 1838; *Desperate Affray...* (1838), p.17.
21. ibid, p.14.
22. *Times*, June 4 1838; *A Canterbury Tale* (1888), p.47, 59.
23. *Globe*, June 5 1838; *Desperate Affray...* (1838), p.24.
24. *A Canterbury Tale* (1888), p.59.
25. *Canterbury Journal*, June 2 1838; *Times*, June 2 1838; *Maidstone Journal*, June 5 1838; *Desperate Affray...* (1838), p.30.
26. *Times*, June 9 1838; *Desperate Affray...* (1838), p.15.
27. Liardet (1839), p.15, 17; 'Canterburiensis' (1838), p.436.
28. *Times*, June 9 1838; *Morning Herald*, June 2 1838.
29. Norton Knatchbull to his father, KA U951/C37/2; *Times*, June 4 1838.
30. *Morning Herald*, June 2 1838. The report calls the officer Captain Minto, but Minter is likely meant; George Minter transferred from the 45th to the 28th Foot the following year.
31. *Weekly Chronicle*, June 10 1838; *Morning Herald*, June 2 1838.
32. *Examiner*, June 10 1838.
33. Liardet (1839), p.13.
34. *Times*, June 9 1838.

Chapter 9

1. *Canterbury Journal*, June 2 1838; *Globe* June 4 1838.
2. Joan White (1983, CCA U3/221/28/18) claims that the heart was 'handed down as a souvenir until it was decently buried a few years ago.' Rogers (1962, p.142 fn) says that it was exhibited in Kent and Canterbury Hospital, and later displayed by a Canterbury watchmaker, before being 'destroyed shortly before the Second World War.' A photograph of the preserved heart survives in the Dawes archive, Mount Ephraim.
3. *Morning Chronicle*, June 6 1838.
4. *Kentish Gazette*, June 5 1838; *Times*, June 2 1838.
5. *Times*, June 9 1838; *A Canterbury Tale* (1888), p.43.
6. *Times*, June 6 1838.
7. *Times*, June 2 1838; *Globe*, June 2 1838.
8. The inquests are reported in the *Globe*, June 4 1838, among other publications, and reprinted in *Desperate Affray...* (1838), pp.7-21.
9. *Times*, June 4 1838; 'Canterburiensis' (1838), p.436.
10. *Times*, June 5 1838; *Globe*, June 5 1838; *Canterbury Journal*, June 9 1838.

11. *Desperate Affray...* (1838), p.23.
12. *Times*, June 6 1838.
13. ibid.
14. *Times*, June 4 1838.
15. *Globe*, June 6 1838; *Times*, June 7 1838.
16. *Times*, June 12 1838.
17. *Globe*, August 11 1838; *Times*, August 11 1838; 'Canterburiensis' (1838), pp.457-482; Rogers (1962), pp.183-93, provides a detailed summary of the trials; see also Reay (1990), pp.161-64.
18. *Canterbury Journal*, Aug 11 1838.
19. Petition, and letter dated Sept 7 1838, NA HO 17/5/117.
20. 'Papers Relative to John Nicholl Thom' PP Vol XLII (1838).
21. *Penny Satirist*, June 23 1838.
22. *A Canterbury Tale* (1888), p.56.
23. CCA U3-235/3/E/3.
24. *A Canterbury Tale* (1888), p.51; Rogers (1962), pp.166-67.
25. Norton and Mary Knatchbull to Sir Edward, KA U951/C37/1; Norton to Sir Edward, KA U951/C37/2.
26. ibid; *Spectator*, June 9 1838; 'Canterburiensis' (1838), p.421; Edward Royle, *Revolutionary Britannia* (2000), p.88.
27. Diary of Fanny Knatchbull (1838), KA U951/F24/35.
28. *Hansard's Parliamentary Debates*, Vol XLIII (1838), pp.1091-1139.
29. *Weekly Despatch*, quoted in *Northern Star*, June 13 1838; *Times*, June 4 1838.
30. *Northern Star*, June 6 1838.
31. Norton Knatchbull to his father, U951/C37/8 (my emphasis); *Times*, June 6 1838.
32. 'Select Committee,' PP Vol XXIII (1838), p.14.
33. *Kentish Gazette*, June 17 1838; *Weekly Chronicle*, June 17 1838.
34. Reay (1990), p.153.
35. Safe (1987), pp.32-33.
36. Reay (1990), p.168.
37. George Rudé, *Protest and Punishment* (1978), pp.212-13; Charles Handley, CCA U3-235/3/E/3.
38. Compiled from online records accessed in the Kent History and Library Centre, Maidstone, and the Beaney Library, Canterbury.
39. White (1983), CCA U3/221/28/18.
40. George Rudé, *The Crowd in History* (1964), p.150.

BIBLIOGRAPHY

Ainsworth, William Harrison. *Rookwood, A Romance*. Richard Bentley, London, 1834.

Anon. *Eccentric and Singular Productions of Courtenay: With his Publication "The Lion", and Trial at Maidstone, for Perjury*. Henry Ward, Canterbury, 1833.

Anon. *Essay on the Character of Courtenay: With Trial... at Maidstone, 1833*. Henry Ward, Canterbury, 1833.

Anon, *The Toilette of Health, Beauty and Fashion*, Allen and Ticknor, Boston, 1833.

Anon. *Account of the Desperate Affray which Took Place in Blean Wood Near Boughton on... the 31st of May, 1838, Between a Party of Agricultural Labourers, Headed by the Self-styled Sir William Courtenay, and a Detachment of the 45th. Regiment of Foot...* William Radcliffe, London, 1838.

Anon. *A Canterbury Tale of Fifty Years Ago: Being the Story of the Extraordinary Career of Sir William Courtenay, Alias John Nichols Thom*. H.J. Goulden, Canterbury, 1888.

Archer, John E. *By a Flash and a Scare: Incendiarism, Animal Maiming, and Poaching in East Anglia, 1815-1870*. Clarendon Press, Oxford, 1990.

Archer, John E. *Social Unrest and Popular Protest in England, 1780-1840*. Cambridge University Press, Cambridge, 2000.

Armytage, W.H.G. *Heavens Below: Utopian Experiments in England, 1560-1960*. Routledge and Kegan Paul, London, 1961.

Barrow, John Henry (ed), *The Mirror of Parliament, for the First Session of the Thirteenth Parliament of Great Britain and Ireland*. Volume VI. Longman, London, 1838.

Belchem, John. *Popular Radicalism in Nineteenth-Century Britain*. Macmillan, London, 1995.

Burridge, Kenelm. *New Heaven, New Earth: A Study of Millenarian Activities*. Blackwell, London, 1969.

Butler, J.R.M. *The Passing of the Great Reform Bill*. Longmans Green, London, 1914.

'Canterburiensis'. *The life and extraordinary adventures of Sir William Courtenay: knight of Malta, alias John Nichols Tom... concluding with an accurate account of the trial of the rioters at the Maidstone assizes*. James Hunt, Canterbury, 1838.

Chase, Malcolm. *The People's Farm: English Radical Agrarianism, 1775-1840*. Clarendon Press, Oxford, 1988.

Chase, Malcolm. *Chartism: A New History*. Manchester University Press, Manchester, 2007.

Colloms, Brenda. *Victorian Country Parsons*. Constable, London, 1977.

Cowtan, Robert, (Reginald FitzRoy Stanley, ed). *Passages from the Autobiography of a "Man of Kent"*. Whittingham and Wilkins, London, 1866.

Crawford, Joseph. *Inspiration and Insanity in British Poetry: 1825–1855*. Palgrave Macmillan, London, 2019.

Dalbiac, Philip Hugh. *History of the 45th: 1st Nottinghamshire regiment (Sherwood foresters)*. Swan Sonnenschein & Co, London, 1902.

Davis, Natalie Zemon. *Remaking Impostors: From Martin Guerre to Sommersby*. Hayes Robinson Lecture Series, Issue 1. Royal Holloway, University of London, 1997.

Dessain, Helen-Frances. 'Resisting mechanisation? Reading Shortshanks' *The March of Intellect* (c. 1828) through the lenses of Daniel and Edward Irving.' *Romance, Revolution and Reform*, Issue 2, pp 36-53. 2020.

Dyck, Ian. *William Cobbett and Rural Popular Culture*. Cambridge University Press, Cambridge, 1992.

Edsall, Nicholas C. *The Anti-Poor Law Movement, 1834-44*. Manchester University Press, Manchester, 1971.

Emsley, Clive. *Hard Men: The English and Violence Since 1750*. Hambledon, London, 2005.

Finn, M; Lobban, M; Bourne Taylor, Jenny (eds). *Legitimacy and Illegitimacy in Nineteenth-Century Law, Literature and History*. Palgrave Macmillan, London, 2010.

Fraser, Antonia. *Perilous Question: The Drama of the Great Reform Bill 1832.* Weidenfeld & Nicolson, London, 2013.

Grande, James; Stevenson, John; Thomas, Richard (eds). *The Opinions of William Cobbett.* Ashgate, Oxford, 2013.

Great Britain. 'Elections: City of Canterbury / Kent Eastern Division.' Accounts and Papers, Volume 3 (Elections, Church, &c). *Parliamentary Papers,* Vol XVII, 1833.

Great Britain. 'Canterbury Convictions: Persons committed to Gaol in Canterbury for riotous Conduct in obstructing Poor Law Commissioners.' Accounts and Papers, Volume 11 (Clergy, Ecclesiastical Revenues, Tithes, Poor). *Parliamentary Papers,* Vol XLVII, 1835.

Great Britain. 'Report from the Select Committee on the Discharge of John Nicholl Thom from the Lunatic Asylum, together with the Minutes of Evidence.' Reports from Committees, Volume 17. *Parliamentary Papers,* Vol XXIII, 1838.

Great Britain. 'Papers Relative to John Nicholl Thom.' Accounts and Papers, Volume 7 (Convicts). *Parliamentary Papers,* Vol XLII, 1838.

Great Britain. *Hansard's Parliamentary Debates,* Vol XLIII, 3rd Series, 1838.

Griffin, Carl James. "Policy on the Hoof': Sir Robert Peel, Sir Edward Knatchbull and the Trial of the Elham Machine Breakers, 1830'. *Rural History,* Volume 15, Issue 2, pp.127-148. 2004.

Griffin, Carl James. 'Affecting Violence: Language, Gesture and Performance in Early Nineteenth-Century English Popular Protest.' *Historical Geography,* 36, pp.139-162. 2008.

Griffin, Carl James. *The Rural War: Captain Swing and the Politics of Protest.* Manchester University Press, Manchester, 2012.

Handley, Major Benjamin. *Facts Illustrative of the Mode by which the Law is Administered by County Magistrates...* James Rigway, London, 1839.

Handley, Robert Clive. *The Handley Family of Newark and Sleaford, U.K. and Australasia.* R.C. Handley, Privately Printed, Merimbula, Australia, 1992.

Harrison, J. F. C. *The Second Coming: Popular Millenarianism, 1780-1850.* Rutgers University Press, New Brunswick, 1979.

Hart, Henry George (ed). *The New Annual Army List... Corrected to 7th February 1840.* John Murray, London, 1840.

Hasted, Edward. *The History and Topographical Survey of the County of Kent.* W. Bristow, Canterbury, 1798.

Hilton, Boyd. *A Mad, Bad and Dangerous People? England 1783-1846.* Oxford University Press, Oxford, 2006.

Hobsbawm, Eric; Rudé, George. *Captain Swing.* Lawrence and Wishart, London, 1969.

Hodder, Edwin, *The Life and Work of the Seventh Earl of Shaftesbury, K.G.* Cassel, London, 1887.

Holmes, Richard. *Redcoat: The British Soldier in the Age of Horse and Musket.* Harper Collins, London, 2001.

Hug, Tobias. *Impostures in Early Modern England.* Manchester University Press, Manchester, 2010.

Huxley, J.E. 'History and Description of the Kent Asylum.' *The Asylum Journal of Mental Science*, pp 39-45. 1855.

Lansberry, Frederick (ed). *Government and Politics in Kent, 1640-1914.* Boydell & Brewer, Woodbridge, 2001.

Lee, Robert. *Unquiet country: voices of the rural poor, 1820-1880.* Windgather Press, Macclesfield, 2005.

Levi, Ken. *Violence and Religious Commitment: Implications of Jim Jones's People's Temple Movement.* Pennsylvania State University Press, Pennsylvania, 1982.

Liardet, Frederick. *Riot in Kent: Report made to the Central Society of Education on the State of the Peasantry (in the County of Kent).* Publications of the Central Society of Education, Vol III, London, 1839.

Linch, Kevin; Lord, Matthew. *Redcoats to Tommies: The Experience of the British Soldier from the Eighteenth Century.* Boydell & Brewer, Woodbridge, 2021.

Lockley, Philip. *Visionary Religion and Radicalism in Early Industrial England: From Southcott to Socialism.* Oxford University Press, Oxford, 2013.

Major, Alan. *Kentish as She Wus Spoke: A Guide to the Kentish Dialect.* S.B. Publications, Seaford, 2001.

Marsh, Joss. *Word Crimes: Blasphemy, Culture and Literature in Nineteenth-Century England.* University of Chicago, Chicago, 1998.

Marshall, John. *Royal Navy Biography, or Memoirs of the Services of all the Flag Officers* (etc). Longman and Hurst, London, 1833.

Matthews, Ronald. *English Messiahs: Studies of Six English Religious Pretenders, 1656-1927.* Methuen, London, 1936.

McCalman, Iain. *Radical Underworld: Prophets, Revolutionaries and Pornographers in London, 1795-1840.* Cambridge University Press, Cambridge, 1988.

Mingay, Gordon E. *The Victorian Countryside.* Routledge, London, 1981.

Morison, Alexander. *The Physiognomy of Mental Diseases.* Longman, London, 1840.

Muir, Rory. *Tactics and the Experience of Battle in the Age of Napoleon.* Yale University Press, New Haven, 2008.

Oakes, Len. *Prophetic Charisma: the Psychology of Revolutionary Religious Personalities.* Syracuse University Press, Syracuse, 1997.

O'Gorman, Frank. *Voters, Patrons, and Parties: The Unreformed Electoral System of Hanoverian England, 1734-1832.* Clarendon Press, Oxford, 1989.

Oliver, William Hosking. *Prophets and Millennialists: The Uses of Biblical Prophecy in England from the 1790s to the 1840s.* Auckland University Press, Auckland, 1978.

Parish, W.D. & Shaw, W.F. *A Dictionary of Kentish Dialect and Provincialisms in use in the county of Kent.* Trübner & Co, London, 1888.

Pearce, Edward. *Reform!: The Fight for the 1832 Reform Act.* Jonathan Cape, London, 2003.

Pearl, Sharrona. *About Faces: Physiognomy in Nineteenth-Century Britain.* Harvard University Press, Cambridge Mass., 2010.

Phillips, John A. *The Great Reform Bill in the Boroughs: English Electoral Behaviour, 1818-1841.* Clarendon Press, Oxford, 1992.

Poole, Robert. *Peterloo: the English Uprising.* Oxford University Press, Oxford, 2019.

Reay, Barry. *The Last Rising of the Agricultural Labourers: The Battle in Bossenden Wood, 1838.* Clarendon Press, Oxford, 1990.

Reay, Barry. *Microhistories: Demography, Society and Culture in Rural England, 1800-1930.* Cambridge University Press, Cambridge, 2002.

Reay, Barry. *Rural Englands: Labouring Lives in the Nineteenth-Century.* Palgrave Macmillan, London, 2004.

Richardson, T.L. 'The Labourers' Standard of Living in Lincolnshire, 1790-1840: Social Protest and Public Order.' *The Agricultural History Review*, Volume 41, Part I, 1993.

Robinson, Beverley. *The Red Lion: A Re-assessment of the Leader of the Tomists of Kent, 'Sir William Courtenay' / John Nichols Tom, Killed in Bossenden Wood, 1838.* People's Publications, Newcastle upon Tyne, 1980.

Rogers, Philip George. *Battle in Bossenden Wood.* Oxford University Press, London. 1962.

Rowland, Christopher. *Blake and the Bible.* Yale University Press, New Haven, 2008.

Royle, Edward. *Revolutionary Britannia?: Reflections on the Threat of Revolution in Britain, 1789-1848.* Manchester University Press, Manchester, 2000.

Rudé, George. *The crowd in history: a study of popular disturbances in France and England 1730-1848.* Wiley, London, 1964.

Rudé, George. *Protest and Punishment: The Story of the Social and Political Protesters Transported to Australia, 1788-1868*. Clarendon Press, Oxford, 1978.

Safe, Wendy. *The Courtenay Affair, 1838*. Faversham Society Heritage Centre, 1987.

Smeyers, Kristof. 'When Immortals Die: Excavating the Emotional Impact of the Death of Prophets in Nineteenth-Century England'. *Pakistan Journal of Historical Studies*. Vol. 2.2, pp 1-32. 2017.

Smith, Leonard. *Cure, Comfort and Safe Custody: Public Lunatic Asylums in Early Nineteenth-Century England*. Leicester University Press, London, 1999.

Snell, K.D.M. *Annals of the Labouring Poor: Social Change and Agrarian England, 1660-1900*. Cambridge University Press, Cambridge, 1987.

Somerville, Alexander. *The Whistler at the Plough*. James Ainsworth, London, 1852.

Stevenson, John. *Popular Disturbances in England 1700-1870*. Longman, London, 1979.

Turner, Barry. *The Victorian Parson*. Amberley, Stroud, 2016.

Vernon, James. *Politics and the People: A Study in English Political Culture, c.1815–1867*. Cambridge University Press, Cambridge, 1993.

Ward, Henry, *The Canterbury Guide*, Canterbury, 1833.

White, Joan. *Boughton-under-Blean*. Faversham Society, 1983.

Wilson, Margaret. *Almost Another Sister: The Family Life of Fanny Knight, Jane Austen's Favourite Niece*. Kent Arts and Libraries, 1990.

Wise, Sarah. *Inconvenient People: Lunacy, Liberty and the Mad-Doctors in Victorian England*. Bodley Head, London, 2012.

Wordworth, Charles Favell Forth, *The Law and Practice of Elections (for England and Wales) as altered by The Reform Act &c*. Saunders and Benning, London, 1832.

Young, George Malcolm. *Early Victorian England, 1830-1865*. Oxford University Press, Oxford, 1934.

Zeiders, Charles; Devlin, Peter. *Malignant Narcissism and Power: A Psychodynamic Exploration of Madness and Leadership*. Routledge, Oxford, 2019.

ACKNOWLEDGEMENTS

My background is in novel-writing, and I was aware as I began this project that I was entered a new and different field. So I am profoundly grateful to all those real historians who have offered me help, inspiration and encouragement as I found the right path.

Without the work of Barry Reay, in particular his 1990 study *The Last Rising of the Agricultural Labourers* and his later *Microhistories*, I could never have contemplated attempting this book. Professors Steve Poole and Elaine Chalus provided helpful advice at the beginning of the project, and Professor Carl Griffin very kindly read and commented upon a draft chapter. My thanks also go to Melanie Backe-Hansen and to Kristof Smeyers.

In the course of my research, I received invaluable assistance from the archives staff at the Kent Library and History Centre in Maidstone, and at the Canterbury Cathedral Archives, who helped in tracking down and in several cases deciphering some very strange old documents, along with those at the Beaney House of Art & Knowledge in Canterbury, the National Archives in Kew, the British Library, and the Mary Evans Picture Library.

I am sincerely grateful to Sandys Dawes of Mount Ephraim, who gave liberally of his time and hospitality on more than one occasion and allowed me to browse at length through his collection of original Courtenay-related artefacts and documents. He also introduced me to the late Mr Guy Gibb, then owner of Bossenden Farm, who very obligingly showed me over his property in 2018.

Richard Mummery, Gary Tong and Dan Brice gave me some illuminating insights into the battle and its true location; I am also grateful for their efforts in getting the site marked on the maps and properly memorialised. I would like to thank Peter Willcock, churchwarden of St Michael's in Hernhill, both for his informative tour of the church and the historical material kept in the vestry, and for his campaign, alongside the Reverend Cathrine Ngangira, priest in charge at Boughton under Blean, to commemorate more fittingly those who died in the conflict.

Arts Council England provided vital support for this project, which differed so greatly from anything I had attempted before. My thanks go to Connor Stait at Icon Books for trusting in my initial proposal and for guiding me in the editorial process. Most of all, I would like to thank Narmi, for her generosity of spirit and confident reassurance throughout the writing of this book.

INDEX

Adams, Thomas and Peter 172
Admiral Hood (smuggling vessel) 43, 60
Ainsworth, William Harrison 83-84, 257
Anatomy Act (1832) 105
Apollonian Club 52
Armstrong, Major Elliott 199-204, 208-214, 216, 223, 226, 264
Army, British xx-xxi, 1, 54, 142, 198-199; 45th Foot xxii, xxvi, 198-200, 210-213, 218, 223, 244, 247, 264-265; 28th Foot 108, 265; 3rd Foot 155; Rifle Brigade 50-51: 9th Light Dragoons 142; Yeomanry xx, 102, 108, 143, 179, 197
Arnold, Elizabeth 132, 144, 183
Austen, Jane xxiii, 31
Australia, transportation to 8, 65, 81, 113, 233-235

Baker, Mary 8
Baker, Stephen 217, 224, 231
Baldock, Richard xxii, 198, 200, 202, 219
Banks, John Waters 6, 21, 61
Barming, *see* Kent County Lunatic Asylum

Beards 1-2, 4, 9, 35, 59, 99, 130, 136, 221, 223
Beckett, Thomas 87
Beckford, William 4
Belchem, John 20, 253, 256
Benbow, William 128
Bennett, Lt Henry Boswell xxii-xxiii, 200, 208-209, 211, 213-214, 219, 223, 225, 233
Bible, the 59, 112, 133, 146, 220; Book of Job 146-147; Book of Matthew 141; General Epistle of St James 146-147; Revelations 127, 132-133, 154
Blake, William 81, 260, 271
Blanchard, William 148, 150, 160, 261
Blean Wood ix, xiv, xxii, xxvii, 34, 88-89, 95, 134, 145, 148, 158, 173, 197
Boar Shields (William Elliot) 16, 31
Bossenden Farm xiv, xix, xx-xxi, xxvi-xxvii, 88, 134-135, 159, 169-170, 173-174, 181, 202, 202-205, 207, 225, 246, 273
Bossenden Wood ix-xvi, 93, 95, 148, 159, 164, 192, 202-204, 215, 223 battle in 207-218, 224, 232, 236, 238, 241, 243-244, 247-248, 259

Branchett, George 110, 121, 126, 145, 148, 155, 164, 166, 176, 210, 217, 219, 231
Brenley House 157, 187
Brothers, Richard 129, 172
Brown, Alderman 13, 50
Brown, Thomas 145, 148
Browning, Edward 251
Browning, John 93, 95, 96
Brunsdame, Elizabeth 145-147
Burford, Edward 85, 109, 206, 246
Burford, Emily 85-89, 91-92, 98, 102, 113, 145, 155, 174, 176, 182, 204, 207, 215, 226-228, 230
Burford, William 85-86, 93-96, 98-99, 101, 109-111, 119, 126, 145, 148, 163, 174, 177, 180, 206, 211, 213, 217, 219, 225, 231, 245-246
Burma xxii, 198, 200, 203, 216
Burridge, Kenelm 137
Butcher, Edward xvii-xviii, xxv, 139

'Canterburiensis' (author) xxxvi, 6, 68-69, 99, 129, 173, 252
Canterbury, Archbishop of 13, 81, 91, 236
Catt, George xxi, 180, 187, 195, 204, 213, 224-225, 237
Chadwick, Edwin 103
Champ, William 213
Chapman, John 32, 36
Charity (anthem, Dr William Boyce) 141
Chisholm, Dr Robert 222, 243
Clarendon Hotel 69, 71-72
Clark, Joseph Henry 245-246
Cobbett, William xxviii, 30, 46-48
Collard, John 3-4, 6-7, 49, 234
Cosway, Sir William 30, 32-33, 36
Couchworth, William 214-215, 232
Courtenay, Sir William, *see* Tom, John Nicholls
Courtenay, Viscount William 4-5, 8-9, 147

Crowther, Reverend James 6
Culver, Sarah 135-138, 154, 176, 182, 192, 206, 215-217, 226, 229, 235, 246
Culver, William xx, 93, 135, 138, 170
Cumberland, Duke of 6, 8
Curling, Edward xxi-xxii, 110, 140, 162, 169-170, 177, 181, 186, 190, 197, 230, 236, 262
Curling, Edward Jr xxii, 197, 208
Curling, Edward Rigden 181, 215, 233
Czernowski, Captain 9

Dalton, Thomas 148
Dawes family 124, 151, 189
Delasaux, Thomas 224, 234
Denne, George 6-7, 36, 61, 131
Dickens, Charles xxxviii, 2, 83
Dove (public house) 88, 158, 182, 190
Ducrow, Andrew 52
Dunkin, John 162

Edwards, Daniel xix, 173, 175-177, 180, 186-187, 193, 204, 225
Emancipation, Catholic 11, 29, 127
Evangelism xxxi-xxxii, 19, 130

Fairbrook Farm xxiv, 38, 40, 53, 87-88, 118-120, 122, 149-150, 184-193, 242
Fanaticism xxx-xxxii, 119, 129, 131
Faversham Farmers' Club 39, 53, 117, 246
Fitzgerald, Mr (entertainer) 42-43
Foad, Alexander 125-126, 153, 166-167, 176, 183-184, 192, 214, 217, 225, 233, 237
Fordwich, Viscount, MP for Canterbury 13, 21-26
Foreman, Edmund 107, 207, 215, 226
Foreman, John 131, 139
Foreman, Richard 233
Foster, William 217, 219, 231

Index

Francis, Eliza Jane xxiv, 40, 43, 117, 122, 184-185, 193, 235, 246
Francis, George xxiv, 38-40, 43-44, 48, 50, 53, 61, 75-76, 78-79, 115-120, 122, 143-146, 149-150, 157-158, 162, 178, 184-186, 188, 236, 241-243, 246
Fuller, John 194
Fulpit, Catherine, *see* Tom, Mrs Catherine

Gate, the (public house) 88, 159, 201, 218
Gipps, George 93, 135
Glover, James 107
Goodwin, James 158, 182, 190-191, 232
Gordon, Commander James Gabriel RN 24, 61, 75-76, 242
Gorham, James 144-147, 159-160, 173, 182, 194, 204, 215, 225
Gorham, Stephen 172, 175
Gosselin, General Gerard 85-85, 107-108, 161, 179
Gosset, Captain John 51
Great Reform Act, the (Representation of the People Act, 1832) xxi, 11-12, 33, 54, 71
Greenwood, Mr (watchmaker) 6-7, 22
Griffin, Carl 101
Griggs, George 170, 212, 216-217, 224
Griggs, Thomas 217, 233
Groves, Colonel Percy xviii, xxv, 155-158, 162, 179, 186

Hadlow, Charles 170
Hadlow, Henry xxv, xl, 177, 217, 232
Hadlow, John 153, 183
Hadlow, Lydia xxv-xxvi, 122, 131-132, 220, 229, 233-235
Hales, Sir Edward 6
Halford, William Henry xxii, 198, 200, 202
Handley, John Jr 142, 189-190, 192, 195, 204, 211

Handley, Major Benjamin 142-143, 189-192, 195, 204, 209
Handley, Cassandra 123-124, 212
Handley, Reverend Charles xiv, xviii, xxiv, xxxvii, 10, 21, 33, 37-39, 89, 91, 94, 111, 120, 123-127, 140-142, 145-146, 155-157, 169, 189-192, 204, 216, 226-227, 229-232, 235-237, 244-245, 248, 251, 254
Harvey, Phineas 110, 158, 210, 217, 219, 231
Hawkins, George 170, 176
Hetherington, Henry 47
Honywood, Sir John Courtenay 3
Horne, Mary 40, 117-118, 120, 122, 149, 184-185, 192-193, 235, 246
Hugo, Mr (brother in law of Mrs Tom) 75
Hunt, Henry 'Orator' 20, 54, 71
Huxley, James 77
Huxtep, William 36

Irving, Reverend Edward xxxii, 48, 71, 80, 128-129

Jarman, Edward 157, 187-188, 195
Jerusalem 5, 10, 68, 152, 154, 184
Jews, Judaism 2, 48, 71, 80, 128, 130, 256

Kay, William xxv, 143
Kennett, William 41-43, 92, 119, 144-145
Kent Assize Court (Maidstone) 49, 59-62, 72, 232
Kent County Lunatic Asylum 52, 76-84, 112-116, 118-119, 130-131, 158, 242
King's Bench, Court of the 51, 56
Knatchbull, Lady Fanny xxiii, 31, 239
Knatchbull, Mary xix, 30, 178-179, 238-239

Knatchbull, Norton xix-xx, xxxvii, 30, 110, 119, 156, 177-180, 186-189, 192-195, 201-202, 207-208, 211-213, 218, 226-227, 238-239, 242
Knatchbull, Sir Edward, MP 12, 29-33, 36, 93, 101, 119, 124, 127, 177, 238-241
Knight, William 170, 192

Langley, Sergeant 208-209
Lavender Farm xxv, 153, 155, 183
Lazarus, Elijah 6, 49
Lewin, Mrs (widow) 25
Liardet, Frederick xxxv, xxxvii-xxxviii, 47, 86-87, 94, 110-111, 123, 125, 134, 165, 220, 244
Lion, the (journal) xxxvii, 45-48, 53-55, 71, 73, 83, 130, 198
Lively (revenue cutter) 43-44, 60

Machine breaking 99-101
Maidstone Prison 65, 75-76, 225, 233, 242
Marsh, Reverend George Pierce xviii, 157, 162, 186, 238
Matthews, Ronald 82
McWilliam, Rohan 18
Mears, John xix, xx, 107, 109-110, 148, 173-177, 180, 187
Mears, Nicholas xvii, xix, xx, 145-146, 173-177, 179, 182-183, 204, 213, 216, 224-225, 237
Mears, Thomas Tyler 107, 126, 133, 144, 172, 174, 180-181, 192, 214, 225, 233, 245
Melbourne, Lord xxvii-xxviii, 114
Methodists 48, 150, 163
Miles, Noah 125, 182, 192-193, 228
Millenarianism xxvi, 73, 127-131, 172, 182
Millgate, Thomas 207, 210
Minter, Captain George 218, 264-265

Morpeth, Lord 127
Mount Ephraim xiv, xviii, 37, 88-89, 124, 142, 151, 189, 194, 212, 262, 265
'Murphy's Frost' 121

Napoleonic War 42, 100, 121, 199
Nash Court 87-88
Naylor, James 172
Neame, Charles 187, 194-195, 204, 208
Newman, Edward 119, 151, 153, 162, 173
Noah's Ark (public house) 125, 182, 228
Nutting, William 225, 232

O'Brien, James Bronterre 240-241
O'Connor, Feargus 241
Orton, Arthur ('Titchborne Claimant') 8
Ovenden, Thomas 182-183, 215, 232

Packman, George 40, 107, 159
Packman, Henry and William (arsonists) 102, 152
Packman, John 92-94
Parke, Mr Justice James 62-65
Parliamentary Select Committee (1838) xxx, xxxvi, 38, 68, 118, 185, 241, 256
Patteson, Sir John 51
Pay, Charles 144
Payne, Alfred 148-150, 152-153, 155, 160-162, 215
Percy, the Honourable Sydney, *see* Tom, John Nicholls
'Peterloo' Massacre xxi, xxvii, 20, 47, 70, 243
Phrenology, Physiognomy xxxiii, 42, 252
Plumptre, John Pemberton, MP for East Kent 30-33, 36

Index

Poor Law (Poor Law Amendment Act, 1834) xxviii, xxix-xxx, 93, 103-106, 108-109, 121, 156, 163, 197, 206, 237, 240, 245-246
Poore, Dr John xix-xxii, xxxvii, 107-108, 145, 156-158, 161-163, 169, 179, 186-190, 194, 201-202, 208-210, 216, 226-228, 235-238
Powderham Castle 3-4, 6, 23, 36, 49, 114
Poynder, George 78-82, 114-116, 158, 239
Prendergast, Lt Thomas 200, 213-214, 219
Preston, Thomas 70
Price, Robert 112
Price, William 144-145, 152-153, 174, 177, 180, 225, 233, 245
Pyramus (convict ship) 245

Reay, Barry 81, 91, 136, 148
Red Lion, the (public house, Dunkirk) xxvii, 88, 92, 99, 147, 160, 170, 195, 201-205, 218-219, 221-225, 228-229
Red Lion, the (public house, Hernhill) xvii, 88-89, 123, 139, 251
Reid, Captain James 200, 202-205, 207-208, 218, 264
Riot Act, the 201-201, 241
Riots xxiii, 11; 'Swing' (1830) 99-102, 112, 144, 239, 246; Bristol (1831) xxi, 11, 50; Anti-Poor-Law (1835) xxviii, 106-109, 111, 123, 163, 197; Newport (1840) 243-244
Robinson, George 6, 32, 62
Rogers, Philip George xxxvii, 135-136, 154, 265
Rookwood (novel) 83-84
Rose Inn (hotel) 2-3, 19, 23, 27, 49, 107, 147
Rothschild, Count Moses Rostopchein, *see* Tom, John Nicholls

Russell, Lord John xxx, 114-115, 229, 237, 239, 241
Rye, William 182, 210, 217, 219, 231

Senior, Nassau 103-104
Serres, Olivia 8
Sessions Court, Canterbury 86, 93, 101, 111
Shaftesbury, Earl of 96
Shambler, Lieutenant RN 60
Shepherd, Julius xxv, 153, 157, 229-230, 234
Slavery, abolition of 11, 142
Sidmouth, Lord 70
Smith, Henry, of Pentonville 49, 69
Snoulton, Osborn 143, 158
Somerville, Alexander 39, 97
Sondes, Lord 244
Southcott, Joanna 129, 172
Southee, Mr (grocer) 22
Spankie, Mr Serjeant 60
Spence, Thomas 69-70, 128
Spencean Philanthropists, Society of 69-70
Stanhope, Lady Hester 68
Stroud, Thomas 49, 52, 54, 56

Thistlewood, Arthur 70
Thomas, John Morris 61
Three Horseshoes, the (public house) 152, 194
Titchborne Claimant, *see* Orton, Arthur
Tocqueville, Alexis de 15
Tom, John Nicholls; family background of 66-68, 75; name of xviii, 59, 75, 115-116; as 'Sir William Courtenay' 3-8, 10, 59, 65-66, 68, 74-75, 80-81, 83-84, 115-116; as 'Count Rothschild' 2-4, 9-10, 14, 48-49, 71, 130; as 'Sydney Percy' 49, 69; as 'Squire Thompson' 69; as 'Mad Tom' x, xxx, xxxix, 231,

243; publications of see *Lion, the*;
religious ideas of 19, 48, 55, 61,
72-73, 129-131, 132-133, 147,
150, 154-155, 165-166, 171-172,
176; political ideas of 17-18,
32-33, 44, 46, 48, 53-55, 69-70,
126, 143; mental health of 67-68,
72-74, 76, 78-82, 176, 241;
Canterbury election campaign
14-15, 17-27, 31, 142; East Kent
election campaign 33-36, 38;
trial in Canterbury 55-57; trial in
Maidstone 59-65; imprisonment
50-51, 65, 75-76; committal to
asylum 77-83, 113-114; death of
210, 215; autopsy of 221-222;
burial of 229-230
Tom, Mrs Catherine 66, 68, 75-76, 114-115, 242
Tom, Mrs Susan 68, 113, 242
Turner, Edmund, MP for Truro 66, 113-115, 240
Turpin, Dick 84

Victoria, Queen x, xvii, xxiii, xxviii, xxx, 113, 115, 198, 241
Vivian, Sir Hussey, MP for East Cornwall 113-115, 239-240

Ward, Henry xxvii, xxxvi, 65, 201, 219
Ward, John 'Zion' 129, 172

Watson, the Hon. Richard, MP for Canterbury 13, 21-24, 26
Watts Russell, Mary, *see* Knatchbull, Mary
Wellington, Duke of 12, 29
Westgate Gaol 49-51
Wheatsheaf, the (public house) 161
White Horse, the (public house) 149, 218, 224, 226
Wills, Helen Courtenay 41, 122, 245
Wills, Lucy 119-120, 122-123, 143, 150, 245
Wills, William 41, 118-120, 126, 131-133, 139, 141, 144-146, 151-153, 162-163, 171, 173, 210, 213-214, 218, 232-233, 245
Winchelsea, Lord xxvii, 11
Woodman's Hall (public house) 110, 144-145, 261
Workhouses xxix, xxxiv, 103-105, 108-109, 121, 166, 184, 206, 210, 231, 245-246
Wraight, Edward, the elder 125-126, 153, 158, 182, 192, 214, 217, 219, 231
Wraight, Edward, the younger 110, 125, 133, 167, 180-181, 183, 192, 214-217, 233
Wraight, Sarah 125, 133-134, 166-167, 181, 183-184, 220
Wroe, John 130, 136-137, 172